Toward a Social History
of the American Civil War

Toward a Social History of the American Civil War

Exploratory Essays

Edited by

MARIS A. VINOVSKIS

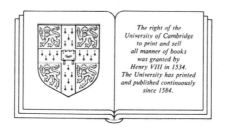

The right of the
University of Cambridge
to print and sell
all manner of books
was granted by
Henry VIII in 1534.
The University has printed
and published continuously
since 1584.

CAMBRIDGE UNIVERSITY PRESS

Cambridge

New York   Port Chester   Melbourne   Sydney

Published by the Press Syndicate of the University of Cambridge
The Pitt Building, Trumpington Street, Cambridge CB2 1RP
40 West 20th Street, New York, NY 10011, USA
10 Stamford Road, Oakleigh, Melbourne 3166, Australia

First published 1990

Printed in the United States of America

Library of Congress Cataloging-in-Publication Data

Toward a social history of the American Civil War : exploratory essays
/ edited by Maris A. Vinovskis.
p.   cm.
Includes index.
ISBN 0-521-39523-2. – ISBN 0-521-39559-3 (pbk.)
1. United States – History – Civil War, 1861–1865 – Social aspects.
I. Vinovskis, Maris.
E.468.9.T75   1990
973.7 – dc20   90-36367

British Library Cataloguing in Publication Data

Toward a social history of the American Civil War :
exploratory essays.
1. American Civil War.   Social aspects
I. Vinovskis, Maris A.
973.71

ISBN 0–521–39523–2 hardback
ISBN 0–521–39559–3 paperback

Contents

Introduction

MARIS A. VINOVSKIS

Despite the popularity of military history, little effort has been made to study the demographic and socioeconomic impact of war on society. A prime example is the neglect of the American Civil War by social historians. Although thousands of articles and books have been written about the military experiences of its participants, not much attention has been paid to their lives. Indeed, most of the so-called new social historians have ignored the possible influence of the Civil War on the life course of nineteenth-century Americans.

In order to begin to explore the social history of the Civil War, seven essays have been solicited for this volume. Because of the scarcity of materials on the social history of the Civil War, it was decided to focus only on the experiences of the North, to allow coverage in greater depth. It is hoped that in the near future a similar volume can be assembled on the South, for of course the wartime and postwar experiences of the two sections were by no means identical. One of the essays, "Have Social Historians Lost the Civil War?", is reprinted from the *Journal of American History,* but the other six were written especially for this volume. The fact that the six original essays for this collection are by scholars in their twenties and thirties suggests that the next generation of scholars will pay more attention to the social history of the Civil War than have their predecessors.

Though one cannot hope to cover all of the major social developments in the North during the Civil War or the impact of that conflict on the survivors in one volume, these essays do illustrate the type of studies that can and should be done. They are intended to supplement, but not replace entirely, the current focus on political and military events of the Civil War, as both perspectives are needed.

The first essay, "Have Social Historians Lost the Civil War? Some Preliminary Demographic Speculations," places the war in the broader context of other American wars by comparing casualty rates. Whether measured by the aggregate number of deaths or the rate of deaths per 10,000 population, the Civil War is by far the bloodiest experience in our history.

The essay then goes on to examine the demographic characteristics of the war in the North and the South, and finds significant differences. A much higher proportion of the white military-age population in the South enlisted and died in the Civil War than in the North. A detailed analysis of the characteristics of those who fought in the Civil War from the Massachusetts seaport city of Newburyport follows, with the unanticipated finding that a higher percentage of the native-born population enlisted than of the foreign-born population and that the Civil War was less of a "poor man's fight" than most contemporaries believed. Far from being a relatively unimportant event, as earlier studies of Newburyport had implied, this analysis shows that a high percentage of young white men participated and that many were either wounded or killed.

Finally, the essay looks at Civil War pensions for Union soldiers and finds that this is a relatively neglected area of research that deserves more analysis. Large numbers of Union veterans or their widows and dependents benefited from an increasingly generous pension system, which, by 1890, provided in effect an old-age assistance program. The magnitude of the federal involvement in this program was sizable: About 40 percent of the federal budget in the early 1890s was spent on Union pensions.

The second essay, "Community and War: The Civil War Experience of Two New Hampshire Towns," by Thomas Kemp, investigates the course of the war in two small rural New England communities. Kemp finds more support for the Union cause in Republican Claremont than in Democratic Newport. This difference in political orientation is reflected to some degree in the likelihood of subgroups of the population to enlist in the war effort and in the overall willingness of their communities to support the war effort.

Kemp makes the important point that individual and community responses to the war varied over time. Initially, both Claremont and Newport citizens responded enthusiastically, but as the costs of that conflict became more visible and personal over time, the local residents became reluctant to volunteer. It then became necessary to use the threat of the draft to fulfill the Union quotas set for those two communities and for the towns to offer sizable bounties to attract new recruits.

As in Newburyport, the ranks of the Union soldiers were filled with residents from all social classes – though men from the skilled and unskilled occupations were somewhat overrepresented. Foreign-born residents of Claremont and Newport did not enlist in excessive numbers, but Kemp points out that they were overrepresented among the nonresidents who were recruited in the latter part of the war. As in Newburyport, the

Civil War had a profound effect on the citizens: Large numbers participated, and a significant proportion of them were killed or incapacitated by the war.

Whereas the first two essays rely heavily on quantitative data, the next one, "The Northern Soldier and His Community," by Reid Mitchell, draws upon the letters and diaries of Union soldiers to explore the meaning of the wartime experiences for its participants. Like the preceding essay on the New Hampshire towns, this one is concerned with the effect of the local community on the lives of the soldiers.

To understand the nature of Civil War military units, it is essential to recognize how much they were influenced by the values and culture of the nineteenth century. Mitchell points out, for example, that although the military leaders wanted to maintain a distance between the officers and the enlisted men, it was difficult to achieve this separation in practice, since companies were often organized locally and the men had known each other before entering the service.

The close and constant communication between the soldiers and their families at home led frequently to local rumors and gossip affecting the troops in the field or their loved ones at home. Unlike the situation in World War II or Vietnam, soldiers usually were unable to escape the scrutiny of their neighbors and relatives in their war conduct. As Mitchell observes, the Civil War experience for the Union soldiers made sense only within the broader context of their domestic and community lives.

If the Civil War affected the life course of soldiers, it also had an impact on the civilians who volunteered their time and money to help those at the front. J. Matthew Gallman's essay, "Voluntarism in Wartime: Philadelphia's Great Central Fair," analyzes a fair held to benefit the U.S. Sanitary Commission, in 1864, to reveal the nature of voluntarism in one large Northern city, as part of a larger study of the home front in Philadelphia.

The Great Central Fair of 1864 was one of the outstanding successes in raising funds for helping soldiers. Like most other wartime relief activities, the fair relied upon the donation of money and goods. Over 250,000 people visited the fair, and the event raised over $1 million. It also allowed Philadelphians from many different social and ethnic groups to participate more directly in the war effort.

Yet Gallman cautions us about inferring that wartime benevolence necessarily had a profound and lasting impact. Though the Great Central Fair of 1864 seemed to indicate a more centralized and more organized approach to charitable work, in fact the entire operation was highly decentralized and often quite chaotic. Similarly, although other scholars have seen the wartime experiences of women in charitable work as pre-

paring them and their male counterparts for a more central role in postwar charity work, Gallman suggests that many of the old, unflattering
gender stereotypes persisted. Looking beyond the Civil War to 1876, when
Philadelphia hosted the nation's Centennial Exhibition, Gallman finds
that the three-week fair in 1864 had relied much more on traditional
practices than its successor twelve years later.

Robin Einhorn, in "The Civil War and Municipal Government in Chicago," traces the impact of the war on the politics of this major midwestern city. She analyzes changes in the structure and practice of Chicago politics, as local residents reshaped their government from a
decentralized, segmented system aimed at direct service to property owners into the more familiar late nineteenth-century urban pattern of machine politics.

In the antebellum period, Chicago's local politics was nonpartisan and
largely apolitical, especially in the way it financed the physical construction projects that constituted its chief business. Einhorn shows how both
decision-making power and financial liability for public-works projects
such as street improvements were limited to those property owners who
were directly affected, rather than decided by the city's full council and
financed by the community as a whole.

With the growing polarization between Republicans and Democrats
over both slavery and the conduct of the war, Chicago's city elections
were repoliticized. At the same time, the war emergency allowed city
officials opportunities to tax and spend on a larger scale than ever before.
These opportunities stemmed from two wartime needs: first, for assistance in the recruitment of volunteer soldiers, and second for the payment of municipal bounties to avoid a local draft. Surprisingly, Einhorn
found that neither Republicans nor Democrats exploited public support
for the war to expand patronage resources with which they might have
courted the political loyalties of large numbers of voters by building political machines. But they did authorize another kind of new spending.
The war stimulated a huge expansion of Chicago's meat-packing industry and, therefore, a huge increase in the amount of pollution this industry poured into the local river. Rather than levying a special assessment
against these wealthy businessmen to finance a cleanup, as might have
been done earlier, the city now used general property-tax revenue to abate
the pollution. While the Civil War did not "cause" machine politics in
Chicago, Einhorn finds that the war experience shaped the form that
machine politics would take when it did emerge soon afterward. This
shape differs from the one historians often portray in stories of the "kindly
boss" as the "poor man's friend."

If little has been written about the social history of the Civil War, even less has been done on the impact of that conflict on the survivors. Stuart McConnell's essay, "Who Joined the Grand Army? Three Case Studies in the Construction of Union Veteranhood, 1866–1900," begins to provide some information by looking at those who joined the major national organization of Union veterans after the war.

The Grand Army of the Republic (GAR) reached a membership of 427,981 in 1890 and became a formidable lobby on behalf of pension funds for Union veterans and their dependents. McConnell examines in detail the membership of the GAR in three different communities: the city of Philadelphia; the industrial town of Brockton, Massachusetts; and the farming and lumber center of Chippewa Falls, Wisconsin.

His analysis suggests that GAR leaders were drawn disproportionately from former officers and from those who had served their country longer. Though some blacks and immigrants were represented in the GAR posts that he studied, most members were native-born whites. The GAR posts served in large part as fraternal institutions that met the needs of high-status professionals and businessmen, though the posts also provided a setting for the socially and economically less-advantaged members who made up the bulk of the membership. Finally, despite its elite leadership orientation, the GAR membership cut across socioeconomic lines and probably helped, like many other fraternal orders, to mute class tensions in post–Civil War America.

In the final essay, " 'Such Is the Price We Pay': American Widows and the Civil War Pension System," Amy Holmes looks at the impact of the Civil War on Union widows in urban Grand Rapids and rural Kent County, Michigan, and in urban Salem and nonurban Essex County, Massachusetts, in 1883.

Historians of nineteenth-century women have paid scant attention to the impact of the Civil War on Union or Confederate widows. This oversight is unfortunate, because a significant proportion of all widows in the post–Civil War era were widows of Civil War soldiers and sailors, and the federal government provided substantial pensions for widows in the North. As these widows aged and as immigration levels rose in the late nineteenth and early twentieth centuries, widows who received federal support as a result of Civil War deaths became an increasingly exclusive group.

Comparing Northern widows in Michigan and Massachusetts who received a federal pension with comparably aged widows in the same communities who did not receive such assistance, Holmes found some intriguing differences. Although widows receiving pensions were less likely to be employed than widows who did not receive payments, Massachusetts widows used pension payments to maintain their own households, whereas in Michigan pension payments helped support widows in households headed by their children. Surprisingly, Holmes discovered that while the North mourned the loss of its fathers and sons with parades and speeches on Decoration Day (now Memorial Day), the war widows and their families were rarely mentioned.

All of these essays point to the need to reconsider the social history of the Civil War. Although none of the results so far can be considered definitive, since almost all of them rely on case studies of a few communities, they demonstrate our need to rediscover the effect of the Civil War on nineteenth-century society. The essays also suggest that the impact of the Civil War did not end abruptly in 1865 but continued to influence the survivors throughout the remainder of their lives. Finally, we are reminded that the study of wars cannot be left only to military historians but must also be undertaken by other scholars, so that we can better appreciate the costs and meanings of warfare in our past as well as today.

1

Have Social Historians Lost the Civil War? Some Preliminary Demographic Speculations

MARIS A. VINOVSKIS

Few events in American history have received as much attention as the Civil War. Almost every battle and skirmish has been thoroughly examined and reexamined, and several scholarly and popular journals specialize in analyzing the conflict. Over eight hundred histories of Civil War regiments have been published, and more are under way. More than fifty thousand books and articles have been published on the Civil War. Indeed, much excellent work has been done on that conflict – especially on the military aspects of the war.[1]

Despite this vast outpouring of literature, we do not know much about the effects of the Civil War on everyday life in the United States. Surprisingly little has been written about the personal experiences of ordinary soldiers or civilians during that struggle. The best studies of the lives of common soldiers are still the two volumes written over thirty years ago by Bell I. Wiley. Very little has been published on civilian life in the North

This chapter is reprinted with permission from the *Journal of American History*, 76, no. 1 (June 1989), 34–58. An earlier version was presented at the American Sociological Association Annual Meeting, New York City, August 1986, and at the Soviet-American Committee on Quantitative History Conference on Political and Social History, New Orleans, December 1986. Financial support was provided by a Guggenheim Fellowship and a grant from the Rackham School of Graduate Studies, University of Michigan. The author would like to thank the large number of individuals who have generously contributed their time and ideas to improving the quality of this manuscript. Among them are Susan Armeny, Allan Bogue, Glen Elder, David Hollinger, Gerald Linderman, James McPherson, Yuri Polyakov, Roger Ransom, John Shy, David Thelen, Mary Vinovskis, and Olivier Zunz.

1　One of the best critical bibliographies of the Civil War is still J. G. Randall and David H. Donald, *The Civil War and Reconstruction* (Lexington, Mass., 1969), 703–834. For an excellent, detailed bibliography, see Eugene C. Murdock, *The Civil War in the North: A Selective Annotated Bibliography* (New York, 1987). The best one-volume study of the Civil War is James M. McPherson, *Battle Cry of Freedom: The Civil War Era* (New York, 1988).

or the South during the war years, and almost nothing is available on the postwar life course of Civil War veterans.[2]

If scholars analyzing the Civil War have neglected the lives of common soldiers and civilians, social historians of the nineteenth century appear to have ignored the Civil War altogether.[3] Almost none of the numerous community studies covering the years from 1850 to 1880 discuss, or even mention, the Civil War. The classic study of Newburyport, Massachusetts, by Stephan Thernstrom and the investigation of Poughkeepsie, New York, by Clyde Griffen and Sally Griffen, for example, do not analyze the effects of the Civil War on the lives of the individuals in those communities. Similarly, three recent overviews of demographic and family life in America mention the Civil War only in passing.[4]

2   Bell I. Wiley, *The Life of Johnny Reb: The Common Soldier of the Confederacy* (Baton Rouge, 1943); Bell I. Wiley, *The Life of Billy Yank: The Common Soldier of the Union* (Baton Rouge, 1952). A less satisfactory volume intended for the popular market is Bell I. Wiley, *The Common Soldier of the Civil War* (New York, 1973). The major study of life in the North during the Civil War remains Emerson D. Fite, *Social and Industrial Conditions in the North during the Civil War* (New York, 1910). Recently, four new books addressing some of these issues have been published: Randall C. Jimerson, *The Private Civil War: Popular Thought during the Sectional Conflict* (Baton Rouge, 1988); Reid Mitchell, *Civil War Soldiers: Their Expectations and Their Experiences* (New York, 1988); Philip Shaw Paludan, *"A People's Contest": The Union and Civil War, 1861–1865* (New York, 1988); and James I. Robertson, Jr., *Soldiers Blue and Gray* (Columbia, S.C., 1988).

3   Several factors have led social historians to neglect the Civil War. Scholars working on the nineteenth century generally study either the pre–Civil War or the post–Civil War period rather than analyzing the middle third of the nineteenth century as a whole. Most historians have neglected the social-history aspects of all wars, instead focusing mainly on military strategy and battles. Finally, interest in nineteenth-century social structure led to studies based upon cross-sectional analyses of population just before and after the Civil War, with little attention to demographic changes in between. For examples of the recent interest in the social history of wars, see Fred Anderson, *A People's Army: Massachusetts Soldiers and Society in the Seven Years' War* (Chapel Hill, 1984); Myron P. Gutmann, *War and Rural Life in the Early Modern Low Countries* (Princeton, 1980); and J. M. Winter, *The Great War and the British People* (Cambridge, Mass., 1986).

4   Stephan Thernstrom, *Poverty and Progress: Social Mobility in a Nineteenth-century City* (Cambridge, Mass., 1964); Clyde Griffen and Sally Griffen, *Natives and Newcomers: The Ordering of Opportunity in Mid-nineteenth-century Poughkeepsie* (Cambridge, Mass., 1978). For an important exception, see Michael H. Frisch, *Town into City: Springfield, Massachusetts, and the Meaning of Community, 1840–1880* (Cambridge, Mass., 1972). A few labor historians discuss the impact of the Civil War on the labor movement, but they do not consider its overall effect on the lives of individual workers. See Alan Dawley, *Class and Community: The Industrial Revolution in Lynn* (Cambridge, Mass., 1976); Daniel J. Walkowitz, *Worker City, Company Town: Iron and Cotton Worker Protest in Troy and Cohoes, New York, 1855–84* (Urbana, 1978). The demographic overviews are Walter Nugent, *Structures of American Social History* (Bloomington, 1981); Robert V. Wells, *Revolutions in Americans' Lives: A Demographic Perspective on the History of Americans, Their Families, and Their Society* (Westport, 1982); and Steven Mintz and Susan Kellogg, *Domestic Revolutions: A Social History of American Family Life* (New York, 1988).

Yet the Civil War probably affected the lives of most mid-nineteenth-century Americans, either directly or indirectly. Unusually high proportions of white males enlisted in the Union and the Confederate forces, and many of them were wounded or killed. Large numbers of soldiers on both sides deserted; they carried a stigma the rest of their lives. The survivors not only faced the inevitable problems of reentering civilian society; some undoubtedly continued to have vivid memories of the bloodiest war in the history of the United States. Memories of the war were shared by a large percentage of the entire population, as almost everyone had a loved one, close friend, or relative who fought in that conflict. Nevertheless, most social historians have paid little attention to the impact of the Civil War on the lives of nineteenth-century Americans.

As a first step toward an assessment of the Civil War's influence, this chapter explores its demographic impact. By looking at the number of Union and Confederate soldiers who died and comparing the results with mortality in other wars, one can gauge the magnitude of the Civil War. Having established that a very high proportion of military-age white males fought and died in the Civil War, the chapter considers how the peculiarities of that conflict may have affected the participants' wartime experiences. Then, preliminary results from an in-depth study of Newburyport, Massachusetts, during the Civil War, are used to sketch the social and economic background of those who fought and died in that conflict. Finally, the chapter examines the impact of the Civil War on the survivors. Given the paucity of research on the influence of the Civil War on the postwar lives of ordinary Americans, I offer a preliminary demographic analysis of the federal pension program, using aggregate statistics as one indication of the type of studies that might be done. These few and brief examples do not adequately cover the wide range of topics that should be addressed in future studies, but they do illustrate, at least from a demographic perspective, why we must pay more attention to the social impact of the Civil War on the lives of nineteenth-century Americans.

Civil War Casualties among Union and Confederate Soldiers

There are many ways of assessing the relative impact of wars on a population. One of the most obvious and simplest is to calculate the number of military casualties – a method particularly suitable in cases such as the American Civil War, where relatively few civilians were killed during wartime. Although it is difficult to obtain accurate information on even military deaths in the Civil War era, such data are more readily available

Maris A. Vinovskis

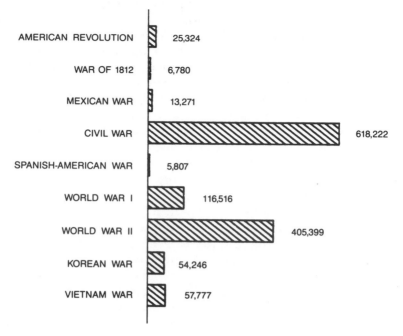

Figure 1.1. American military deaths in wars, 1775–1973. *Source:* For the Mexican War, Civil War, World War I, World War II, and the Korean War, see Claudia D. Goldin, "War," in *Encyclopedia of American Economic History*, ed. Glenn Porter, 3 vols. (New York, 1980), 3:938–9. For the American Revolution, see Howard Peckham, *The Toll of Independence: Engagements and Battle Casualties of the American Revolution* (Chicago, 1974), 130. For the War of 1812, see Bell I. Wiley, *The Common Soldier of the Civil War* (New York, 1973), 118. For the Spanish-American War, see Gerald F. Linderman, *The Mirror of War* (Ann Arbor, 1974), 110. For the Vietnam War, see U.S. Department of Commerce, Bureau of the Census, *Statistical Abstract of the United States, 1987* (Washington, 1986), 328.

and more reliable than estimates of civilian casualties or estimates of the economic costs of the war.

Was the Civil War an important event in our history from the perspective of the number of soldiers killed? The best estimate is that about 618,000 Union and Confederate soldiers and sailors died during the Civil War (see Figure 1.1). The military deaths for the Civil War exceed by more than 50 percent the military deaths in World War II – the American war responsible for the second highest number of service-related deaths.

Indeed, before the Vietnam conflict, the number of deaths in the Civil War almost equaled the total number killed in all our other wars combined.[5]

Another perspective on the extent of casualties in the Civil War can be achieved by computing the number of military deaths per 10,000 population (see Figure 1.2). During the Civil War, 182 individuals per 10,000 population died; the comparable estimate for the next highest-ranked war, the American Revolution, is only 118. The United States suffered many military deaths during World War II, but the much larger population base at that time meant that the number of deaths per 10,000 population was 30 – only about one-sixth the Civil War ratio. The Vietnam War, which has caused such great emotional and political anguish in our times, inflicted only 3 military deaths per 10,000 population. Whether we consider the total number of military deaths or the ratio of deaths to the total population, the American Civil War was by far the bloodiest event in our history.

Since the two sections were very unequal in population and resources, a clearer picture of the impact of Civil War deaths emerges from comparing Union and Confederate losses. The North, with its much larger population, was able to field considerably larger armies than the South, and the North sustained greater military losses. It is estimated that about

5 Information about military casualties is limited and often highly unreliable. For a useful summary, see Claudia D. Goldin, "War," in *Encyclopedia of American Economic History,* ed. Glenn Porter, 3 vols. (New York, 1980), 3:935–57. Goldin's estimates of casualties for the Mexican War, Civil War, World War I, World War II, and the Korean War were used. Her numbers for the other wars appear too small and were replaced by data from other sources. For the American Revolution, see Howard Peckham, *The Toll of Independence: Engagements and Battle Casualties of the American Revolution* (Chicago, 1974), 130. For the War of 1812 estimate, which includes a crude estimate of military deaths from nonbattle causes, see Wiley, *Common Soldier of the Civil War,* 118. For the Spanish-American War, see Gerald F. Linderman, *The Mirror of War* (Ann Arbor, 1974), 110. The figure for the Vietnam War is considerably higher than Goldin's estimate because it includes 10,449 Vietnam servicemen who died in accidents or from disease. U.S. Department of Commerce, Bureau of the Census, *Statistical Abstract of the United States, 1987* (Washington, 1986), Table 549, p. 328. The reader should regard some of these estimates as intelligent approximations rather than definitive figures.

   Robert Fogel and his associates are reanalyzing mortality in the nineteenth-century United States – including military deaths during the Civil War. For a preliminary analysis of their work on nutrition and mortality trends, see Robert W. Fogel, "Nutrition and the Decline in Mortality Since 1700: Some Additional Preliminary Findings," in *Long Term Factors in American Economic Growth,* ed. Stanley L. Engerman and Robert E. Gallman (Chicago, 1986). On antebellum mortality, see Maris A. Vinovskis, "Recent Trends in American Historical Demography: Some Methodological and Conceptual Considerations," *Annual Review of Sociology,* 4 (1978), 603–27; and Maris A. Vinovskis, *Fertility in Massachusetts from the Revolution to the Civil War* (New York, 1980), 25–39.

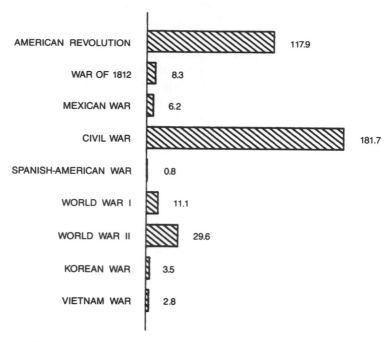

Figure 1.2. American military deaths in wars, 1775–1973 (per 10,000 population). *Source:* On the Mexican War, Civil War, World War I, World War II, and the Korean War, see Claudia D. Goldin, "War," in *Encyclopedia of American Economic History,* ed. Glenn Porter, 3 vols. (New York, 1980), 3:938–9. On the American Revolution, see Howard Peckham, *The Toll of Independence: Engagements and Battle Casualties of the American Revolution* (Chicago, 1974), 130. On the War of 1812, see Bell I. Wiley, *The Common Soldier of the Civil War* (New York, 1973), 118. On the Vietnam War, see U.S. Department of Commerce, Bureau of the Census, *Statistical Abstract of the United States, 1987* (Washington, 1986), 328. Population estimates for all wars are from Goldin, "War," 938–9.

360,000 men died in service to the Union; 258,000 died in service to the Confederacy.[6]

Though military losses in the North during the Civil War exceeded those in the South by nearly 40 percent, the relative impact of that struggle on the South was much greater, because of its smaller population

6 Goldin, "War," 938. Goldin's figure of 360,222 Union deaths includes both white and black soldiers. An estimated 36,000 black Union soldiers died in the Civil War. Ira Berlin, Joseph P. Reidy, and Leslie A. Rowland, eds., *Freedom: A Documentary History of Emancipation, 1861–1867. Series II: The Black Military Experience* (Cambridge, 1982), 633n.

base. Looking at the North and South together, approximately 8 percent of the estimated population of white males aged 13 to 43 in 1860 (the individuals most likely to fight in the war) died in the Civil War. Considering the North and the South separately, about 6 percent of Northern white males aged 13 to 43 died in the Civil War, and about 18 percent of their Southern counterparts died. Young white men in the South were almost three times as likely to die during the four war years as young men in the North.[7]

The heavy casualties experienced by military-age whites in the mid-nineteenth century are unparalleled in our history. Many young men died in the Civil War, leaving dependent widows, and grieving parents and friends. Many who survived were wounded or disabled during the war and carried visible reminders of the conflict with them for the rest of their lives.[8] Given the war's magnitude, most Americans who were adults in the second half of the nineteenth century probably either participated in the war or had close friends or relatives who fought in it.[9]

7   The estimate of white males aged 13 to 43 is based on data from the published federal census. Tennessee was divided on the basis of the secession vote in June 1861. The population of Virginia was subdived into Virginia and West Virginia, using county divisions from 1870. The Confederate and Union populations for Delaware, Kentucky, Maryland, Missouri, and West Virginia were apportioned using James M. McPherson's estimates of the division of military recruits from those areas. It was assumed that all individuals in the other Confederate and Union states and territories supported their own side. The result of these estimates is a crude approximation, but it provides an adequate basis for preliminary comparisons. U.S. Department of Interior, *Population of the United States in 1860: Compiled from the Original Returns of the Eighth Census under the Direction of the Secretary of the Interior* (Washington, 1964); James M. McPherson, *Ordeal by Fire* (New York, 1982), 149–62.

8   The figures on the wounded are even less reliable than those on the dead. Goldin estimates 275,175 wounded in the North, but she does not even try to provide such data for the South. Goldin, "War," 938–9. It is difficult to evaluate the effect of wounds and war-related disabilities on the lives of veterans. William H. Glasson lists the causes of the 467,927 Union disabilities for which pensions had been granted by 1888, but it is impossible to ascertain their seriousness from the categories provided. William H. Glasson, *Federal Military Pensions in the United States* (New York, 1918), 138. Goldin and Lewis assume that wounded veterans lost one-half their potential earning ability, but they do not explain how they arrived at that estimate. Claudia D. Goldin and Frank D. Lewis, "The Economic Cost of the American Civil War: Estimates and Implications," *Journal of Economic History*, 35 (June 1975), 299–326.

9   Although the Civil War is the bloodiest experience in United States history, it is less extraordinary when viewed from a European perspective. The number of deaths per 10,000 population in the Civil War was slightly higher than the losses the British and Irish suffered in World War I but only two-thirds the losses experienced by the Germans and one-half those of the French in the same war. Winter, *The Great War and the British People*, 74. Civil War casualties can also be compared to those in other modern civil wars. Among the 106 civil wars between 1815 and 1980 that resulted in at least 1,000 military deaths a year, the American Civil War is tied with the Spanish civil war (1936–9) for fourth place, based on the total number of deaths, and is ranked eighth in deaths per capita. Melvin Small and J. David Singer, *Resort to Arms: International and*

Characteristics of the Civil War

For many Americans the death of a close friend or relative was the central event of the Civil War, yet reactions to the conflict were shaped not only by personal experiences but also by communities' responses to the war. Although there was considerable division within the North and South over the desirability of secession and the proper federal response to it, once the Confederates had fired on Fort Sumter support for the war solidified in both sections. The early calls for volunteers were quickly answered. Most communities in both the North and South responded enthusiastically by pledging to help the dependents of those who left for the front and by even raising money to purchase uniforms and weapons. Unlike the many who criticized American involvement in the Vietnam War from the start, few questioned the wisdom or necessity of supporting the war effort early in the Civil War.[10]

Everyone expected that the war would be very short, and therefore volunteers were enlisted only for a few months. Soon it became clear that neither the Union nor the Confederate forces could gain a decisive victory, and the news of heavy casualties at battles such as Antietam dampened the enthusiasm for volunteering. As a result, both sides had to resort to the draft to supply their armies with sufficient recruits. Draft riots in the North testified to the unpopularity of conscription. Although relatively few men were actually drafted, the threat of conscription induced states and communities to raise the requested troops by offering bounties. The setbacks on the military field and the increasing sacrifices demanded of the population led many, particularly in the North, to question the wisdom of continuing the war. Thus the initial enthusiasm for the war slackened, as the casualties mounted and all hope for a quick victory vanished.[11]

Civil Wars, 1816–1980 (Beverly Hills, 1982). See also Jack S. Levy, *War in the Modern Great Power System, 1495–1975* (Lexington, Ky., 1983).

10 On the initial responses to secession, see Kenneth M. Stampp, *And the War Came: The North and the Secession Crisis, 1860–1861* (Baton Rouge, 1950); and David Potter, *The Impending Crisis, 1848–1861* (New York, 1976). On the role of local communities in providing assistance for the war, see Frisch, *Town into City,* and Emily J. Harris, "Sons and Soldiers: Deerfield, Massachusetts, and the Civil War," *Civil War History,* 30 (June 1984), 157–71.

11 On the draft in the North, see Eugene C. Murdock, *One Million Men: The Civil War Draft in the North* (Westport, 1971). Only 6% of the Union enlistments "can be attributed to the direct effects of the draft," according to Marvin A. Kreidberg and Merton G. Henry, *History of Military Mobilization in the United States Army, 1775–1945* (Washington, 1955), 108. For an interesting quantitative analysis, see Peter Levine, "Draft Evasion in the North during the Civil War, 1863–1865," *Journal of American History,* 67 (March 1981), 816–34. On the draft in the South, see Albert Burton

Despite the increasing difficulty of recruiting troops as the war continued, both sides raised large armies. Altogether, more than 3,000,000 men (including about 189,000 blacks, who fought for the Union) served in the Civil War. Nearly 2,000,000 whites joined the Union forces and 900,000 the Confederate cause.[12] In the North and South combined, about 40 percent of whites of military age (age 13 to 43 in 1860) served in the armed forces. Although the North fielded more than twice as many men as the South, a much smaller percentage of whites of military age participated from the North (35 percent) than from the South (61 percent).

As the preceding section indicates, large numbers of soldiers and sailors were killed in the Civil War. Therefore the chances of someone enlisted in the war dying was high. More than one out of every five whites participating died. Again, the casualty rates were much higher in the South than in the North. Approximately one out of six white males in the Union forces died, whereas more than one out of four of their counterparts in the Confederate armies perished. In part the higher mortality rate among Southern troops reflects the fact that many Confederate soldiers were forced to remain in the armed forces throughout the war, while Northern soldiers were allowed to return home after completing their scheduled tours of duty.[13]

Death rates during the Civil War were much higher than those in twentieth-century wars, partly because participants were more likely to die of disease. Disease caused more than one-half the deaths among Union soldiers. Furthermore, due to the relatively primitive nature of medical

Moore, *Conscription and Conflict in the Confederacy* (New York, 1924). For a case study of class divisions within the Confederacy, see Paul D. Escott and Jeffery J. Crow, "The Social Order and Violent Disorder: An Analysis of North Carolina in the Revolution and the Civil War," *Journal of Southern History,* 52 (August 1986), 373–402. For a thoughtful, well-balanced account of the Democratic Party in the North, see Joel H. Silbey, *A Respectable Minority: The Democratic Party in the Civil War Era, 1860–1868* (New York, 1977).

12   The estimates of white males in the Union and Confederate forces are from McPherson, *Ordeal by Fire,* 181. Recently he has revised his estimate of Confederate soldiers and sailors to 900,000. See McPherson, *Battle Cry of Freedom,* 30n. Even the latter figure may underestimate the total whites in the war by excluding some who served in state militia units – particularly in the South. James M. McPherson to Maris A. Vinovskis, June 24, 1987 (in Maris A. Vinovskis's possession). The traditional figure for blacks in the Union armies is 179,000. See Berlin, Reidy, and Rowland, eds., *Freedom,* 633n1. As many as 10,000 blacks may have served in the Union navy. See McPherson, *Ordeal by Fire,* 355.

13   On the differences in experiences of Confederate and Union soldiers, see Wiley, *Life of Johnny Reb,* Wiley, *Life of Billy Yank.* For an excellent review of the recent studies of Civil War soldiers, see Marvin R. Cain, "A 'Face of Battle' Needed: An Assessment of Motives and Men in Civil War Historiography," *Civil War History,* 28 (March 1982), 5–27. About 33,000 of the estimated 179,000 black soldiers died in the Civil War, or approximately 18%. Berlin, Reidy, and Rowland, eds., *Freedom,* 633n1.

care in the Civil War era, a much higher percentage of those wounded eventually died than in subsequent wars.[14]

Many soldiers and sailors abandoned the war, deserting their units. It is estimated that 200,000 Union soldiers deserted (80,000 of whom were caught and returned) and that at least 104,000 Confederate soldiers deserted (21,000 of whom were caught and returned). War-weariness and concern about their families induced nearly one out of ten Union soldiers and nearly one out of eight Confederate soldiers to desert. If we assume that soldiers who died had not previously deserted, approximately 12 percent of surviving Union soldiers and 16 percent of surviving Confederate soldiers deserted. The many veterans who had once deserted may have experienced considerable difficulty in readjusting to civilian life as the stigma of desertion haunted them.[15]

The nature of Civil War recruiting also influenced the experience of those who volunteered or were drafted. Groups of soldiers were often recruited from one locale and were usually formed into companies consisting of individuals from the same geographic area. At the beginning of the war, they sometimes elected their own officers, choosing popular political leaders or prominent individuals within the community.[16]

The practice of creating units from the same locality had important implications for soldiers' life courses. Rather than being separated from their peers and getting a new start in the armed forces, as American servicemen did in World War II and do today, most men served with friends and neighbors who were familiar with their social background and earlier experiences. Those who distinguished themselves in the Civil War were considered local heroes, and those who deserted might not dare to return to their former homes. Indeed, how soldiers dealt with each other in the army often had repercussions on how their spouses or relatives

---

14   William F. Fox, *Regimental Losses in the American Civil War, 1861–1865* (Albany, 1889); Thomas L. Livermore, *Numbers and Losses in the Civil War in America, 1861–1865* (Boston, 1901). The estimate of those who died from disease is low, since it does not include approximately 30,000 Union soldiers who died of disease in Confederate prisons. McPherson to Vinovskis, June 24, 1987. Despite efforts by both the North and the South to reduce deaths from disease, more men on both sides died from disease than from battle wounds. On deaths from disease on the Union side, see Paul E. Steiner, *Disease in the Civil War: Natural Biological Warfare in 1861–1865* (Springfield, Ill., 1968).

15   For the estimates on desertion, see McPherson, *Ordeal by Fire*, 468. Since approximately 40% of Union and 20% of Confederate deserters were caught and returned to their units, some of them undoubtedly died from disease or were killed in battle. In addition, some soldiers may have deserted more than once. Therefore, the number of surviving Union and Confederate soldiers who deserted was lower than the estimates presented in the text. For a discussion of contemporary attitude toward and treatment of deserters, see Ella Lonn, *Desertion during the Civil War* (New York, 1928).

16   On Civil War recruiting, see Murdock, *One Million Men*, 276–83, and Moore, *Conscription and Conflict in the Confederacy*, 1–10.

treated each other at home during the war. Furthermore, since there was great variation in the mortality experiences of units, some communities lost relatively few of their loved ones, while others must have suffered staggering losses. Thus, the manner of recruiting and assembling soldiers reinforced their previous experiences and sometimes dramatically altered the life of a whole local community.[17]

Certain characteristics of the Civil War – high rates of participation, high rates of disability and death, widespread desertion, service in locally based units – may have affected soldiers and sailors. But what about their personal experiences in that conflict? How did military service affect them at the time and after the war? The few works published on the lives of ordinary soldiers suggest that individuals reacted to military life and the war in many different ways. Some relished the opportunity to participate in a great undertaking and welcomed the danger and excitement that accompanied battles. Many others quickly tired of long marches and short rations and dreaded the terror of facing death at the next encounter.[18] How their wartime experiences shaped their subsequent lives in unknown, since little research has been done on Civil War veterans.

While there are a few general studies of the soldiers in the Civil War, there is even less information about the lives of civilians. Most historians assume that few civilians were wounded or killed during the fighting. The great majority of battles occurred in the South, so most Northern communities escaped direct physical damage. One might speculate that the devastation of crops and farm animals in the South during the later stages of the Civil War created severe hardships that weakened civilians and made them more susceptible to disease. Furthermore, soldiers who were exposed to new diseases such as malaria may have brought them back to their own communities after the war.[19]

The economic impact of the war on the North was quite different from

17 For example, Samuel Cormany's part in helping to demote an inefficient noncommissioned officer poisoned his wife's formerly close relationship to that man's spouse at home. See James C. Mohr and Richard E. Winslow III, eds., *The Cormany Diaries: A Northern Family in the Civil War* (Pittsburgh, 1982), 369; Fox, *Regimental Losses*, 1–10; Livermore, *Numbers and Losses*, 63–6, 70–139.

18 On the varied experiences of combat in the Civil War, see Gerald F. Linderman, *Embattled Courage: The Experience of Combat in the American Civil War* (New York, 1987). On the differences between Union and Confederate soldiers, based on a content analysis of diaries and letters, see Michael Barton, *Goodmen: The Character of Civil War Soldiers* (University Park, 1981). Numerous published letter collections and diaries of individual soldiers provide useful information about Civil War experiences. For an annotated introduction to such materials, see Murdock, *Civil War in the North*, 529–65.

19 Steiner, *Disease in the Civil War*, 12–36. It is difficult to obtain figures on civilian casualties in the Civil War. McPherson has guessed that about 50,000 civilians in the South perished because of the war. McPherson, *Battle Cry of Freedom*, 619n53.

that on the South. While Southerners experienced more scarcity of goods and more war-related destruction of property, many Northerners benefited from economic growth. Both sides, however, suffered from high rates of inflation that reduced the real incomes of workers and from new wartime taxes that drained their resources. Some historians have argued that overall the Civil War stimulated economic growth and prosperity in the North, but more recent scholarship emphasizes the negative economic impact of the war on the North. For example, the rate of industrialization and the growth of per capita wealth slowed during the Civil War decade, marking a major departure from earlier decades.[20] In addition, the growth of population by immigration was severely curtailed. Claudia D. Goldin estimates that the Civil War reduced immigration by approximately 1.3 million people – nearly twice the number lost in the armed conflict itself. She speculates that the combined effect of the losses in immigration and military deaths was to reduce the population by 5.6 percent from what it would have been without the Civil War; however, that figure is probably too high, because Goldin overestimates the decline in immigration.[21]

Newburyport and the Civil War

A sizable proportion of military-age white males fought in the Civil War, and many of them died, suffered wounds, or deserted. But did the Civil War affect everyone equally, or were there large differences in the experiences of participants from different ethnic and socioeconomic back-

20   Stephen J. DeCanio and Joel Mokyr, "Inflation and the Wage Lag during the American Civil War," *Explorations in Economic History,* 14 (October 1977), 311–36. On scarcity and poverty in the South, see Paul D. Escott, "Poverty and Governmental Aid for the Poor in Confederate North Carolina," *North Carolina Historical Review,* 61 (October 1984), 462–80. Goldin and Lewis, "Economic Cost of the American Civil War"; McPherson, *Battle Cry of Freedom,* 816. McPherson argues that the Civil War had a positive economic impact on the North, but his assessment is not so well grounded as the work done by economic historians. For example, he does not calculate what the per capita income of the North would have been if the Civil War had not occurred.

21   The source for Goldin's estimate of immigrants is the work of Chester W. Wright. Wright, however, estimates a total decrease of some 1.3 million people (3.8%) – 635,000 due to Civil War deaths and 500,000 due to reduced immigration – not a 1.3 million decrease in immigration. I am indebted to James M. McPherson for raising questions about Goldin's estimate of the decrease in immigration. Goldin, "War," 947–8; Chester W. Wright, "Economic Consequences of War: Costs of Production," *Journal of Economic History,* 3 (December 1943), 1–26, esp. 11; McPherson to Vinovskis, June 24, 1987. The Civil War did not have a more profound long-term demographic impact partly because increased immigration after the war replaced many of those killed. On nineteenth-century immigration to the United States, see U.S. Department of Commerce, Bureau of the Census, *Historical Statistics of the United States: Colonial Times to 1970,* 2 vols. (Washington, 1975), series C89–119, 1:105–6.

grounds? If it was a "poor man's" fight, for example, as many contemporaries complained, then the human costs of the war would have been disproportionately borne by those in lower-class occupations.

Since there are no detailed national statistics on the characteristics of those who fought and died in the Civil War, it is convenient to pursue those questions on the local level, where participants' characteristics can be determined.[22] Although no city is representative or typical of the North as a whole, Newburyport, Massachusetts, provides a useful setting for such an investigation. In 1860 Newburyport was a small maritime community of 13,000 individuals, with an ethnically diverse population (almost entirely white but about one-fifth foreign-born). The construction of five steam-powered cotton mills had revitalized the city economically in the 1840s and early 1850s, but it suffered hard times after the panic of 1857. During the Civil War itself, the city recovered, as the demand for its goods and services increased.[23]

One of the major reasons for selecting Newburyport is the availability of excellent military records describing the role of its citizens in the Civil War. Although the city, like most other communities, did not keep complete and detailed records on the townspeople who contributed to the war effort, George W. Creasey, a Civil War veteran himself, devoted nearly three and a half decades of his life to meticulously tracing and recording the Civil War experiences of Newburyport soldiers. He consulted military records in Boston and Washington, D.C., and interviewed many survivors of the war. Although some errors may exist in his work, his compilation provides a more complete and comprehensive record than could be assembled today by someone relying only on surviving written documents.[24]

22   Few scholars have studied the characteristics of those who fought in the Civil War, but a few historians have analyzed the backgrounds of soldiers in small units. Earl J. Hess, "The 12th Missouri Infantry: A Socio-Military Profile of a Union Regiment," *Missouri Historical Review*, 76 (October 1981), 53–77; David F. Riggs, "Sailors of the U.S.S. *Cairo*: Anatomy of a Gunboat Crew," *Civil War History*, 28 (September 1982), 266–73. On soldiers from a small western Massachusetts community, see Harris, "Sons and Soldiers." The only comparison of those who enlisted with those who did not is W. J. Rorabaugh, "Who Fought for the North in the Civil War? Concord, Massachusetts, Enlistments," *Journal of American History*, 73 (December 1986), 695–701.

23   An additional advantage of using Newburyport is the availability of useful monographs about it. See, for example, Benjamin W. Labaree, *Patriots and Partisans: The Merchants of Newburyport, 1764–1815* (Cambridge, Mass., 1962); Susan Grigg, *The Dependent Poor of Newburyport: Studies in Social History, 1800–1830* (Ann Arbor, 1984); Thernstrom, *Poverty and Progress;* E. Vale Smith, *History of Newburyport from the Earliest Settlement of the Country to the Present Time* (Newburyport, 1854); John J. Currier, *The History of Newburyport, Massachusetts, 1764–1905,* 2 vols. (Newburyport, 1906–9).

24   George W. Creasey, *The City of Newburyport in the Civil War, from 1861 to 1865*

As part of a larger study of Newburyport during the Civil War, the data compiled by Creasey from military records were linked to demographic and socioeconomic information in the federal manuscript census of 1860. In addition, high school attendance records were linked to the two data sets. Although the results reported here are only a preliminary assessment of the impact of the Civil War on Newburyport residents, they provide a more detailed analysis of participation in the Union forces than heretofore available and suggest the information that can be gleaned from community studies.

Compared with Northerners in general, Newburyport residents were more likely than men from other places to enroll in the army or navy. The 1,337 different servicemen credited to the city represent 45 percent of the total number of males aged 13 to 43 listed in the 1860 Newburyport census, whereas throughout the North an estimated 35 percent of men of that age group enrolled.[25] To gather background information on the servicemen from Newburyport, a subset of all of the soldiers and sailors who could be identified in the 1860 federal census for that city was created. The number of soldiers and sailors from Newburyport who could be linked to the 1860 census, however, was only 728 – about 55 percent of individuals credited to the city throughout the war and 48 percent of those listed in Creasey's compilation. Although some biases may have been introduced by using the linked set of military and census data, overall this sample provides a fairly accurate picture of the characteristics of men from Newburyport who served in the war.[26]

(Boston, 1903). Creasey found that many servicemen's records were inaccurate and had to be corrected from other sources. Indeed, the reliance on any single set of data can be problematic, due to reporting errors; therefore studies drawing on several sources of information are more reliable. Creasey gathered information on everyone in the military whose enlistment was credited to the city of Newburyport or who was a resident of that community but enrolled in another area. In addition, he included the military activities of some former Newburyport citizens who had moved elsewhere before the Civil War. He found information on 1,562 soldiers and sailors – 225 of whom were credited to other communities.

25 The percentage estimates for Newburyport and the North are based on the total number of servicemen, divided by the number of white male residents aged 13 to 43. Since some of the servicemen were under age 13 or above age 43 in 1860, the estimates are slightly higher than the figures would be if we used only the enlistees aged 13 to 43 in 1860. Unfortunately, we do not have complete and comprehensive national information on the ages of enlistees in the Union army and navy.

26 There are several possible explanations for the difficulty in linking enlistees with Newburyport residents enumerated in the federal manuscript census of 1860. First, perhaps a few individuals could not be matched because of inadequate or incorrect information. More likely, some 1860 residents of Newburyport moved elsewhere during the war, and some enlistees migrated to Newburyport after the census was taken. Given the high population turnover of antebellum cities, it is difficult to match residents in any community with individuals described in records generated two to five years later – particularly men in their twenties, who were especially mobile. Some soldiers and

The ages of Newburyport men serving in the Civil War ranged from 11 to 63 years in 1860. Most were in their late teens or twenties. Only one boy aged 11 in 1860 enrolled later, and very few aged 50 and above ever enrolled. This analysis focuses on those aged 12 to 49 in 1860 (that category includes 98 percent of all soldiers or sailors identified in the manuscript census). Information on the military experiences of New-buryport servicemen comes from Creasey. The census provides data on age, ethnicity, occupation, wealth, and enrollment in school. School records report high school attendance.

In the only other study of those who joined or did not join the Union forces, W. J. Rorabaugh used cross tabulation to analyze his Concord, Massachusetts, data. Using that technique, Rorabaugh calculated the percentage of men enlisting by some other variable, such as their property ownership or occupation. That approach does not allow the analyst to make reasonable inferences about the relative importance of each of the independent variables (for example, property ownership or occupation) in predicting whether or not someone enlisted – especially when tests of the strength of those relationships are not calculated.[27] This study improves on Rorabaugh's statistical analysis by employing multiple classification analysis (MCA), which permits assessment of the relationship between each independent variable and whether or not someone from Newburyport enlisted. Thus, it is possible to determine not only the relationship between enlisting and ethnicity, separate from the effects of the other variables, but also the relative ability of the different variables to predict the likelihood of an individual's enlisting.[28]

sailors credited to Newburyport may have lived elsewhere in 1860 but decided to enlist there because of the relatively generous municipal bounties that Newburyport offered to avoid resorting to the draft. In a comparable study of enlistments from Concord, Massachusetts, W. J. Rorabaugh matched 47.8% of those on the military list for that community with the manuscript census data for 1860. Rorabaugh, "Who Fought for the North in the Civil War?", 697.

   It is not clear what biases may result from the failure to find many Newburyport soldiers and sailors in the federal manuscript census of 1860. I have used information from Creasey on the age, nativity, and rank at first muster of all soldiers and sailors in a multiple classification analysis (MCA) of individuals who were linked compared with those who were not. It reveals that those aged 19 and under in 1860 were more apt to be found in the 1860 census than men in their early twenties; individuals in the army (especially noncommissioned officers) were more apt to be found than those in the navy; and the native-born were more apt to be found than the foreign-born. On most indicators of what happened to someone during the war (such as being wounded or killed), there was little difference between the matched and unmatched records. On the issue of desertion, however, there was a significant difference. Only 2% of those linked, but 13% of those not linked, deserted.

27 Rorabaugh, "Who Fought for the North in the Civil War?"

28 Due to limitations of space, the MCA results reported in this chapter will not be reproduced in detail. A more comprehensive analysis of the Newburyport soldiers in the Civil War will be published elsewhere later. Anyone interested in the specific tables

Since many of the young teenagers who reached military age during the war had not yet entered the labor force or accumulated any personal property in 1860, the sample was separated into two groups. For individuals aged 12 to 17, the occupations and wealth of their parents were used as the indicator; for those aged 18 to 49, their own occupations and wealth were used. To minimize any distortions introduced by using different criteria for the two subgroups, separate multiple classification analyses were run on each group. The two groups were analyzed for the influence of six variables on the enlistment of Newburyport men: age, ethnicity, occupation, wealth, school attendance, and educational attainment.[29]

As expected, age was the best predictor of whether or not someone enlisted in the armed forces. About one-half of those aged 16 to 17 in 1860 fought in the Civil War, as did nearly four-tenths of those aged 18 to 24. Only one-sixth of men in their thirties in 1860 joined the Union forces, and only one-twentieth of those in their forties joined.[30]

There is considerable controversy over the participation rate of foreign-born men in the Union army. Many scholars claim that foreign-born soldiers predominated in Northern units, but more recent work suggests that foreign-born men were represented at a rate equal to, or less than, that of native-born men. In Newburyport the foreign-born were much less likely to enlist in the Union forces than the native-born. Aliens who had not taken out naturalization papers were not subject to the military draft, and many foreigners in the North were hostile to the entire war effort – especially those who perceived it as an unnecessary crusade to free slaves. Somewhat surprisingly, second-generation Americans were even more likely to serve than children of native-born parents. Perhaps second-generation youth, who were subject to the draft, wanted to display and prove their attachment to the United States, despite any misgivings their parents may have had about the war. Alternatively, or in addition, second-generation Americans may have been less able to avoid military service by hiring substitutes or paying the $300 commutation

referred to in this chapter should consult the longer, preliminary version of this essay available from the author. For a clear and lucid introduction to the use of MCA, see Frank Andrew, N. J. Morgan, John A. Sonquist, and Laura Klem, *Multiple Classification Analysis* (Ann Arbor, 1973).

29   The division of Newburyport males into two subgroups (aged 12 to 17, and 18 to 49) is based on an analysis of the pattern of school attendance in the town on the eve of the Civil War. See Maris A. Vinovskis, "Patterns of High School Attendance in Newburyport, Massachusetts, in 1860," paper presented at the American Historical Association Meeting, New York City, December 1985 (in Vinovskis's possession).

30   Rorabaugh found a similar pattern in Concord: 35% of those aged 16 to 20 in 1860 enlisted, 22% of those aged 21 to 29, 13% of those aged 30 to 39, and 8% of those aged 40 to 49. Rorabaugh, "Who Fought for the North in the Civil War?", 696.

fees. Ethnicity was the second-best predictor of participation in the Civil War.[31]

Many contemporaries portrayed the Civil War as a "poor man's" fight, since the well-to-do could afford to hire substitutes or pay commutation fees.[32] Therefore one might expect that in Newburyport unskilled workers or their children would have enlisted in disproportional numbers. Yet the results of the MCAs reveal that among those in the 12 to 17 age group the sons of fathers employed at high-status white-collar or skilled jobs joined at much higher rates than the sons of unskilled workers. Among adults, the skilled workers were also more likely to enlist than the unskilled workers, but in that age group the few individuals in high-status white-collar occupations were particularly averse to serving and enrolled at a very low rate (although most of that differential disappears once we control for the effects of the other independent variables).

With regard to wealth, the expected pattern of greater wealth predicting lower enrollment is confirmed but with a surprising similarity in the two rates. The rate of enrollment for youths with parents having less than $100 total wealth was 29 percent, and the rate for those with the wealthiest parents was 24 percent. Adult males whose total wealth was $1,000 or more were less likely to enlist than those with less wealth. Therefore, although there were differences in the rates of enrollment by occupation and wealth, those differences are not large enough to justify describing the war as a "poor man's" fight.[33]

31 The most detailed study of foreigners in the Union forces emphasizes the disproportionately high rate of enlistment by the foreign-born. Ella Lonn, *Foreigners in the Union Army and Navy* (Baton Rouge, 1951). For recent questions about that interpretation, see McPherson, *Ordeal by Fire*, 358–9. Rorabaugh also found that the Irish were less likely to enlist than the native-born population. Rorabaugh, "Who Fought for the North in the Civil War?", 697. Unfortunately, he did not distinguish between the participation of second-generation Americans and that of young men with native-born parents. Since very few men from either Newburyport or Massachusetts as a whole were drafted, it is unlikely that large numbers of second-generation Americans there who lacked funds to hire substitutes or pay commutation fees were drafted. The draft, however, may have induced such individuals to "volunteer" (and thus secure generous bounties), since otherwise they were likely to be drafted. Creasey, *City of Newburyport in the Civil War*, 124–5, 135–6.

32 Murdock, *One Million Men*, 178–217.

33 Rorabaugh, looking only at the native-born population, found that the propertyless were much more likely to enlist than the propertied. Enlistees were also underrepresented among the mercantile and professional elite but overrepresented among propertied small shopkeepers, clerks, and skilled workers in their twenties and skilled workers in their thirties. He speculates that "a combination of economic and social malaise" on the eve of the Civil War may explain the socioeconomic differentiation he found in enrollments. Rorabaugh, "Who Fought for the North in the Civil War?", 699. Although Rorabaugh's suggestions are intriguing, they are limited by the small cell sizes in his analysis and his inability to adequately control for the effects of other potentially important variables. Nevertheless, his call for more attention to the socio-

The effect of education on enlistment can be gauged by asking two questions: Did attendance at school deter enlistment? How did the level of education attained affect enlistment? Since most children in nineteenth-century Newburyport completed their education well before they were likely to enlist, few would have declined to join in order to complete their schooling.[34] Those who indicated in the census of 1860 that they were still enrolled in school (either common school, high school, or college) were less likely to enlist than those who had already entered the labor force – even after one controls for the effects of other factors, such as the age of the child. Current enrollment in school was the weakest predictor of military participation.

A better indicator of the influence of education on enlistment was high school training. That measure of education was the third best predictor of enlistment. A great swell of patriotic fervor swept through the Newburyport high schools after the war began, yet former high school students were less likely to enroll than those who had not attended any high school. One out of every five former high school students enrolled, but almost one out of every three who never attended high school enrolled.[35]

Thus far we have examined some factors that might predict which Newburyport residents would participate in the Civil War. We now turn to a consideration of the effects of that experience on the participants. Four important measures of the impact of military service are the likelihood of dying, being wounded, being discharged as disabled, or deserting. Many of the studies of the effects of twentieth-century wars on the life course of individuals focus on experiences such as marriage, education, or job mobility, without adequate attention to those more direct outcomes of participation in a war.

Of the Newburyport servicemen identified in the manuscript census and aged 12 to 49 in 1860, 13 percent died of wounds or disease during the Civil War. That percentage is somewhat lower than the aggregate estimate that 17 percent of all white Union soldiers and sailors died in the Civil War. To a large degree the lower mortality rate for Newbury-

economic differentials in enlistment, as well as his attempt to relate them to larger developments in antebellum society, are to be commended.

34 Vinovskis, "Patterns of High School Attendance in Newburyport."

35 We have no measure of the years of schooling received by adult males. However, the federal manuscript census of 1860 did indicate the literacy of adults. Many nineteenth-century commentators and twentieth-century historians assumed that illiterates were disproportionately likely to serve in the Union forces. The results of the MCA on men aged 20 to 49 in 1860 present a different picture. In Newburyport, 19% of literate men enlisted, but 6% of the illiterate did. Even after the effects of age, ethnicity, occupation, and wealth are controlled for, illiterates were still likely to enlist – although the differential between the two groups was considerably narrowed. Overall, an adult male's literacy was the weakest predictor of his participating in the Civil War.

port reflects the high proportion of Newburyport men who served in the navy, since the navy suffered fewer losses than the army.

Approximately 16 percent of Newburyport soldiers and sailors were wounded but survived. Altogether, 29 percent of the town's servicemen were either wounded or killed during the Civil War. Only 2 percent of those in the military who could be identified in the federal manuscript census deserted, but, as indicated earlier, a much higher proportion of those who could not be identified deserted. Adding the small number who deserted, 31 percent of all Newburyport soldiers in the sample either died, were wounded, or deserted. Thus one out of every eight servicemen from Newburyport who fought for the Union died, and one out of every five who survived the war was either wounded or had deserted.

Many Newburyport soldiers and sailors, including some of the wounded, were discharged from the armed forces as disabled. Almost one out of every five servicemen was discharged due to a disability.[36] Altogether, at least 42 percent of those who fought in the Civil War from Newburyport were killed, wounded, deserted, or discharged as disabled. Thus, the immediate adverse effects of the war on many participants' life courses are evident.

Newburyport soldiers' and sailors' chances of being killed or wounded during the Civil War varied, depending on their age and socioeconomic status.[37] As before, the sample was subdivided into those aged 12 to 17 in 1860 and those aged 18 to 49 in 1860, so that young teenagers without occupation or personal wealth could be assigned to appropriate social and economic categories. Each group was analyzed to determine the extent to which age, ethnicity, occupation, wealth, and service experiences can predict casualty outcomes, but space limits us to only a brief discussion of the results.

Servicemen aged 12 to 14 in 1860 were less likely to be killed or wounded than those aged 15 to 17. The obvious explanation for the differential is that many of them became old enough to join only late in the war and therefore served shorter times. Among soldiers and sailors aged 18 to 49 in 1860, the youngest and the oldest were the most likely to be killed or wounded.[38] Although age is the strongest predictor of enlistment in the

36 Since Creasey did not always indicate whether or not someone discharged for wounds was disabled, the actual percentage of discharged servicemen who were disabled was probably higher than the 20% figure.

37 Separate MCAs were run on whether or not someone was killed, was wounded, or deserted and whether or not someone was killed, was wounded, was disabled, or deserted. The results of the latter two analyses were generally similar to the one based on whether or not a serviceman was killed or wounded (although the percentage of servicemen affected was higher).

38 Future investigations will calculate the likelihood of being killed or wounded, taking into consideration the total months enrolled in the armed forces.

Civil War, it is the weakest predictor of whether or not a serviceman died or was wounded.

Foreign-born and second-generation American soldiers and sailors were more likely to die or to be wounded than servicemen with native-born parents. Perhaps foreign-born soldiers were more susceptible to disease, since then tended to be less affluent than their native-born comrades. Although foreign-born youths and adults were the least likely to enlist in the Union forces, they were much more likely to be casualties then native-born troops of either age group.

Servicemen from disadvantaged backgrounds were more likely to be killed or wounded during the Civil War than servicemen with higher-ranking jobs or greater wealth. The generally inverse relationship between socioeconomic status and the probability of dying or being wounded, even when the effects of the other independent variables are controlled for, raises intriguing questions. Was the health of Newburyport's lower-status citizens generally poorer at enlistment, leaving them more susceptible to disease? Or were they assigned to units that were given particularly dangerous missions?

The last factor to be considered is the particular branch of service that a Newburyport enlistee joined. This variable was subdivided into three categories: the experience of army privates, of army officers, and of those who enlisted in the navy. Among the younger enlistees, army officers were more likely to be killed or wounded than army privates or those who joined the navy. Among servicemen aged 18 to 49 in 1860, however, army officers were less likely to be wounded or to die than army privates or those in the navy. Overall, this variable was the best predictor of whether or not a serviceman was killed or wounded in the Civil War.

Our examination of Newburyport servicemen indicates widespread participation in the war effort among males aged 13 to 49 in 1860. Although there were some occupational and wealth differences in the rates of enlistment, Union soldiers and sailors were not disproportionately recruited from the lower socioeconomic groups in Newburyport. Second-generation Americans were the most likely to enlist, and the foreign-born were the least likely. Despite the strong support for the war in the secondary schools, those Newburyport youths who received more education were less likely to enlist – even though most of them had already completed their education. However, among adult males Newburyport illiterates were underrepresented in the Union forces.

If the likelihood of a Newburyport resident's participating in the Civil War differed only moderately depending on his occupation, wealth, or level of education, the likelihood of his being killed or wounded differed considerably depending on those variables. Servicemen from the lower socioeconomic segments of Newburyport society were much more likely to be killed or wounded than those from the more privileged segment. In addition, the foreign-born servicemen experienced a particularly high casualty rate, even though they had been less willing to enlist initially. The relative casualty rates among privates and officers in the army were mixed for the two age groups, but in both groups those in the navy were much less likely to be killed or wounded.

Civil War Pensions and Union Veterans

Almost nothing has been written about the postwar experiences of Civil War veterans. Although considerable work is available on the aggregate economic impact of the Civil War, social historians have ignored the impact of that conflict on the large number of veterans who survived. Undoubtedly, wounds and war memories affected many Union and Confederate soldiers decades after the war and helped determine their employment opportunities. Well after the war itself had ended, the Civil War experience continued to shape the outlook of some, such as Oliver Wendell Holmes, Jr.[39]

But the influence of the Civil War went beyond the devastation caused by the loss of lives and property or by the memories imprinted on the minds of the survivors. The pension programs created for Union soldiers had a profound and longlasting impact on the lives of veterans. On July 14, 1862, President Abraham Lincoln signed into law an act that became the basis for all subsequent federal pension legislation until 1890. It provided for monthly payments to men totally disabled and to the widows

39 On the economic impact of the Civil War, see Ralph Andreano, ed., *The Economic Impact of the American Civil War* (Cambridge, Mass., 1967); Stanley L. Engerman, "The Economic Impact of the Civil War," in *The Reinterpretation of American Economic History*, ed. Robert W. Fogel and Stanley L. Engerman (New York, 1971), 369–79; Goldin, "War"; Goldin and Lewis, "Economic Cost of the American Civil War"; and Patrick O'Brien, *The Economic Effects of the American Civil War* (Atlantic Highlands, N.J., 1988). We have no general studies of how being a Civil War veteran affected a man's employment after the war. But see Daniel E. Sutherland, "Former Confederates in the post–Civil War North: An Unexplored Aspect of Reconstruction History," *Journal of Southern History*, 48 (August 1981), 393–410. For an analysis of 1,250 Tennessee Confederates, based on questionnaires administered between 1915 and 1923, see Fred A. Bailey, *Class and Tennessee's Confederate Generation* (Chapel Hill, 1987). For an intriguing interpretation and an introduction to the literature on the postwar effects of the Civil War on Southerners, see Gaines M. Foster, *Ghosts of the Confederacy: Defeat, the Lost Cause, and the Emergence of the New South* (New York, 1987). On the lifelong impact of Civil War experiences, see Hiller B. Zobel, "Enlisted for Life," *American Heritage*, 37 (June / July 1986), 56–64, and George M. Fredrickson, *The Inner Civil War: Northern Intellectuals and the Crisis of the Union* (New York, 1965). Unfortunately, nothing comparable to Fredrickson's work on intellectuals has been done on the postwar experiences of common soldiers.

of those killed during service. Before the end of the war, further legislation granted higher compensation to veterans suffering specific disabilities (such as the loss of both hands or both feet). After the war, Union veterans or their dependents received additional payments, whereas their Confederate counterparts received neither federal nor state aid. Only after Reconstruction did some of the Southern states provide even minimal help for Confederate veterans.[40]

From 1861 to 1885, 555,038 pension claims were filed alleging the existence of service-caused disabilities, and 300,204 of them were allowed. Likewise, 335,296 claims of widows, minor children, or dependent relatives were filed during the same period for deaths of soldiers due to war-related causes, and 220,825 of them were allowed. Many of the claims were judged invalid, because the pension law required claimants to prove that the serviceman's disability or death was due to military service. As a result, there was great political pressure in the late 1880s to provide Civil War pensions for all who had served in the Union forces. On June 27, 1890, Congress passed a new pension act, providing that anyone who had served in the Union forces for ninety days or more during the Civil War, had received an honorable discharge, and was disabled for any cause whatsoever was entitled to a pension. The Act of 1890 eventually provided assistance to thousands of Union veterans as they became incapacitated by illnesses associated with aging.[41]

Some analyses of the legislative and administrative aspects of federal pension aid in the nineteenth century are available, but virtually nothing has been done from the vantage point of the veteran or his dependents.[42] It is very difficult even to speculate about the probable impact of the program on individual veterans or their families, since the necessary data have never been compiled or analyzed. Nevertheless, using very fragmentary published statistics, the contours of the federal pension program for Union veterans can be sketched.

40 On the federal legislation affecting Civil War veterans, see William Henry Glasson, *History of Military Pension Legislation in the United States* (New York, 1900), 20–106; Glasson, *Federal Military Pensions*, 123–42; Gustavus A. Weber and Laurence F. Schmeckebier, *The Veterans' Administration: Its History, Activities, and Organization* (Washington, 1934); and Gustavus A. Weber, *The Bureau of Pensions: Its History, Activities, and Organization* (Baltimore, 1923).

41 Glasson, *Federal Military Pensions*, 125–42; Heywood T. Sanders, "Paying for the 'Bloody Shirt': The Politics of Civil War Pensions," in *Political Benefits: Empirical Studies of American Public Programs*, ed. Barry S. Rundquist (Lexington, Mass., 1980), 137–59.

42 On Northern veterans' agitation for more federal pension support, see Mary R. Dearing, *Veterans in Politics: The Story of the G.A.R.* (Baton Rouge, 1952). On the composition of the Grand Army of the Republic at the local level and the types of individuals who joined it, see Stuart Charles McConnell, "A Social History of the Grand Army of the Republic, 1867–1900," Ph.D. diss., Johns Hopkins University, 1987.

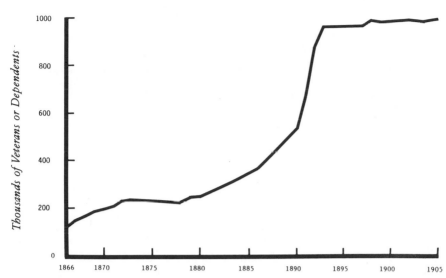

Figure 1.3. Veterans or their dependents receiving federal pension benefits, 1866–1905. *Source:* William H. Glasson, *Federal Military Pensions in the United States* (New York, 1918), 273.

The number of Union veterans and veterans' dependents receiving federal pension benefits immediately after the Civil War was rather small, but it grew rapidly in the late nineteenth century – especially after the passage of the act of 1890, which relaxed eligibility requirements (see Figure 1.3). The number of veterans or their dependents receiving federal pensions rose from 126,722 in 1866 to a high of 999,446 in 1902 (at the later date a few pensioners were veterans of the Spanish-American War). The last Union veteran survived until 1956, and in 1987, 66 widows and children of men who had fought for the Union or the Confederacy remained on the federal pension rolls.[43]

Initially, many of the recipients of veterans' benefits were widows or children of deceased Union soldiers – 58 percent in 1866. But as the eligibility requirements for pensions were relaxed and as more veterans

43 Glasson, *Federal Military Pensions*, 273. Since 1862, federal policy had stated that those who were not loyal to the Union during the Civil War were not eligible to receive the benefits of the national pension laws. In 1958 a new law was passed that extended Civil War pension benefits to both Confederate and Union veterans and their dependents (Act of May 23, 1958, Pub. L. no. 85–425, 72 Stat. 133–4). The 1987 figures are from U.S. Veterans Administration, Office of Public Affairs, "America's Wars," Jan. 1988 (in Vinovskis's possession).

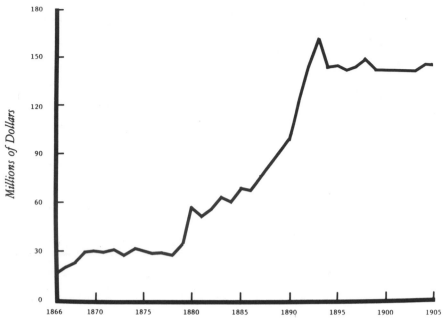

Figure 1.4. Federal veteran benefits, 1866–1905. *Source:* Calculated from William H. Glasson, *Federal Military Pensions in the United States* (New York, 1918), 144, 271; and U.S. Department of Commerce, Bureau of the Census, *Historical Statistics of the United States: Colonial Times to 1970,* 2 vols. (Washington, 1975), series Y960, 2:1145.

themselves applied for them, the proportion of widows or other dependents who received such benefits dropped to 19 percent in 1891.[44]

The percentage of surviving Union soldiers receiving a federal pension also changed dramatically over time (see Figure 1.4). In 1866 only 2 percent of Union veterans received any financial assistance from the federal government for their services in the war. By 1895 that figure had jumped to 63 percent – largely as the result of the changes in pension legislation. In fact, by 1900 the Pension Bureau began to treat the disability pensions as old-age assistance to Union veterans. Commissioner H. Clay Evans instructed the examining doctors, "A claimant who has reached the age of 75 years is allowed the maximum rate for senility alone, even when there are no special pensionable disabilities. A claimant who has attained the age of 65 is allowed at least the minimum rate, unless he appears to have unusual vigor and ability for the performance

44 Glasson, *Federal Military Pensions,* 144, 271.

of manual labor in one of that age."[45] Thus, by 1900 the United States government had in effect developed a very extensive and expensive old-age assistance program for veterans.

It is difficult to estimate exactly how important veterans' pensions were for nineteenth-century Americans, but some general statements can be made. Overall, only a small proportion of the adult white population received veterans' pensions – about 1 percent in 1870 and 4 percent in 1900. Thus, one might speculate that federal pensions had relatively little impact on Americans.

But such a conclusion does not take into account the age distribution of veterans. Since most soldiers in the Civil War were quite young, we need to follow the cohort of individuals who were in their late teens and early twenties during the Civil War. We find that 56 percent of all white males aged 25 to 29 and 34 percent of those aged 30 to 34 in 1870 were Union veterans. Similarly, 48 percent of all white males aged 55 to 59 and 29 percent of those aged 60 to 64 in 1900 were Union veterans. (Since Union veterans constituted only about 70 to 75 percent of all veterans from the North and South together, an even larger proportion of white males in certain age cohorts had fought in the Civil War on either the Union or the Confederate side).[46]

To understand nineteenth-century Americans' experience with federal pensions, we need to bear in mind both the widespread military participation by men of certain cohorts and the increasing availability of pensions as those cohorts aged. One can roughly guess, given the percentages of Union veterans and the overall proportion of them who received federal pensions, that in 1870 only about 1 percent of white males aged 25 to 34 received such pensions. But by 1900, 30 percent of all white males aged 55 to 59 and 18 percent of those aged 60 to 64 were receiving federal pensions.[47] Thus a surprisingly high percentage of Civil War vet-

---

45 Ibid., 243.
46 Calculated from Bureau of the Census, *Historical Statistics of the United States,* series A119–34, 1:15–18, and series Y943–56, 2:1144. Since an estimated 5% of Union veterans were blacks, the data have been adjusted. The estimate that 70% of all veterans were Union veterans is from the federal census of 1890, which inquired about the veteran status of the population. See U.S. Department of the Interior, *Report on the Population of the United States at the Eleventh Census: 1890,* 2 vols. (Washington, 1895), 1, Pt. 1, 803–4. If one calculates the estimated number of Union and Confederate soldiers and sailors and subtracts the number killed, then Union veterans made up about 75% of all veterans in 1865.
47 This estimate, which is only approximate, relies on the calculations of the percentage of white males in 1870 and 1900 who were veterans. Using additional data from William H. Glasson on the number of Union veterans receiving federal pensions in 1870 or in 1900 and assuming that the likelihood of having a federal pension was uniform for all age groups of veterans, the percentage of white males receiving a federal pension could be calculated. Glasson, *Federal Military Pensions,* 144, 271.

Figure 1.5. Veteran benefits as a share of federal budget, 1866–1905. *Source:* Calculated from U.S. Department of Commerce, Bureau of the Census, *Historical Statistics of the United States: Colonial Times to 1970,* 2 vols. (Washington, 1975), series Y336, Y971, 2:1104, 1115.

erans received a form of old-age assistance from the federal government. Finally, if we take into consideration the pensioned widows and dependents of deceased Union soldiers, a high proportion of Americans of the cohorts that reached adulthood about the time of the Civil War benefited from federal aid in their old age, thirty or forty years before the creation of the federal Social Security system.

The financial aspects of the federal veterans' pension program also need to be examined. How much money was involved overall, what percentage of the federal budget went to veterans' pensions, and how much did the average claimant receive? The amount of money provided through the federal veterans' pension program started low and rose sharply. In 1866 the federal government spent $15.9 million on veteran benefits. By 1893 it was spending $165.3 million – an increase reflecting the rapid expansion of the number of veterans eligible for the benefits. As a percentage of the federal budget, expenditures for Civil War veterans greatly exceeded those for veterans today (which consume less that 3 percent of that budget) (see Figure 1.5). In fact, the percentage of the federal budget allocated to veterans' pension benefits rose steadily throughout the nineteenth century, until the expenses associated with the Spanish-American

War greatly expanded the total budget and thereby reduced the veterans' percentage. In 1893 veterans' benefits to former Union soldiers or their dependents constituted more than 40 percent of the overall federal budget.[48]

Finally, we need to consider the financial impact of the federal pension program on the recipients. If the amount of money received by each recipient was very small, then the influence of the program, despite the large number of people it reached, may have been minimal. On the other hand, if the sum of money provided for veterans or their survivors was large, then the program played an important role in supporting significant numbers of Americans in the second half of the nineteenth century.

In real dollars, the amount of money per recipient from the federal veterans' pension programs was substantial, and it grew rapidly in the 1880s. In current dollars, the average recipient received $122 annually in 1866 ($64 in 1860 money) and $139 annually in 1900 ($136 in 1860 money). Considering that the average annual earnings of all employees in 1900 was $375, the average of $139 provided by the federal pension program was substantial – especially by nineteenth century standards.[49] Furthermore, since the act of 1890 did not make veterans' pension payments conditional on economic destitution, some recipients may have used those funds as supplementary income.

In 1890 there were 195,000 white Civil War widows – approximately 10 percent of all white widows at that time. Since 69.3 percent of white Civil War widows in 1890 were those of Union soldiers, many of them were eligible for federal assistance. Civil War widows, like veterans, were particularly concentrated in certain age groups. In 1890, of white widows 65 and older, only 4.5 percent had been married to Civil War soldiers or sailors, but of those aged 45 to 54, fully 18.8 percent had been married to Civil War soldiers or sailors.[50]

We know very little about the effects of the availability of federal benefits on the lives of the widows of Union soldiers or sailors. One intriguing analysis of rural and urban widows in Kent County, Michigan, in 1880, found that women who received a federal pension were slightly

48 Calculated from Bureau of the Census, *Historical Statistics of the United States*, series Y336, Y971, 2:1104, 1145–6.
49 The average amount of money received per recipient is calculated from Glasson, *Federal Military Pensions*, 273. The average annual earnings, adjusted for unemployment during the year, is from Bureau of the Census, *Historical Statistics of the United States*, series D723, 1:164.
50 Calculated from Census Office, *Report on the Population of the United States at the Eleventh Census: 1890*, vol.1, Pt. 1, p. 831, and U.S. Department of Interior, Census Office, *Compendium of the Eleventh Census: 1890*, Pt. 2 (Washington, 1897), 576–9.

more likely to be living in their own households and much less likely to be working than widows who received no federal assistance.[51]

Although the federal pension program for Union veterans and veterans' widows has been mentioned in some accounts of American life in the second half of the nineteenth century, it has not received the attention it deserves. Just as social historians have ignored the impact of the Civil War on the life course of their subjects, so have they failed to investigate how the pensions granted veterans and widows benefited Americans after the war. Similarly, although researchers analyzing changing attitudes and behavior toward the elderly have noted the existence of the federal pension programs for Union soldiers, they have not attempted to investigate their scope and their importance to older Americans in the late nineteenth and early twentieth centuries.[52] Thus the influence of the Civil War on the lives of Americans between 1865 and 1920 remains to be considered.

Conclusion

During the past twenty-five years, the study of the lives of ordinary Americans, based on sources such as the federal manuscript censuses, has been one of the most exciting and productive areas of research in American history. Employing sophisticated statistical and demographic techniques, social historians have revolutionized our knowledge of the experiences of individuals in the nineteenth century. Whereas the study of the American past had earlier been dominated by analyses of political, diplomatic, and military events, today attention has shifted to the investigation of social history.

Although the recent interest in social history has opened unexplored areas for study and introduced new social science techniques for analyzing the past, it has sometimes resulted in the neglect of the more traditional themes and events in our past. Unlike military, intellectual, political, or economic analysts, social historians have lost sight of the centrality of the Civil War. As we have seen in this chapter, the Civil War directly affected the lives of most Americans at that time and left behind a legacy

51 Amy E. Holmes, " 'Such Is the Price We Pay': American Widows and the Civil War Pension System," Chapter 7 in this volume.

52 For example, see W. Andrew Achenbaum, *Old Age in the New Land: The American Experience since 1790* (Baltimore, 1978); William Graebner, *A History of Retirement: The Meaning and Function of an American Institution, 1885–1978* (New Haven, 1980); Carole Haber, *Beyond Sixty-Five: The Dilemma of Old Age in America's Past* (Cambridge, 1983). For a useful discussion that appreciates the importance of Civil War pension programs, see Ann Shola Orloff, "The Politics of Pensions: A Comparative Analysis of the Origins of Pensions and Old Age Insurance in Canada, Great Britian, and the United States," Ph.D. diss., Princeton University, 1985.

that continued to influence them many years after Appomattox. Indeed, it is difficult to imagine how any of us studying the life courses of Americans in the second half of the nineteenth century could have overlooked such a major and tragic experience.

The Civil War was the bloodiest experience in United States history. Almost as many Americans died in that conflict as in all the nation's other wars combined. Nearly one out of five white males of military age died in the South and one out of sixteen in the North. There was widespread participation in the war, but perhaps servicemen from lower socioeconomic backgrounds were particularly likely to be wounded, disabled, or killed.

Perhaps the experiences of men from a wide variety of backgrounds fighting together in the Civil War eased some of the class and ethnic tensions that plagued antebellum society. The camaraderie on the battlefield often continued after the war as veterans gathered in organizations like the Grand Army of the Republic to remember an idealized version of their wartime experiences. Like the fraternal orders of the period, which also cut across class lines, postwar veterans' organizations may have reduced the growing class tensions of an urbanizing and industrializing America during the last third of the nineteenth century.[53]

The impact of the Civil War on the lives of Americans did not end in 1865 but continued throughout the nineteenth and early twentieth centuries. The war left many survivors physically disabled, and some emotionally scarred. While large numbers of Union soldiers or their widows received generous federal pensions, their Southern brethren struggled unassisted to reconstruct their lives after being vanquished. The heritage of the war remained with many – from both sides – for the rest of their lives. There can be little doubt of the importance of the Civil War to that generation, but the exact nature of the war's impact is yet to be specified and analyzed.

The failure of social historians to study the impact of the Civil War on the lives of those who participated in it is not an isolated phenomenon. In general, we have ignored the effect of wars on the life courses of citizens. American scholars and readers have shown great interest in the nation's military heroes and exploits, but very little attention has been paid to the terrible costs of the conflicts to those who lived through them. Yet there is a resurgence of scholarly interest in the effects of wars on

53   On the way local and national activities of the Grand Army of the Republic helped to integrate the North across ethnic and class lines, see McConnell, "Social History of the Grand Army of the Republic." On the role of fraternal orders in transcending class divisions, see Mary Ann Clawson, "Fraternal Orders and Class Formation in the Nineteenth-century United States," *Comparative Studies in Society and History,* 27 (October 1985), 672–95.

soldiers and civilians. As we pursue those questions further, we will be in a better position to understand the consequences of wars and appreciate the importance of specific historical events in the life course of individuals.[54]

54   On the effects of wars, see Glen H. Elder, Jr., "Military Times and Turning Points in Men's Lives," *Developmental Psychology*, 22 (March 1986), 233–45; Glen H. Elder, Jr., "War Mobilization and the Life Course: A Cohort of World War II Veterans," *Sociological Forum*, 2 (Fall 1987), 449–72; Glen H. Elder, Jr., and Yoriko Meguro, "Wartime in Men's Lives: A Comparative Study of American and Japanese Cohorts," *International Journal of Behavioral Development*, 10 (December 1987), 439–66; and John Modell and Duane Steffey, "A People's War to Protect the American Family: Military Service and Family Formation, 1940–1950," paper presented at the Social Science History Association annual meeting, Chicago, November 1985 (in Vinovskis's possession). On the use of life-course analysis to study the impact of historical events, see Glen H. Elder, Jr., "History and the Life Course," in *Biography and Society: The Life Course Approach in the Social Sciences*, ed. D. Bertaux (Beverly Hills, 1981), 77–115; Glen H. Elder, Jr., "Family History and the Life Course," in *Transitions: The Family and the Life Course in Historical Perspective*, ed. Tamara K. Hareven (New York, 1978), 17–64; Maris A. Vinovskis, "From Household Size to the Life Course: Some Observations on Recent Trends in Family History," *American Behavioral Scientist*, 21 (November / December 1977), 263–87; and Maris A. Vinovskis, "The Historian and the Life Course: Reflections on Recent Approaches to the Study of American Family Life in the Past," in *Life-span Development and Behavior*, ed. Paul B. Baltes, David L. Featherman, and Richard M. Lerner (Hillsdale, 1988), 33–59.

2

Community and War: The Civil War Experience of Two New Hampshire Towns

THOMAS R. KEMP

The Civil War was America's bloodiest war, leaving nearly as many dead as all our other wars combined. The significance of this conflict in the minds of Americans is reflected by the vast number of titles on the war, making the Civil War the most written-about subject in American history. The interest in the war is not surprising, because the conflict was, and is, seen as a fight for freedom and a test of whether the American system of government could succeed. Yet despite the importance of the conflict and the interest in it, little has been written about the impact that the war had on the lives of nineteenth-century Americans. Military aspects of the war have drawn the attention of many Civil War historians, but the lives of the common soldier and citizen have been virtually ignored.[1]

My intention in the present chapter is to measure the effect of the Civil War on nineteenth-century America by analyzing the war experience of the soldiers and citizens of two New Hampshire towns: Claremont and Newport. The war's impact on these neighboring communities will be assessed by examining civilian life during and after the war. First I analyze the communities' reaction to the war as it unfolded for the citizens and soldiers of both towns. After showing that the war altered community life and changed attitudes toward warfare, I then examine the socio-

This chapter is a revised version of my "Community and War: The Civil War Experience of Claremont, New Hampshire, and Newport, New Hampshire," senior honors thesis, University of Michigan, 1988.

1 For a discussion of the Civil War being America's bloodiest war, see Maris A. Vinovskis, "Have Social Historians Lost the Civil War? Some Preliminary Demographic Speculations," Chapter 1 of this volume. On the absence of works focusing on the social history of the Civil War, see Vinovskis, Introduction to this volume. For a brief discussion of the relative popularity of the Civil War among American historians, see James M. McPherson, *Battle Cry of Freedom* (New York, 1988), vii–ix.

economic characteristics of individuals from Claremont and Newport who did and did not fight in the war, comparing and contrasting the socioeconomic backgrounds of participants and nonparticipants. I conclude by analyzing the effect of the war on the individuals who fought and on the community as a whole after the war had ended.[2]

Claremont and Newport were selected for this study because of the large number of Civil War–era records that still exist for both towns. Each was settled as an agricultural community in the mid-eighteenth century, but later generations of inhabitants capitalized on the Sugar River, which flows through both towns, by harnessing its power for mills and factories. In 1860 Claremont had a population of 4,026; Newport had a population of 2,077. A contemporary observer considered farmers as having the highest social position in both towns, reflecting the fact that in 1860 farmers owned nearly one-half the total wealth in Claremont and Newport, although they composed only 15 percent of the adult male population. Manufacturing in the two towns also played a significant role in their economies. More than a dozen mills existed in the two towns prior to the outbreak of war, and over one-half of the men aged 18 to 45 had a manufacturing occupation. While having similar economies, the two towns differed politically. Claremont was staunchly Republican: 71 percent of the voters voted Republican in the 1860 March gubernatorial election, and only 29 percent voted Democratic; in Newport, 52 percent voted Democratic and 48 percent Republican in the same election.[3]

2   Very few studies look at a Northern community's Civil War experience. Three that I have found useful for comparison are Emily J. Harris, "Sons and Soldiers: Deerfield, Massachusetts, and the Civil War," *Civil War History*, 30 (June 1984), 157–71; Michael Frisch, *Town into City: Springfield, Massachusetts, and the Meaning of Community, 1840–1880* (Cambridge, Mass., 1972); Dale Prentiss, "Troy, Michigan, in the Civil War Draft," seniors honors thesis, University of Michigan, 1981. By combining data from town records, newspapers, letters, and histories with data from quantitative sources such as military and census records, I have tried to provide a larger picture of the Civil War community experience than has previously been given.

3   Claremont and Newport background information is from Otis F. R. Waite, *History of the Town of Claremont, New Hampshire, for a Period of One Hundred and Thirty Years from 1764 to 1894* (Manchester, N.H., 1895), 167; Edmund Wheeler, *The History of Newport, New Hampshire, from 1766 to 1878, with a Genealogical Register* (Concord, N.H., 1879); George H. Moses, "By the Beautiful Mountain: A Sketch of Claremont," *Granite Monthly*, 16 (1894), 103–23. Claremont and Newport 1860 population figures are from U.S. Census Bureau, "Eighth Census of United States, Sullivan County, New Hampshire, 1860." By recording all data found in the 1860 census for each male between the ages of 13 and 45, I created a census data base of military-age males in Claremont and Newport. This census data base was primarily used for comparing socioeconomic differences between the soldiers and citizens of the two towns. In this essay, "total wealth" is the value of an individual's real estate added to the value of his personal wealth, both of which are provided in the 1860 census. The occupational models used in this study are based on those models found in Theodore Hershberg et al., "Occupation and Ethnicity in Five Nineteenth-century Cities: A Collaborative In-

In analyzing the Civil War experience of Claremont and Newport, it is important to look at the mood and expectations of the two towns at the outbreak of the war, in order to understand their later reactions. The expectations of any community going into war often differ from what actually occurs, and the difference between the two can be used as a measure of the psychological impact of the event. For Claremont and Newport, the expectations of the Civil War created a sense of community identification with the war and a perception that the war was "their" war. As will be shown, the realities of war turned out to be very different from the initial perceptions, not only for the soldiers who fought but for the communities far away from the battlefield.[4] This difference between the expectation and the reality of war led to varying degrees of disillusionment with the war itself, occurring first among the soldiers in the field and then eventually spreading to civilian society. Whether the towns' preconceptions about the war and their sense of identifying with it remained after combat ceased will be explored at the conclusion of this essay.

"The Union is too precious": Claremont and Newport, 1861–1865

The firing on Fort Sumter (located off of Charleston, South Carolina) on April 12, 1861, was met with jubilation in both the North and South. The attack on Fort Sumter unleashed a "popular torrent" on both sides that leaders could not resist or subdue. Hundreds of miles north of Fort Sumter, the immediate reaction of Claremont and Newport was an intense feeling of excitement. Both towns had felt powerless as the secession crisis unfolded, and the firing on Fort Sumter finally allowed the two towns an opportunity to act. The state of national affairs that the Newport *New Hampshire Argus and Spectator* considered "dark and gloomy" on April 12 was now bright and clear on April 19: "The Die is Cast! . . . To Arms, Ye Brave!"[5]

quiry," *Historical Methods Newsletter*, 7 (June 1974), 187–9. My breakdown of occupations into classes and sectors-of-the-economy can be found in Kemp, "Community and War: The Civil War Experiences of Claremont, New Hampshire, and Newport, New Hampshire," senior honors thesis, University of Michigan, 1988, 119–22. Election results were tabulated from Claremont Town Proceedings, 1857–66, and Newport Town Proceedings, 1857–66 (records located in the respective town halls).

4   This theme of expectation differing from actuality, as it applies to combat soldiers of the Civil War, is discussed in Gerald F. Lindermann, *Embattled Courage: The Experience of Combat in the American Civil War* (New York, 1987).

5   Jacob D. Cox, *Military Reminiscences of the Civil War*, 2 vols. (New York, 1900), 1:4–5; *New Hampshire Argus and Spectator*, April 12, April 19, 1861. During the war Claremont had two newspapers, the *National Eagle* and the *Northern Advocate*, that

34 *Thomas R. Kemp*

Claremont's reaction to the firing on Fort Sumter and to President Lincoln's April 15 call for 75,000 three-month volunteers was loud and joyous. "The excitement in Claremont since the rebel thunder . . . has been intense — and we are glad and proud to say that the popular current is rushing on in loyalty, with a patriotic determination to sustain the Flag and the Honor of the country," boomed the Claremont *Northern Advocate*. Claremont was "all on fire to do her share in putting down the rebellion." By April 18 a recruiting officer for the town had been appointed, young men were flocking "in faster than they could be examined and sworn," and notices were posted for a town meeting the next evening.[6]

On April 19 the town hall "was filled to overflowing, ladies occupying the galleries." A town historian reported that "it was such a meeting of the citizens of Claremont, without distinction of party, as had seldom been held." Patriotic speeches filled the hall, and a fund was created for the support of those Claremont men who would enlist. Before the meeting was adjourned a committee was appointed to "prepare and report resolutions expressive of the sentiments in regard to the rebellion," which were to be reported at a town meeting to be held the very next evening. The next day the "town hall was again crowded, and the excitement on the increase. . . . The young men just enlisted by William P. Austin were marched into the hall, where front seats had been reserved for them, and met with an enthusiastic reception. As they entered the audience rose to their feet and gave them three hearty cheers." The committee that had been formed the night before presented their resolutions to the town, which were "unanimously adopted." Patriotic speeches once again filled the hall, and the meeting was adjourned to April 23.[7]

Newport was not far behind Claremont in its reaction to the outbreak of war. The Democratic *Argus* called on the citizens to rally to the flag, and an enthusiastic town meeting, held on April 22, was "filled to overflowing." A town historian reported that "substantially the whole adult population of the town" attended the meeting, "without distinction of party." That evening the town voted to raise $1,500 "for the fitting out and support" of any volunteers. In just one week after President Lincoln's call for volunteers, 44 residents of Claremont had enlisted, and 23 residents of Newport had done the same. By the end of the month, a total of 66 Claremont and 26 Newport men had enlisted for the war. The

both supported the Republican party. The Newport *Argus* was strongly Democratic at the time.
6 *Advocate*, April 23, 1861; Otis F. R. Waite, *Claremont War History: April, 1861, to April, 1865; with Sketches of New-Hampshire Regiments, and a Biographical Notice of Each Claremont Soldier, etc.* (Concord, N.H., 1868), 16.
7 Waite, *Claremont War History*, 16–19.

enlistments from the two towns in the first month of the war were so high that they accounted for 12 percent of the men initially requested from the entire state by Lincoln, even though the two towns' combined populations only accounted for less than 2 percent of the population of New Hampshire.[8] In fact, enlistment throughout the North was high during the first year of the Civil War, to the point that more men had volunteered than could be accommodated.[9]

What created this outpouring of emotion and the rushing of men, both young and old, to go off to war? The answer is found in popular opinion leading up to the secession crisis. It is safe to say that prior to the outbreak of war, opinion in the North had been crystallizing, first "against the expansion of slavery and then against the institution itself and the South."[10] The Republican Party had always stood firmly against the "Slave Power," perceiving it as a threat to American liberties, and by 1860 even Northern Democrats were suspicious of their Southern counterparts. In July of 1860 the Newport *Argus* had decried the "villainous measures" by Southern Democrats that had split the party and declared that the Breckenridge slave-code platform was "not only repugnant to [the electorate's] feelings but . . . inconsistent with the theory of our government and the acknowledged rights of the people." A sense of crisis had gradually overtaken Northern communities like Claremont and Newport, and many feared for the existence of republican self-government.[11] The rationale behind the North's reaction to the outbreak of war was expressed in an *Argus* editorial: "The union is too precious and has conferred too many blessings not only upon the American people, but upon mankind, to go down at this time." The resolutions that were "unanimously passed" in Claremont's town meeting of April 20, 1861, emphasized the same theme. One went as follows: "Resolved, That for the maintenance and perpetuity of the priceless boon of civil and religious liberty, bequeathed

8 *Argus*, April 26, 1861; Wheeler, *History*, 28. The names and military records of Claremont and Newport soldiers are in Augustus D. Ayling, *Revised Register of the Soldiers and Sailors of New Hampshire in the War of Rebellion, 1861–1866* (Concord, N.H., 1895). Data found in the military records of those soldiers connected with Claremont and Newport was used to create a soldier data base for this study. All military statistics were compiled from this data base, unless otherwise noted. The number of men that composed the first New Hampshire regiment called for by Lincoln is tabulated from Waite, *Claremont War History*, 15–16. New Hampshire census data is from the census data base and Stanley B. Parsons, *U.S. Congressional Districts and Data, 1843–1883* (Westport, Conn.), 22.

9 James W. Geary, "Civil War Conscription in the North: A Historiographical Review," *Civil War History*, 32 (September 1986), 208; Eugene Murdock, *Patriotism Limited, 1862–1865: The Civil War and the Bounty System* (Kent, Ohio, 1967), 5.

10 Frisch, *Town into City*, 54.

11 *Argus*, July 27, 1860; Michael F. Holt, *The Political Crisis of the 1850s* (New York, 1978), vii–viii.

by our forefathers in the Constitution of this Union and the free institutions it guarantees, we would imitate their example in unitedly and unreservedly tendering to the Government, if need be, 'Our lives, our fortunes and our sacred honors.' "[12] Since Claremont and Newport believed that republican government ensured their individual liberties, the destruction of the federal government would be the destruction of their personal liberty.[13] This idea of what the war meant – the preservation of personal liberties ensured by the Constitution – became the primary foundation for identifying with the war by the citizens of both communities, for residents saw themselves as being fundamentally linked to the Union cause.

The two towns' vision of war also became a part of their identification with the conflict. To the citizens and soldiers of Claremont and Newport, the war itself was to be a test of courage, a chance to fight for one's honor and an opportunity to win glory. "The cause" had reduced itself to a "manifestation of courage," and the force that had struck them was "so overwhelming that it seemed to suppress all reservations regarding war, to remove all complications," and to "melt all moral ambiguities."[14] These notions of courage and war had a chivalrous tone to them, as evidenced by this letter from an officer to the sister of a Claremont soldier, informing her of the death of her brother in South Carolina in June 1862: "But his death furnished the most fitting eulogy of his life, and records the strongest testimony of his indomitable will, undaunted courage and unflinching zeal in the perilous hour of battle, receiving his death-wound squarely facing the foe." This notion of war was exemplified by Claremont soldier George Nettleton, whose last words to his wife, in a letter that he wrote to her before the battle of Fredericksburg, were: "I may fall, but ever remember it was at the post of duty, and in a noble cause." Nettleton did fall in a heroic manner, when "several men carrying the colors of his regiment were shot down," and Nettleton "had but just raised them when he was hit."[15] War and warfare were noble and positive concepts at the beginning of the war, thus making it easy for a community to identify itself with the cause.

The martial spirit that emerged in both towns had become contagious

12 *Argus*, September 13, 1861; Waite, *Claremont War History*, 17–19.
13 Linderman, *Embattled Courage*, 82; Eric Foner, *Free Soil, Free Labor, Free Men: The Ideology of the Republican Party before the Civil War* (New York, 1970), 1–39; Eric Foner, "The Causes of the American Civil War: Recent Interpretations and New Directions," *Civil War History*, 20 (September 1974) 213–14.
14 Linderman, *Embattled Courage*, 80.
15 The letter to Martha Moore, sister of Horatio, is from the *Advocate*, July 1, 1862. George Nettleton's letter to his wife and the description of his death are from Waite, *Claremont War History*, 128.

by the end of April 1861. Claremont and Newport volunteers marched through the streets, giving each village "quite a military appearance." The firefighters of Newport eventually were referred to as "Fire Zouaves" in the *Argus,* the name taken from regiments that patterned themselves after French infantry units known for their colorful uniforms and precise drilling. The upcoming departure of the volunteers fueled this spirit. In a special ceremony in Claremont on April 29, each Claremont recruit was presented with a revolver, a dirk knife, a "handsomely bound pocket Testament," and clothing ranging from flannel shirts to wool socks.[16] As Michael Frisch notes in his study of Springfield, Massachusetts, Northern "towns themselves did most of the work in this first mobilization, with little direction or instruction from the state." This approach "resembled the old militia procedures where localities received enlistments and equipped their own volunteer units," all in the " 'true patriotic and working spirit of '76.' "[17] This independence in mobilizing and outfitting soldiers became another source of identification with the war. Claremont's and Newport's ability to motivate men to enlist and organize them into military units made the communities feel it was "their" war to control in some manner, with the war effort a reflection on both towns.

On April 30 the "Claremont Volunteers" left for Concord, New Hampshire, in order to be mustered into government service. Prior to leaving, the company had elected its officers, and William Austin, a former selectman of the town, who had enlisted the troops, was chosen captain. In Newport, Ira McL. Barton, a "promising young lawyer," was elected captain.[18] This practice of electing local leaders as officers was common during the Civil War and is one way in which the community reappeared within the different units.

As the Claremont recruits boarded the train, a crowd of over 300 cheered them off. As the train neared Concord, "at every considerable railway station multitudes of people were assembled, who gave the men their blessing and cheered them on their way." Newport's soldiers enjoyed the same joyous receptions. Captain Barton wrote to the *Argus:* "Our journey . . . was one continual ovation through the entire length of the free states." Barton's men were later mustered into the First Regiment, New Hampshire Volunteer Infantry, a three-month regiment. The Claremont Volunteers were eventually sent to Portsmouth, since there were enough men to form one regiment in Concord, and another was forming in Portsmouth. On May 3 Lincoln issued a call for 20,000 three-year men, and the Claremont Volunteers were given the option of reenlisting for three

16   *Argus,* April 26, July 12, 1861; Waite, *Claremont War History,* 23.
17   Frisch, *Town into City,* 61.
18   Waite, *Claremont War History,* 21–3; Wheeler, *History,* 28.

years or being discharged after three months. Most took the option of reenlisting, and the Claremont Volunteers unit was disbanded, its members being dispersed to various companies within the Second Regiment.[19]

A town meeting was held in Claremont on May 8, and it was voted to appropriate a sum of $2,500 for the benefit of the families of Claremont soldiers. In the first year of the war alone, Claremont paid out over $3,000 to aid the families of soldiers, and Newport paid out over $1,300 (see Table 2.1). Throughout the war, the women of both communities met regularly to make various articles needed by soldiers and hospitals. Moreover, work for the U.S. Sanitary Commission and other charities gave women an "escape valve for wartime anxiety." The shock of the first battle of the war exacerbated this anxiety. On July 16, 1861, the Second Regiment, containing over 45 residents of Claremont and Newport, marched toward the "disastrous field" of Bull Run. As Claremont town historian O. F. R. Waite reports, "Men who had been upon the sick-list for weeks reported for duty, fondly believing that our troops were about to strike the death-blow to the rebellion. The world knows the sanguinary character and result of this battle." The first death of a resident of Claremont or Newport occurred at Bull Run, when a young Claremont soldier had a leg shot off by a cannonball and died as a prisoner of rebel troops.[20]

Shortly after the first battle of the war the Newport volunteers returned home, after serving their three-month tour of duty in the First Regiment. A welcome-back reception was given for the men in the town hall in mid-August. The enlistment of men for only three months at the start of the war symbolized the belief that the war was to be a painless, heroic outing, over within a few months. It was also a reflection of the initial perception that the enemy was weak in resolve and would quickly be defeated by the Northern armies. This perception was expressed in a letter from Captain Barton to the *Argus,* written shortly before the battle of Bull Run: "I never was so fully impressed with the perfect cowardice and incompetency of southern men and troops as I was when I saw Harper's Ferry [deserted]."[21]

The South's victory at Bull Run showed Southern resolve and a willingness to fight; Lincoln and the North soon realized that more than three-month enlistments would be needed to defeat the South. Commonly held perceptions of warfare also began to be tested. The hard

19 Waite, *Claremont War History,* 21–6; *Argus,* June 28, 1861. Out of the 66 men from
    Claremont who enlisted in April, 58 would later reenlist, while 24 out of the 26 April
    enlistees from Newport would later reenlist..
20 Frisch, *Town into City,* 59; Waite, *Claremont War History,* 23–7, 46.
21 *Argus,* July 19, 1861.

Table 2.1. *Financial burden of the Civil War on Newport and Claremont*

Year ending (Month/year)	Aid to families of soldiers		Bounties		Town assets (+) or liabilities (−)	
	Newport	Claremont	Newport	Claremont	Newport	Claremont
3/59					$ 5,953−	$ 910+
3/60					6,697−	1,871+
3/61					4,969−	2,104+
3/62	$ 1,356	$ 3,064			4,666−	3,523−
3/63	3,726	7,895	$ 7,100	$ 3,550	13,730−	11,249−
3/64	5,669	5,557	11,437	28,258	22,212−	28,931−
3/65	5,365	7,043	35,571	41,710	56,060−	70,862−
3/66	2,238	2,797	9,100	950	56,506−	63,167−
Total	$18,354	$26,356	$63,208	$74,468		

Source: Financial Report of the *Proceedings of the Annual Town Meeting in Claremont* (Claremont, N.H.), 1859–1866; Newport Town Proceedings, 1859–1866 (Newport Town Hall, Newport, N.H.).

reality of war soon became apparent to the soldiers out in the field, but,
as will be shown, it was slow to reach the people far removed from the
battle. The newspapers in Claremont and Newport, for the first year of
the war, always had Union troops "covered with glory," regardless of
the outcome of a battle.[22] But the towns' soldiers soon had a different
viewpoint, one far removed from the glorious notions of war that they
and their communities had entertained in April 1861. This new attitude
was expressed in a July 26, 1861, letter from Charles Putnam of Claremont to his brother George, concerning "that great disaster" at Bull Run:

> I tell you what it is, George, that was the hardest day's of work I
> ever did. We started at 2 o'clock in the morning, marched eighteen
> miles, and right on the battle-field without any rest or breakfast, and
> many of the men had no waters in their canteens. . . . It was an awful
> sight to see such brave men slaughtered as they were, and what looked
> almost as bad, to see the noble horses cut to pieces by the cannon
> balls. . . . During thirty-six hours we marched over sixty miles, be-
> sides being on the field seven hours, with nothing to eat but hard
> bread, and nothing to drink but muddy water.[23]

Putnam was later killed in Virginia, in May 1862. The hardships he described were not enough to convince his brother George to avoid enlistment, for George joined up in October 1861 and was killed in the battle
of Cold Harbor, in June 1864. Not until later did both communities
realize that war was not a glorious and noble affair, as they initially had
thought.

Following Bull Run, the state governor called for the formation of new
regiments. By late August, Claremont had appointed several recruiting
officers for the Fifth Regiment, while recruiters in Newport were looking
for men for the Fourth and Sixth Regiments. From August to the end of
November 1861, 145 men from Claremont had enlisted, compared to 39
from Newport. The claremont recruits eventually formed Company G of
the Fifth Regiment, and Charles H. Long, a moderately wealthy farmer
from Claremont, was elected captain. The bulk of Newport's recruits
joined a company in the Sixth Regiment. Having a large number of residents in the same unit caused an extension of the community into the
unit, as did the election of local leaders as officers. Soldiers who distinguished themselves became local heroes, while deserters were probably
not willing to reappear at home to face the stigma associated with aban-
doning comrades. Having the communities represented in the field helped
the two communities identify the war with themselves, and "this made
the war more personal, immediate and exciting for the home commu-

22   See also Frisch, *Town into City*, 57.
23   Waite, *Claremont War History*, 59–61.

nity." This, however, proved to be a "double-edged sword," for whenever a community's unit fought a "bloody battle, the casualty lists would carry one familiar name after another." Thus in the beginning of the war each community thought of a particular unit as theirs and an extension of themselves, and in turn the soldiers in the field thought of their unit as representing their community.[24]

Compared to the noise created after Fort Sumter, the winter of 1861 and spring of 1862 passed quietly for Claremont and Newport, and both communities were filled with the hope that the rebellion was on its last legs. Claremont had every reason for being proud of its contribution to the war effort, for 221 men from its community had enlisted in the first year of the war, accounting for 278 total enlistments (which includes 57 men who reenlisted). The 221 men represented 33 percent of the male population in Claremont between the ages of 20 and 45 in 1860. Newport contributed 63 men in the first year of the war and had 13 men reenlist, totaling 76 enlistments. The 63 men represented 18 percent of the 20- to 45-year-old male population of Newport in 1860, proportionally almost one-half as many men as Claremont contributed (see Figure 2.1).

What explains this difference between the two towns' first-year enlistments? Residents in the two communities had the same opportunity to enlist, for there were numerous recruiters in each town, and neither town had offered monetary inducements to attract men to enlist. The difference can best be attributed to the two communities' political orientations. Democrats throughout the North tended to blame "ultraists" in the North (and South) for the tension leading to the war. Even while calling on men to enlist after the firing on Sumter, the *Argus*, on April 19, 1861, said, "When the republicans now call upon us to defend our country, can we close our eyes to the fact that their twenty years 'war upon the slave power' has provoked the war which is now declared?"[25] Hence it is very possible that Newport, with its Democratic tendencies, was not as enthusiastic about fighting a "Republican" war as was Claremont. Newport's stronger Democratic affiliation raises a question concerning its willingness to support the war effort when disillusionment with the war later pervaded the North, and this will be addressed later in this chapter.

But enthusiasm for the war was high initially, and successive Union victories in the spring of 1862 led to a consensus in the North that the

24 See Vinovskis, "Have Social Historians Lost the Civil War?", Chapter 1 of this volume, section entitled "Characteristics of the Civil War"; Frisch, *Town into City,* 57; Linderman, *Embattled Courage,* 36, 225.

25 *Argus,* April 19, 1861.

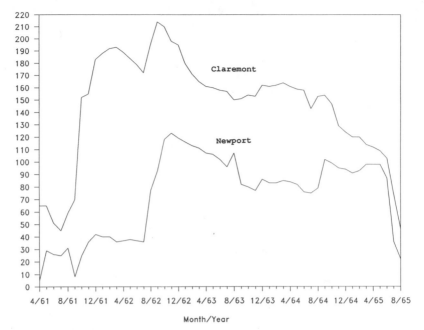

Figure 2.1. Number of residents in the field, by month (from date of mustering in until date of mustering out, discharge, death, or desertion). Data compiled from Augustus D. Ayling, *Revised Register of the Soldiers and Sailors of New Hampshire in the War of Rebellion, 1861–1866* (Concord, N.H., 1895).

war was soon to be over. In mid-February 1862, the bells in Claremont and Newport rang loudly to celebrate the news of a capture of Fort Donelson, and support for the war effort led to a "complete triumph of the Republican party" in the March state elections. By May, the *Advocate* confidently stated that "victory after victory has crowned the Union arms, and at this present writing everything appears to foreshadow a speedy winding up of the rebellion."[26] But battles such as Fair Oaks, the second battle of Bull Run, Antietam, and Fredericksburg would reveal, in the second half of 1862, that the war was not yet over. As noted by Frisch, the "shock of the summer and fall of 1862 [in the North] still leaps from the pages" of century-old newspapers. The Union setbacks unleashed a great deal of frustration with the war in Claremont and Newport, as

26 Ibid., February 21, March 14, 1862; Waite, *Claremont War History*, 28; *Advocate*, May 13, 1862. The Democrats in Newport posted their worst showing of the war in the 1862 gubernatorial election, with slightly over one-fourth the vote. The Republicans and the third-party War Democrat (Union) Party split the rest of the vote. *Argus*, March 14, 1862.

witnessed by the bitter editorials appearing in the two towns' newspapers.[27] If the realization that the war was not going to end quickly was not enough, the letters from Claremont and Newport soldiers that filled the newspapers with the news of the deaths of friends and loved ones made the war even more shocking.

Added to this shock was the growing recognition that warfare was not what the communities had initially perceived. For the first time, the harsh realities of war made itself known to the people back in New Hampshire through each week's newspaper. The same letters that filled the newspapers with news of the deaths of residents also contained unflattering accounts of war. Captain Barton, the "promising young lawyer" who had criticized Southern troops prior to the first battle of Bull Run, wrote the following account to newspapers in Claremont and Newport:

> I came out of the fight with sixteen men – went in with sixty one, officers included. . . . I will not attempt a description of the horrors of the battlefield, and the hospital. A heartless heart would bleed to see what I have seen. . . . Let me have a few thousand of those "on-to-Richmond" thorough-blood fellows out here – I would like to have them put through.

Many accounts were graphic, as evidenced by this letter "from a wounded soldier to his friends at Newport":

> Frank Hersey was shot through the head and died instantly. The bullet entered his eye and passed through, the blood spirting in jets. Henry Stockwell was also shot through the head and lived a day or two – even after his brains had partly run out. Albert Miner's tall brother was also shot through the head.

While it would take a little longer for both communities seriously to question their initial conceptions of war, the effect of letters like these would soon become evident when residents were sought after to enlist.[28]

On June 22, 1862, Claremont held a meeting in the town hall "as a demonstration of respect for the brave Claremont men who had been killed at Fair Oaks and in other battles." The Claremont *National Eagle* commented that a "deep feeling brooded over the entire assembly" and noted that the number of relatives of the departed soldiers seated in the front of the town hall "was by no means small." Fourteen soldiers were commemorated at the meeting, and by the end of the month a total of 21 soldiers from Claremont had died during the first fourteen months of the war, compared to 5 from Newport.[29]

27 Frisch, *Town into City*, 58; *Eagle*, July 3, 1862.
28 *Argus*, June 13, 1862; *Advocate*, June 17, 1862; *Eagle*, June 26, 1862.
29 Waite, *Claremont War History*, 29–30; *Eagle*, July 3, 1862.

While Claremont and Newport were mourning the loss of their fellow citizens, it was becoming evident in the North that the Union was in desperate need of men. Enlistment, in the early summer of 1862, had slowed down, and troops were needed to fill losses and successfully prosecute the war. In New Hampshire the enlistments were such that on June 10 the state "bounty" (a monetary inducement to attract enlistments) was doubled from $10 to $20. On July 3 President Lincoln made a call for 300,000 three-year men, and a draft bill was signed into law on July 17, 1862. The Militia Act created the apparatus that assigned troop quotas for each state to fill. The states were then to break down their quota on a town-by-town basis, thus giving each town a quota of its own to fill. Men enlisting for a community would be "credited" to that community's quota. Witnessing that appeals to citizens' patriotism were not enough to inspire enlistment, states and communities soon began offering bounties to attract men to enlist, so that they could meet their quota. Potential soldiers could now "shop around" for the town offering the most money, and this quickly created a "bounty war" between the various states and communities. The lure of higher bounties did attract 18 Claremont men and 6 Newport men to enlist elsewhere in the second half of 1862, mostly in Vermont.[30]

Meetings were held in July in Claremont and Newport to raise the men needed to fill the quota. If the quota were not met by mid-August, a draft of men between the ages of 18 and 45 would occur to make up the number that the community lacked to fill its quota. Having to eventually resort to the draft to fill one's quota was perceived to be highly unpatriotic, and the most disgraceful event that could befall a community.[31] Meetings were hold in Claremont on July 14 and 19 to encourage enlistment, and both meetings called upon "the people to aid in all practicable ways in raising men" to fill the ranks. But by July 22 no one had enlisted in either Claremont or Newport, and residents from both had already enlisted elsewhere to collect bounties. While applauding the use of the "draft system" to raise men, the *Argus* noted that the "romance of military life has apparently lost its charm." Appeals by the community to citizens' sense of duty were no longer enough, by themselves, to attract residents to enlist. Following the state's increase of its bounty to $50, both towns called informal meetings to offer a bounty to avoid the draft.[32]

Claremont, on July 25, and Newport, on July 26, held informal gath-

---

30   *Eagle,* July 3, July 17, 1862. Vermont's high bounties throughout the war led the *Eagle* to claim that over 1,000 New Hampshire men had already "swelled the ranks of Vermont" by mid-July, 1862. *Eagle,* July 17, 1862.
31   For an analysis of what the draft meant to a community, see Eugene C. Murdock, *One Million Men: The Civil War Draft in the North* (Madison, 1971).
32   Waite, *Claremont War History,* 30; *Argus,* July 11, 1862.

erings, and each town recommended that the community pay recruits $50 upon enlistment. War meetings such as these were "the order of the day," and they seem to have been held throughout the entire state. In Newport a wealthy resident even offered to pay $10 to each of the first 25 soldiers to enlist. At both meetings it was also voted to hold a county war meeting in Claremont on August 2. On that day the town hall in Claremont was "crowded to its utmost capacity," and speakers such as Governor Nathaniel Berry made "stirring and patriotic speeches." The *Eagle* reported that "no circumstance was wanting to its completeness, its harmony, and its moral effect."[33]

Eligible men seemed not to be overtly swayed, for only a handful from both towns enlisted. On August 4 Lincoln issued a call for 300,000 nine-month militiamen, and a few days later the War Department published orders on how the enrollment of military-age men and the draft would be handled.[34] The *Eagle* reported on August 7 that deficiencies in the call for three-year men would be made up in the draft for nine-month men to be held in mid-September. The result of this new call was the doubling of the burden on each community to raise men, which resulted in an even more frantic bounty war between towns to attract men and avoid having to draft its residents. Commenting on the bounty war before the call for nine-month men was made, a reader of the *Advocate* from Maine wrote, "It is surprising to witness the alacrity of our smaller and purely agricultural towns, in adopting measures to fill their quotas." He went on to say that the town of Chelsea, in Maine, was offering a bounty of $125 − $75 more than Claremont and Newport offered.[35]

Not only were Claremont and Newport, by the end of the first week of August, feeling the pressure to raise their bounties, but concern for the overall effect of the war on the communities was voiced for the first time in the town newspapers. The first set of men recruited in response to the president's call for 300,000 three-year men left Claremont on August 4 for Concord. The recruits "appeared to be in excellent spirits, but it is hardly necessary to say that they have left behind them many depressed spirits," an emotion not noticed when the first batch of troops left Claremont in April 1861. In late July the *Advocate* noted that the "enlistments bear somewhat heavily upon our farmers who are now in the midst of their haying," and farm laborers under contract were given up, to be

33 *Eagle,* July 31, August 7, 1862; *Advocate,* July 29, 1862; Waite, *Claremont War History,* 31.
34 Murdock, *Patriotism Limited,* 6. "Enrollment" was the process of recording the name, occupation, and address of each man between the ages of 20 and 45. If a community failed to meet its quota, a draft would occur to make up the number deficient by having a "lottery" that would randomly select names from the enrollment list.
35 *Eagle,* August 7, 1862; *Advocate,* August 5, 1862.

replaced by Claremont's "gallant women and girls," who were "promptly filling up the places thus left vacant in the field." The *Eagle* even stated, "It is true there has been a seeming apathy in some places in regard to enlistments, but it is the result mainly of a feeling of discouragement and disappointment."[36]

The bounty war was undoubtedly another source of dismay for Claremont and Newport. On August 7 Claremont legally ratified the offering of a $50 bounty, but the story reporting this in the August 14 *Eagle* also stated that three neighboring communities were already offering a $100 bounty. By mid-August another town in the area was offering a bounty of $150. On August 20 the citizens of Claremont met in an informal town meeting and recommended that the bounty be raised to $100. This also failed to attract a large number of recruits, as indicated by the *Advocate* on August 26: "Enlistments are going on slowly. The liberal offer of the town . . . has stimulated operations some, but not as much as we should like to see." But two days later the *Eagle* proudly reported that the state had calculated that Claremont's quota had been filled. Residents who were already in the field were allowed to be counted toward each town's quota, thus explaining the delay in figuring out whether each town's quota had been met. Claremont had been able to meet its quota primarily by having a large number of residents enlist in the first year of the war. A surplus of around 50 men was claimed by the town, and Claremont believed that this surplus would be its "credit against the next requisition from the government, if it shall come." The *Eagle* even claimed that the "war spirit has been renewed" in Claremont, and the editor of that paper sent a letter to the *Boston Journal* under the headline "How It Is Done in Claremont."[37]

The number of enlistments during the first year of the war had helped Claremont fill its quota but had worked against Newport. Because of the small number of Newport residents who were in the field in 1862, Newport actually had to raise more men to avoid a draft than did Claremont, despite Newport's smaller population. In an emotional meeting on September 2, it was announced that Newport lacked 31 men to fill its quota. As a result, the town voted to raise its bounty to $100. Two clergymen and a selectman of the town announced their intention to enlist, hoping that they would inspire others to do the same, and the meeting was ended with the warning, "Let nobody await to be 'snaked into the ranks by a

36 *Advocate*, August 5, July 29, 1862; *Eagle*, August 7, 1862.
37 *Eagle*, August 14, August 28, 1862; *Advocate*, August 12, August 19, August 26, September 2, 1862. It is interesting to note that a nine-month volunteer collected a $100 bounty, while a volunteer who had enlisted for three years a few weeks earlier collected only a $50 bounty. This is indicative of what the towns had to do to attract enlistments. See also Frisch, *Town into City*, 62.

draft.' " The state eventually delayed the ordering of the draft, and Newport was able to fill its quota by the beginning of October. Newport was helped to fill its quota in part by the enlistment of 15 members of the Newport Cornet Band in late September.[38]

Claremont and Newport were able to avoid the nation's first draft and the stigma attached to it, but the war and its effects seemed to rage around them. A few neighboring towns had been unable to fill their quotas in October 1862, and the threat of the draft constantly hung over them well into December 1862, due to postponements of the draft by the state. It would not be until after the turn of the new year that the quota set for the state in the middle of 1862 was finally filled. The battle of Fredericksburg, in mid-December 1862, had turned December into the bloodiest month of the war for both Claremont and Newport, with 37 men from the two towns either killed or wounded in that month alone. The Militia Act had "been the handwriting on the wall," for by February 1863 a comprehensive conscription act was starting to take form in Washington, which would signal more calls for men and more quotas to be filled.[39]

In the beginning of March 1863 the communities held their annual town meetings and voted for the various state officers, and it was clear that recent events had had an effect on the ballot box throughout the state. In Newport the Democrats posted their best showing of the war, with 50 percent of the vote. However, the presence of a War Democratic (Union) third party forced the gubernatorial election to be decided by the Republican-controlled state legislature, and the Republicans naturally elected their own man.[40] Both Claremont and Newport also voted to raise money for families of volunteers, and both were forced to raise taxes to pay for the high cost of bounties, which was leading them deeper into debt (see Table 2.1).

By the middle of March both communities were faced with the prospect of a new draft, if 20 percent of their enrolled males did not enlist toward their quota by August. The Enrollment Act was signed into law on March 3 and made every able-bodied male citizen between the ages of 20 and 45 eligible for the draft.[41] The consensus that had finally emerged

---

38 *Argus*, September 5, September 19, 1862; *Eagle*, September 11, 1862.
39 James M. McPherson, *Ordeal by Fire* (New York, 1982), 355. The 37 men killed or wounded from the two towns in December 1862 represented 2.5% of the two towns' male population between the ages of 13 and 45 at the time.
40 McPherson, *Battle Cry of Freedom*, 599–600.
41 Some men were actually more "eligible" than others. The Enrollment Act set up two classes of enrolled men. Class 1 included "single men from 20 to 45 and married men from 20 to 35, while class 2 included married men from 35 to 45. Class 2 was not be called out until the list of names in class 1 were exhausted." Murdock, *Patriotism Limited*, 9.

from Washington was that a conscription plan under federal authority was the only method left to successfully prosecute the war, and seeing that the state governors had poorly administered the militia draft, the new draft system was firmly placed in the hands of the federal government. The new law appointed provost marshals to each congressional district, who directly reported to the provost marshal general in Washington. Quotas were to be assigned on the basis of the number of enrolled military-age males in each congressional district, and quotas were then to be broken down into subdistricts within each district. Each district was immediately given a quota of 20 percent of its enrolled men to fill, because the immediate need of the Union was "putting men right into service." Only if a town's quota was not filled would a draft occur in that town.[42]

The Enrollment Act marked the final wresting of control of the war effort away from Northern states and communities to the federal government. Decisions concerning enlistment and mobilization were not being made in Claremont or Newport but elsewhere – in 1862 by the state and in later years by the national government. The passage of the Enrollment Act also underscored the fizzling out of the enthusiasm for enlisting. Not only had Claremont and Newport lost control over the mobilization of their own residents, but they were finding it more and more difficult to inspire residents to enlist. Now, unlike the first year of the war, appeals to patriotism alone were no longer working, and the communities found that they had to offer large sums of money as an inducement to enlist. As will be shown, even large sums were not enough to entice residents, and the towns had to look elsewhere for men. The war was turning out to be very different from Claremont's and Newport's initial perception, so much so that it was getting harder for the towns to see it as "their" war.

---

42 McPherson, *Ordeal By Fire*, 355–6; Murdock, *Patriotism Limited*, 7, 10. The two most controversial features of the Enrollment act were "substitution" and "commutation." "Substitution" was the hiring of another individual (a "substitute") to take the place of a drafted man. In order to keep the price of substitutes from skyrocketing (which was long "hallowed by tradition"), the Enrollment Act contained a "commutation" clause, which provided that the payment of a fee could free a draftee from the obligation to serve (McPherson, *Battle Cry of Freedom*, 603). Paying a commutation fee exempted a drafted person from that particular draft, but not from any future drafts. By setting the commutation fee at $300 – the yearly wage of an average worker at the time – the act kept the price of substitutes under $300, the logic being that most people would not pay more than $300 for a substitute when they could also avoid service by commuting. The commutation fee led many people – especially many Democrats – to refer to the war as a "rich man's war but a poor man's fight." Those who used this slogan argued that only the wealthy could afford the $300 (and that substitutes were not always easy to get), and the commutation clause became the rallying cry for many opposed to conscription and the war itself. Murdock, *Patriotism Limited*, 9; McPherson, *Ordeal By Fire*, 356; Murdock, *One Million Men*.

A draft in August still seemed far away for the residents of Claremont and Newport, and both communities were filled with the confidence that they could apply their "surplus" credits from the last call to their current quotas. Some of this confidence probably came from the belief that the war was winding down. On May 10 a telegram reached both towns claiming that Richmond had been captured. The telegram was "read in the churches" and "bells rung, cannon fired, and other demonstrations of joy were made." But, like many ideas of the war, it turned out not to be true.[43]

Although Claremont and Newport did little to attract enlistments, many other communities in the state were busy filling their quotas. On July 10 the state legislature passed an act that forced towns to keep their bounties below $300, showing that the bounty war was still in full force.[44] In other Northern states the draft had already begun. On July 13 draft riots broke out in New York City, and the shock waves from the riots caused the acting assistant provost marshal general of New Hampshire to postpone the draft to September, even though "preparations were such that it might have been made a month earlier."[45]

Less than a month before the draft was to have begun, troops from Claremont and Newport returned home on furlough. On August 5, Company G of the Fifth Regiment returned to Claremont. Of the 81 Claremont men who had left with the unit, only 12 returned to Claremont for the furlough. Twenty-four had been "killed in battle or died of disease, and the balance had either been discharged or left behind in hospitals." In late August the Newport men in the Sixteenth Regiment returned to Newport, and the *Argus* reported that a few returned as invalids. The sight of injured and battle-worn friends and neighbors could only dissuade potential enlistees from joining the service, and it seems that a feeling of gloom had settled over both towns.[46]

On August 21, with the draft only two weeks away, Newport offered

43 Waite, *Claremont War History*, 33.
44 *Eagle,* September 10, 1863. There is some debate today over the role of bounties in the raising of men during the Civil War. Geary, in "Conscription in the North," argues that bounties, not conscriptions, were responsible for the raising of men. Geary, "Conscription in the North," 215–16. But this ignores the fact that if there had been no conscription, there would have been no bounties. As the provost marshal of the Third District in New Hampshire noted, "Without the existence of a power which could compel involuntary service . . . neither towns, nor individuals, would have offered the large bounties." "Historical Reports of the State Acting Assistant Provost Marshals Generals and District Provost Marshals, 1865," for the Third District, New Hampshire, 15, found in Records of the Provost Marshal General's Bureau (Civil War) (Record Group 110), National Archives, Washington, D.C. See also Prentiss, "Troy, Michigan, in the Civil War Draft," 18.
45 "Historical Reports," 6.
46 Waite, *Claremont War History*, 34; *Argus,* August 28, 1863.

to pay a total of $300 to those enlisting toward its quota. This measure managed to credit 15 men to Newport's quota by the end of the month, 13 of whom were Newport residents. Newport offered a bounty prior to the draft because it knew that its surplus from the last call could not cover its current quota; however, Claremont made no effort to offer a bounty because it was still confident that its large surplus could be applied to the current quota. Throughout the summer of 1863 and up to the day of the draft, the governor of New Hampshire reassured towns like Claremont that they could apply their previous credits to the current quota; at the same time, he was negotiating with Secretary of War Edward Stanton to find out whether or not towns could actually do this. It was not until nearly the day of the draft that Stanton rejected Governor Gilmore's request, citing the delay in the draft that would be caused by calculating the number of residents out in the field.[47]

The draft for the two towns was held on September 2. A company of the Veteran Reserve Corps had been stationed at the draft site to ensure against any disturbance, but no violence was reported. Ninety-five eligible men were drafted from Claremont and 57 from Newport. The interest in finding out who had been drafted was so great that the issue of the *Eagle* containing the names of those drafted sold over twice the paper's normal circulation.[48] Even after the draft, Claremont was still confident that it could apply its previous surplus of credits. Telegrams to and from the governor, which needed "no comment," went back and forth. The editor of the *Eagle* telegrammed one day after the draft, "Shall you not hold the Govt. to its promise concerning the surplus of towns?", to which the governor replied the next day, "Unless the Govt. back right straight down the draft will be equalized. I have got their written agreement to

47 *Argus,* August 7, July 24, 1863; *Eagle,* October 8, 1863.
48 "Historical Reports," 6–7; *Advocate,* September 8, 1863. There is some debate over whether or not the draft system was "fair." Did the draft discriminate against one class, as many Democrats claimed? By linking the names of those drafted to the census data base, I developed a socioeconomic profile of those drafted. Of these men, exactly 66% were found on the 1860 census list. A cursory glance at the wealth and class of those drafted shows that wealthy farmers and white-collar workers were underrepresented in the draft. But this ignores the factor of age. The majority of those drafted were in their mid-twenties, even though men aged 20 to 45 were eligible for the draft. The reason for the higher "draft level" in the 20 to 29 age group is best explained by the enrollment process. As discussed in note 41, single men aged 20 to 45 and married men aged 20 to 35 would be the first to be drafted and would be called before married men aged 35 to 45. Of the men aged 35 to 45 in Claremont and Newport, approximately 85% were married in 1860. Thus the concentration of men in their twenties among the draftees is explained. Armed with this knowledge, and noting that the bulk of those with wealth and of high social class (farmers and white-collar workers) were aged 35 to 45, it is determined that this draft was in fact "fair." The draft did cut evenly across class and wealth lines, when the age of those drafted is factored in. See Kemp, "Community and War," 136–8.

do so, and I shall do all that mortal man can do to enforce it." When the federal government refused to back down, the shock in Claremont was great, as reflected in the reaction of the two newspapers. The residents of Claremont quickly realized that they had to offer a bounty, and on September 21 Claremont offered to pay drafted men or their substitutes $300. A few drafted men had even begun to look for and hire substitutes, knowing that they themselves would pass the physical examination.[49]

The physical examination of the drafted men took place in the beginning of October, and Claremont still lacked 33 men to fill its quota, while Newport only lacked 4.[50] Newport's determination to fill its quota by offering a bounty two weeks before the draft meant that only 4 men out of the 57 drafted were faced with the prospect of either serving, commuting, or hiring a substitute. Of the 33 Claremont men who passed the examination, 29 eventually bought substitutes, while 4 served as draftees. Three of the 4 Newport men who passed the physical examination hired substitutes, and only 1 commuted. The *Advocate* reported that "the price of substitutes ranged from 125 to 150 dollars." Paying commutation seemed to be unpopular, "owing to the uncertainty of its relation to the next draft." The *Advocate,* on October 6, dismissed the concern about another call for men as "premature," reasoning that the draft at hand had just finished.[51]

But two weeks alter President Lincoln made a call for 300,000 three-year men and gave districts until January 5, 1864, to fill their quotas, or a draft would be held on that date. This call immediately sent both Claremont and Newport scurrying to fill their quotas; raising men had become the "question of the hour." The governor had issued a proclamation setting the state bounty at $100 and recommended to the towns "to take immediate measures for promptly raising their full quota by offering reasonable town bounties," although, given the reaction of Claremont and Newport, this recommendation was probably not needed.[52]

As in the previous draft, Claremont and Newport looked beyond their town borders for men to fill their quotas. Both had come to the conclu-

---

49 It is interesting to note that Claremont's enlistments in the first year of the war had allowed the town to avoid a draft in 1862 but had lulled it into believing that it could avoid the draft in 1863. Newport, at the moment, seemed to be in a better position than Claremont, even though Claremont had given more men to the war effort. "How it is done in Claremont" in 1862 and 1861 did not apply to 1863, like many earlier perceptions of the war.

50 Drafted men were examined in the order in which they were drafted. Each "passing" draftee reduced that community's quota by one, and the examinations continued until the community's quota was reduced to zero. If the quota was not filled by the first group of men drafted, another draft would occur.

51 *Advocate,* October 6, 1863.

52 *Eagle,* November 12, 1863; *Advocate,* November 10, 1863.

sion that their residents were not going to enlist, and they felt it was best to fill their quotas by any means possible. Not only were residents unwilling to enlist, but the two towns also felt that their supply of potential soldiers had run out. Writing in November 1863 about the offering of a higher local bounty to attract nonresidents, the *Eagle* claimed that "Claremont has no need to vindicate her patriotism, and by this means our much needed citizens may remain at home while the army will still be filled." Even as early as October 1862, the *Argus* noted that "able-bodied men in this town are few and far between."[53]

By October 1863 both Claremont and Newport had hired "substitute brokers" in Canada to find men to fill their quotas.[54] The desperation for men was so great that by early December both towns were also offering a local bounty of $300 and advancing the $100 state bounty and the $302 national bounty, thus offering a potential recruit $702.[55] The offering of large bounties in advance by towns like Claremont and Newport not only was leading these towns into greater debt (see Table 2.1) but acted as an encouragement for repeated desertion by men known as "bounty jumpers." These men would collect the bounty in one community and immediately desert, and then they would repeat the process in another community. It was generally agreed upon that the quality of the soldiers who enlisted in 1863–5 was greatly inferior to that of the recruits who enlisted in 1861–2, and criticism especially concentrated on substitutes. According to the provost marshal of the Third District, most substitutes had an "extremely vicious character," and he was of the opinion that "not more than fifty percent of this class so enlisted . . . have been of any value to the service."[56] This posed an interesting dilemma for towns such as Claremont and Newport that hired substitutes to fill their quotas. The towns wanted the war to end quickly, but they did not

53 *Eagle*, November 19, 1863; *Argus*, October 3, 1862. Of the 152 men drafted from the towns in September 1863, nearly one-half (75) failed the medical examination. "Descriptive Book of Drafted Men and Substitutes, September 1863–March 1865, for the Third District, State of New Hampshire" found in the Records of the Provost Marshal General's Bureau (Civil War), (Record Group 110), National Archives, Washington, D.C. See also Harris, "Sons and Soldiers," 165–6.

54 *Eagle*, November 12, 1863; *Argus*, December 4, 1863. "Brokers" were people who supplied substitutes to a community for a fee. The provost marshal of the Third District summed up the general feeling toward brokers by referring to them as "men of suspectable character." "Historical Reports," 17–18.

55 Soldiers received state and national bounties in installments. By "advancing" those bounties to recruits, Claremont and Newport assumed the soldiers' installment payments.

56 "Historical Reports," 8–19. Distrust of substitutes was so great by 1864 that after a substitute's physical examination, he was locked up and kept under guard until his mustering in.

want their citizens to serve, and they knew that the soldiers that they were sending were not of the quality that was needed to win the war.[57]

One result of the large bounties and hiring of substitutes was the weakening of the relationship that the communities had with the soldiers out in the field. Soldiers undoubtedly looked with disgust on their neighbors and friends back home who hired substitutes and avoided service while they risked their lives. The *Advocate,* in August 1864, stated that this had had a "deadening effect all along our lines." In addition, depleted units were being filled by nonresidents, meaning that it was becoming harder for the communities to think of a unit as an extension of themselves, just as it was becoming "more difficult for soldiers to continue to think of a particular unit as representing their community."[58] Thus many communities were gradually coming to perceive that the war was being fought by strangers, and it is likely that these communities felt that they did not have as great a stake in the war as they once did.

While Claremont and Newport were busy trying to fill their quotas by the January 5 deadline, governors and recruiting committees from various states were pleading with Lincoln for more time to fill their quotas. Their pleas eventually led to the draft being postponed to February 1864. Communities throughout the North were, in turn, pleading with their state governments for some relief from the high bounties. In a meeting of New Hampshire mayors and selectmen, held in Manchester on February 8, the convention unanimously resolved that the governor should "assume the entire responsibility of filling the quota of the State," so that "the towns will be relieved of the necessity of offering bounties." This resolution was later rejected by the state government, but it shows that the towns wanted the burden of raising men removed from their shoulders – a reaction markedly different from their initial response to the war.[59]

By early January 1864, Newport had filled its quota, but Claremont still lacked men. Claremont was able to avoid the draft in February only because another call for men was made and the new draft deadline was postponed to March 10. But this draft was also postponed, to be replaced by an April draft deadline that included a call for even more men, and even larger quotas, for both towns. Newport was able to fill its quota by

---

57 The towns also knew that the hiring of substitutes did not diminish the number of enrolled men eligible to be drafted. *Argus,* December 15, 1863.

58 *Advocate,* August 9, 1864; Linderman, *Embattled Courage,* 222–5. For a similar analysis concerning a southern community and its men in the field, see Robert C. Kenzer, *Kinship and Neighborhood in a Southern Community: Orange County, North Carolina, 1849–1881* (Knoxville, 1988), 73–4.

59 *Eagle,* February 11, 1864.

mid-April and thus avoid the draft, but Claremont still had only filled its original quota of 45 from the first call. Claremont failed to meet the April draft deadline, and on May 17, 13 men from Claremont were drafted. This draft still could not fill Claremont's quota, because more men were found exempt by the medical examiner than expected, and it finally took two more drafts and the hiring of more substitutes in early June to fill Claremont's quota.[60]

The constant pressure of having to fill quotas clearly showed in the two towns during the first half of 1864. Quota meetings in Claremont were reported as not being as full as they "ought to have been," and complaints of "croakers" (those critical of the war effort) were appearing in the town newspapers. The seemingly unending draft deadlines had left both communities disheartened, and, to make matters worse, the war had become a bloody war of attrition. News of the deaths of residents were being reported almost weekly, and the battle of Cold Harbor alone, in June 1864, had left 22 Claremont soldiers either dead or wounded. Although it was once again felt that the war was winding down, many people in the North believed that the South would make a last-ditch effort to bring the war into the North. Many towns in the North also sensed that another call for men was imminent, and in late June Claremont voted to offer a bounty to potential recruits in "anticipation of future calls."[61]

This general disillusionment in 1864 with the war in the North raises a question about whether Newport was willing to support the war effort, given its Democratic tendencies. In 1863–4, many Democratic communities throughout the North had switched allegiance away from the goal of one union and had become willing to make peace with the Confederacy. But Newport, like Claremont, supported the war effort throughout, and it seems that both towns' identification with the war in 1863–4 was still strong enough to keep them supporting the war.

What transpired at a town meeting in early 1862 can be seen as a good indicator of Newport's later support for the war effort. A resolution was proposed condemning emancipation and abolitionism as treasonous "heresies." Levi Barton rose in opposition to the resolution and stated that he "was no abolitionist, nor emancipationist, but he was opposed to slavery, and if it got its death blow in the war he should rejoice at the event." By a small majority, the final decision on the resolution was "indefinitely" postponed.[62] Barton's statement reflected the prevailing belief

60   *Advocate*, May 24, June 21, 1864.
61   *Advocate*, March 29, 1864; *Eagle*, October 15, 1864; Waite, *Claremont War History*, 36.
62   *Argus*, February 28, 1862.

that the war was a struggle to preserve the liberty and freedom guaranteed by the Constitution, being waged against a "Slave Power" that was a threat to his and others' personal liberties. While not at first as enthusiastic for the war as Claremont, judging by the initial number of men enlisting, Newport held to its belief that the South's challenge to the North was a greater threat to individual liberty than the cumulative hardship of the war. Furthermore, the towns' identification with their soldiers was still strong, for both Newport and Claremont had a substantial number of residents in the field throughout the later part of the war (see Figure 2.1). For Newport to repudiate the war effort would, in effect, be to repudiate a large number of its own citizens.[63] It seems plausible that communities in the North that did switch allegiance did so because disillusionment had overcome their identification with the war.

The North, however, still needed more men if it was to defeat the South. On July 18 of 1864 Lincoln called for 500,000 men and gave the states fifty days to fill their quotas, or another draft would be held on September 5. A few days later it was announced that Newport's quota had been set at 43; Claremont's was 68. Both communities immediately began to look for substitutes to fill their quotas, although the repeal of commutation in early July had sent the price of substitutes skyrocketing, thus making it more difficult and expensive for towns to fill their quotas.[64] On July 30 Newport voted to raise $43,000 for bounty money and to pay substitutes $300 in gold, but a few days later the selectmen rejected the plan as too expensive. In early August Claremont voted to ask its state representatives to attempt to modify or repeal the state law keeping local bounties below $300, "so that the several towns can pay any sum that may be necessary to fill their respective quotas."[65] The result of the great number of men needed and the high price of substitutes was that both towns were forced to look for new solutions, having already rejected the possibility of filling their quotas with local residents.

Meeting the quota had once again become the dominant subject in both towns, and plans were devised in both, in August 1864, to avoid the draft. Newport's idea was to have the town finance the purchase of substitutes by having an individual seeking a substitute pay the "difference of expense to the town." That differential was estimated to be $100 at a town meeting held on August 13, thus giving a man the opportunity to reduce Newport's quota by one if he gave the town $100. In Clare-

---

63 In March 1864 alone, over 16% of Newport's 1860 male population between the ages of 13 and 45 was in the field.

64 The *Argus* reported the price of substitutes to be between $600 and $700, in June 1864. *Argus,* June 3, 1864.

65 *Eagle,* August 13, 1864.

mont, committees had been appointed to notify every enrolled man to meet at the Town Hall on August 12 to discuss the quota. Claremont finally agreed on a plan whereby 300 enrolled men would pay $15 each, and 20 men $175 each, to help the town purchase the necessary number of substitutes to avoid the draft. The next day committees canvased each Claremont school district, collecting money from enrolled men.[66]

By August 16 the appointed committees were still trying to collect money from Claremont's enrolled men, and a letter appeared in the *Advocate* exhorting enrolled men to "pay up." The letter was signed by "ONE WHO DON'T LIKE DRAFTS," and it read in part:

> So you see, Mr. Editor, that it now remains in the power of a very few men, who so far have held back, to say whether there shall be a draft in C. or not. . . . . It seems to me that it [the plan] will sweeten the slumbers of every man who has a part in it. It seems to me that the thanks and blessings of many wives and children will follow everyone who thus shows his brotherly feeling towards his towns-men. It seems to me that the plan is one which, without argument, will commend itself to the feelings and the judgements of all who have hearts and minds not seared by avarice or hardened by self love; while at the same time *it is the most selfish plan* which an *enrolled* man can adopt, because it will cost him less than any other plan by which he can be sure to be exempt.

On August 20 it was announced in the *Eagle* that the enrolled men had "perfected their arrangements, so as probably to obviate the necessity for a draft." It is not known how many of the enrolled men contributed $15, but exactly 26 enrolled men contributed $175 each to procure substitutes.[67]

The net result of these plans was that both Claremont and Newport were able to avoid the draft, and these actions show how dramatically their conception of war had changed. In four years of war the meaning of patriotism in the two towns had gradually evolved from residents enlisting out of "true" motives to the community being willing to pay non-residents large sums of money to enlist. Community pressure was no longer on men to represent their community in the field but to group together and buy their way out of being drafted.

The most visible result of this change in attitude toward the war was

66 Newport Town Proceedings, July 30, August 13, September 3, 1864 Newport Town Hall, Newport, New Hampshire; *Eagle*, August 13, 1864. Only 14 out of Newport's quota of 43 were filled by substitutes, the rest being filled by Newport residents. The large number of resident enlistments is probably attributable to Newport's total bounty of $600 for one-year enlistments, $100 over the limit allowed by law.

67 *Advocate*, August 16, 1864; *Eagle*, August 20, 1864; "Financial Report for the Year Ending March 8, 1865," Claremont Town Proceedings, 8.

reflected in the large number of nonresidents filling both communities' quotas. After March 1863, 66 percent of Claremont's quota was filled by nonresidents, as compared with 47 percent of Newport's quota. As discussed earlier, many of these nonresidents were bounty jumpers, enlisting for large bounties and then deserting. Sixty percent of the 120 nonresidents who counted toward Claremont's quota deserted, while 34 percent of Newport's nonresidents did the same.

The enormous number of desertions was affecting not only the war effort but the two towns as well. The *Eagle* reported on September 10, 1864, that out of 500 recent recruits of the First New Hampshire Cavalry, 300 had deserted within a week. Every deserter had collected over $1,000 in bounty money, and the *Eagle* reported that this made "a total loss of over three hundred thousand dollars to the government in the space of one week." Twenty-three of these deserters had enlisted toward Claremont's quota, collecting over $10,000 in bounty money from Claremont.[68] In the month of August 1864 alone, exactly 27 nonresidents credited to Claremont deserted. Desertion was not limited only to nonresidents. In September 1864 Claremont resident Selden S. Chandler was shot for desertion, and during the war a total of 23 Claremont residents deserted, compared to 10 Newport men.[69]

But even given the quotas and desertions, the consensus in both communities by the end of 1864 was that the North would eventually triumph. The reelection of President Lincoln revealed that both communities still had faith in the Union cause, with Lincoln taking 75 percent of the vote in Claremont and 52 percent of the vote in Newport. In mid-December the North made another call for men and gave until February 15, 1865, for each state to fill its quota. The Confederacy had begun to crack into pieces, and this call was designed to "finish up the job." Delays once again moved the draft deadline back a month. Claremont was able to fill its quota by February 1865, relying on the method used in the previous draft. Newport could not fill its quota and eventually had to face the draft. Newport was still in the process of procuring substitutes when Richmond was finally captured on April 14.[70]

68 *Eagle*, September 10, 1864 (the *Eagle*'s report was taken from the *Portsmouth Journal*); "Financial Report for the Year Ending March 8, 1865," 7. Claremont "lost" more money on these deserters than it spent on its public schools and its fire department for fiscal year 1865. The state and federal government eventually paid back to the towns all the local bounty money spent during the war.

69 It is interesting to note that Selden Chandler was one of the officers of the Claremont Volunteers who had enlisted in April 1861. Chandler was married and had two children. It should also be pointed out that in many town histories of Newport it is claimed that no residents of Newport deserted. Ten actually did desert, including 4 who were found on the 1860 census for Newport.

70 *Advocate*, November 15, 1864; Murdock, *Patriotism Limited*, 12.

News of the end of the war was met with joy throughout the North. In Claremont, on April 15, "business was immediately suspended, the stores closed," and "men, women and children were upon the streets," and the "church, mill and school bells were rung." Newport celebrated in a similar manner. A town meeting was held in Claremont that evening, and patriotic addresses filled the agenda. The evening was capped off with fireworks and the burning of Jefferson Davis in effigy. The next morning the news of the assassination of Lincoln turned the joy into gloom, and the following day the Claremont town hall was once again filled, but this time for mourning.[71]

It is not surprising that Claremont's and Newport's vision of war changed over the course of the conflict, given the constant demand to meet quotas and the heavy casualties. As noted by the *Argus* in 1862, the "charm" of war had apparently lost its luster for the two towns after one year of war. But it seems that this change in perception only affected the two towns' perception of the means to the desired goal – the goal of the preservation of personal liberty guaranteed by the Constitution – not the goal itself. The direct results of finally attaining this goal will be analyzed later, but this essay will now focus on the actual individuals from Claremont and Newport who did and did not participate in the war.

Who Fought for Claremont and Newport?

What were the socioeconomic characteristics of the actual individuals from Claremont and Newport who fought in the Civil War? Answering this question not only provides a better understanding of the two towns' relationship to the war but also permits us to rest various theories concerning the socioeconomic background of Civil War soldiers. Additionally, analyzing the participation of the two towns' citizens allows for a comparison of two towns that differed politically but had rather similar wartime experiences.[72]

71 Waite, *Claremont War History*, 37–8.
72 There are very few studies that look at the socioeconomic background of soldiers from the same community. Harris, in her study of Deerfield, Massachusetts, does discuss several socioeconomic qualities of enlistees from Deerfield. The two most thorough studies that look at participants and nonparticipants are Maris Vinovskis's study of Newburyport, Massachusetts, and W. J. Rorabaugh's study of Concord, Massachusetts: Vinovskis, "Social Historians," section entitled "Newburyport and the Civil War"; W. J. Rorabaugh, "Who Fought for the North in the Civil War? Concord, Massachusetts, Enlistments," *Journal of American History*, 73 (December 1986) 695–701. References to the data found in the Newburyport and Concord studies are taken from these two sources, respectively, unless otherwise noted. Vinovskis based his study on those aged 12 to 49, while Rorabaugh based his study on those aged 16 to 49. Vinovskis's sample size was 3,200, while Rorabaugh's was 517. This essay looks at those aged 13 to 45 in Claremont and Newport. Selection of the 13 to 45 age group was

For this study, a data base of the two towns' 1860 census roll was created. By linking the names of the communities' soldiers to the federal census – which contained information on an individual's age, occupation, wealth, ethnicity, education, and family status – a picture of the types of individuals who fought in the Civil War for these two communities emerges. Claremont's listing of soldiers is found in O. F. R. Waite's *Claremont War History* (which includes biographical material on 306 Claremont soldiers). Newport's listing of soldiers is found in Edmund Wheeler's history of Newport. Because I noted a few inaccuracies in these sources, I also examined other materials to compile a more accurate listing of Claremont's and Newport's soldiers.[73]

During the Civil War, exactly 338 men from Claremont and 199 men from Newport enlisted. The estimated average number of enlistments for the North as a whole represented 35.8 percent of the total male population aged 13 to 43, and the actual number of people enlisting from Claremont and Newport represented respectively, 37.6 and 40.2 percent of that same-aged population in 1860.[74] If we count reenlistments of residents as individual enlistments, 50.8 percent of Claremont's and 51.7 percent of Newport's 13- to 43-year-old males in 1860 participated. And, by adding the number of nonresidents who were credited toward the two towns' quotas to the number of resident enlistments and reenlistments, it is seen that in 1860 Claremont contributed 64.1 percent of its male population aged 13 to 43 to the war, whereas Newport contributed 63.6 percent.

In terms of matching soldiers to the census, 57.4 percent of Claremont's soldiers were found on the 1860 census, as compared with 66.8 percent for Newport.[75] It is hard to determine what biases were caused

based on the ages of the two towns' soldiers, as found in the military records. The 13 to 45 age group accounted for 99% of the residents found in the military records (based on their age in the military records). Claremont's population for this age group in 1860 was 947, while Newport's same-aged population was 518.

73 In compiling the list of soldiers, I consulted town newspapers, town records, town histories, and the military records of New Hampshire. All information pertaining to military records was compiled from Ayling's *Revised Register*. Unlike many other state registers, the New Hampshire register lists soldier's residence and place of birth.

The reliance on more than one source is important in compiling a relatively accurate list of soldiers from one community. An example of this is provided by the military records, in which much of the information was reported by the soldiers themselves. See also Vinovskis, "Social Historians," section entitled "Newburyport and the Civil War," and Rorabaugh, "Who Fought for the North?," 696–7.

74 Northern average from Vinovskis, "Social Historians," section entitled "Newburyport and the Civil War."

75 In his study of Newburyport, Massachusetts, Vinovskis matched 55% of the soldiers to the census; Rorabaugh, in his study of Concord, Massachusetts, matched 47.8% of the soldiers to the census. By adding the number of nonresidents to the number of resident soldiers, we find that only 46.5% of the soldiers who were either residents of

in this analysis by the fact that not all of the soldiers matched the census. Maris Vinovskis, in his study of Newburyport, Massachusetts, found that those 19 and under had a better likelihood of matching the census, as did native-born soldiers. In looking at the soldiers' military records, Vinovskis found little difference between matchers and nonmatchers in terms of their likelihood to be either killed or wounded, but a substantial difference was found in those who deserted. He determined that 2 percent of those who matched the census deserted, as compared to a desertion rate of 13 percent for nonmatchers. W. J. Rorabaugh, in his study of soldiers from Concord, Massachusetts, claims that the military records of the matchers and nonmatchers were "relatively similar." In analyzing the military records of soldiers from Claremont and Newport, I found that those in Claremont who were 19 years old or younger and those who were over 35 had a better chance of matching than soldiers between the ages of 20 and 34. In Newport, the matching ratio was fairly equal throughout all age groups. Foreign-born men in Claremont had a better matching ratio, while in Newport those of native birth had a better matching ratio. The percentage of deserters in Claremont and Newport for those who matched was 2.4, whereas the percentage of deserters for those who did not match was 12.5 percent. Even with this in mind, the percentage of soldiers matching from Claremont and Newport is higher than in any other similar study performed and should be fairly representative of the residents from Claremont and Newport who enlisted.[76]

As in Vinovskis's and Rorabaugh's studies, age was the best predictor of whether or not someone participated in the war. For Claremont and Newport, the bulk of their enlistments came from those aged 13 to 29 in 1860. The age group with the highest percentage of enlistments in both towns was the 18 to 19 age group, with over one-third of that group participating in the war. Twenty percent of those aged 13 to 17 in Claremont participated, and 26 percent of that population participated from Newport. It is interesting to note that Claremont had a relatively high

Claremont or Newport or nonresidents credited toward the two towns matched the census. Only 3 nonresidents could be found in the census roll for outlying communities. A total of 41 Claremont and Newport soldiers found on the census either were residents of neighboring communities listed in the 1860 census or were above or below the 13 to 45 age range. These soldiers were discarded when analyzing those between the ages of 13 and 45 in the two communities.

76 There are two reasons why a higher percentage of residents did not match. First, there were errors in the census and the military records. Second, soldiers moved to or from the towns between the time when the census was taken (summer of 1860) and when they eventually enlisted. For example, Waite lists 306 resident soldiers in his *Claremont War History,* but I found that 16 "residents" had definitely moved away from Claremont well before 1860 (based on the evidence of the military records and town newspapers).

number of 40- to 45-year-olds who enlisted, most of whom enlisted in the first year of the war.

Increasingly larger percentages of enlistees tended to be in their early twenties or late teens as the war progressed.[77] Over one-half of Claremont's enlistments after 1863 were made by those who were in the 13 to 17 age group in 1860. This also is represented in Newport, with just less than one-half of its enlistments in the same period being made by those in the 13 to 17 age group. This trend is reproduced when the ages of the soldiers are looked at using the military records. The number of 18- to 19-year-olds who enlisted throughout the war remained steady and constituted the largest group enlisting at the end of the war for both towns, while the 20 to 24 age group was the largest group enlisting throughout the first half of the war and the second largest group enlisting in the latter half of the war. As noted, the self-reporting of age led to many errors in the military records. An example of this is the enlistment of Newport soldier Hial Comstock in September 1862. Comstock listed himself as being 44, presumably in order to bring his age under the military age limit of 45, but he was actually around 60 at the time, assuming that his listing as 58 in the 1860 census is correct. For most of the war a person had to be between 20 and 45 years old to enlist, and it seems that very few enlistees who were actually under 20 admitted their real age. Nonetheless, the ages found in the military records give a general idea of the trend of enlistees being concentrated in one age group as the war progressed.[78]

In looking at the wealth and occupations of participants and nonparticipants from Claremont and Newport, mention should be made that there has been much controversy over whether or not poor, unskilled laborers were overrepresented in the Union army. Most of this controversy stems from the practice of substitution and the commutation clause found in the Enrollment Act. As mentioned earlier, many portrayed the war as a "rich man's war but a poor man's fight," because of these two methods of avoiding conscription. A great deal has been written about whether commutation was fair or not, and it is safe to say that many historians have become so preoccupied with commutation as a means of

77 Harris notes the same occurrence in Deerfield. "Sons and Soldiers," 168.
78 This claim that the ages of the soldiers became concentrated in their early twenties or late teens as the war progressed is verified when we look at nonresidents who enlisted for both Claremont and Newport. Most of the nonresidents credited to the two communities were (or at least claimed to be) in their early twenties upon enlistment. Because all nonresident enlistments for both communities occurred after 1863, combining the ages of nonresidents with residents who enlisted in that same period demonstrates that by the second half of the war most of the soldiers associated with the two towns were in their early twenties or late teens.

judging "fairness" in the ranks that they have ignored other valuable topics.[79] But figuring out whether commutation was fair still does not determine whether one class within the soldiery was overrepresented or not. Federal conscription appeared two years after the war had begun, and by that time over 60 percent of Claremont's total enlistments had already occurred, as opposed to 54 percent of the total enlistments from Newport. So to better understand whether or not one class was over-represented, one should look at the soldiers themselves, as opposed to trying to interpret the fairness of a system that only supplied less than one-half of the soldiers for these two communities during the war.

By breaking down Claremont and Newport soldiers between the ages of 18 and 45 by occupational class, it appears that farmers and low-status white-collar workers were underrepresented in both communities, as were high-status white-collar workers in Newport. High-status white-collar workers in Claremont participated at the highest rate within that town, but in Newport they participated at the lowest rate. Unskilled workers participated at the highest rate for Newport, whereas in Claremont they participated at the second-highest rate. Skilled workers in both towns participated at a rate slightly less than that of unskilled workers. Even with a high level of participation by high-status white-collar workers in Claremont, one could still argue that the "upper" classes in both communities—farmers and white-collar workers—for the most part avoided the war.[80] But this information is deceptive, because it does not show that the majority of white-collar workers and farmers tended to be in the age group that was least likely to serve (the 30 and over age group).[81] By dividing the classes into age groups, we get a clearer picture of who served and who did not from each class (see Tables 2.2 and 2.3).

The data suggest that the supposed underrepresentation of the "upper classes" is not as clear-cut when age is included in the calculation with class. For example, low-status white-collar workers in Claremont showed a high level of participation in the 20 to 24 age group. The most consistent enlistment patterns in both towns were those of skilled and unskilled workers, throughout all age groups. The general enlistment patterns shown in both communities are confirmed when individuals between the ages of 18 and 45 whose occupations were not listed in the census are analyzed according to the occupation of their fathers. The majority of these "un-

79 Peter Levine, "Draft Evasion in the North during the Civil War, 1863–1865," *Journal of American History,* 67 (March 1981), 818.
80 As noted earlier, farmers in the two towns owned nearly one-half the total wealth of both towns, although they comprised only 15 percent of the male population between the ages of 18 and 45 in 1860.
81 McPherson notes the same when he looks at occupations of Northern and Southern soldiers. *Ordeal By Fire,* 357.

Table 2.2. *Age and class of Claremont soldiers*

Class	15–19		20–24		25–29		30–34		35–39		40–45		Total	
	N	%E	N	%E	N	%E	N	%E	N	%E	N	%E	N	%E
High-status white-collar (merchant, physician, etc.)			3	33	8	63	8	13	7		17	12	43	21
Low-status white-collar (clerk, teacher, etc.)			14	28	11		13	8	9		12		59	9
Skilled worker (blacksmith, machinist, etc.)	4	75	35	20	47	21	33	21	35	6	39	18	193	19
Unskilled worker (farm laborer, factory worker, etc.)	10	20	71	20	35	23	28	25	22	5	31	26	197	20
Farmer			4		10	10	20		17		30	3	81	3
Unknown (occupation not given in census)	69	35	46	9	16	6	22	9	12		7		172	19
Total	83	35	173	17	127	20	124	15	102	3	136	13	745	17

Note: Age = age in 1860; N = number of cases; %E = percentage enlisting.
Source: Compiled from U.S. Census Bureau, "Eighth Census of the United States, Sullivan County, New Hampshire, 1860," and Augustus D. Ayling, *Revised Register of the Soldiers and Sailors of New Hampshire in the War of Rebellion, 1861–1866* (Concord, N.H., 1895).

Table 2.3. Age and class of Newport soldiers

Class	18–19		20–24		25–29		30–34		35–39		40–45		Total	
	N	%E	N	%E	N	%E	N	%E	N	%E	N	%E	N	%E
High-status white-collar (merchant, physician, etc.)			1	100	1		6		6		5		19	5
Low-status white-collar (clerk, teacher, etc.)	2		7	14	7		5	20	9	11	7		37	8
Skilled worker (blacksmith, machinist, etc.)	6	50	20	35	22	55	8		11	18	15		82	31
Unskilled worker (farm laborer, factory worker, etc.)	13	30	38	44	16	38	12	25	17	18	10	30	106	34
Farmer			2		19	16	21	5	26	15	28		96	8
Unknown (occupation not given in census)	35	43	25	32	9	11	5	40	4		4		82	32
Total	56	39	93	37	74	30	57	12	73	14	69	6	422	23

Note: Age = age in 1860; N = number of cases; %E = percentage enlisting.
Source: Compiled from U.S. Census Bureau, "Eighth Census of the United States, Sullivan County, New Hampshire, 1860," and Augustus D. Ayling, *Revised Register of the Soldiers and Sailors of New Hampshire in the War of Rebellion, 1861–1866* (Concord, N.H., 1895).

knowns" tended to be young, especially between the ages of 18 to 24. When we analyze this group, we find that sons of farmers in Claremont participated at the same low level that farmers in Claremont did, while sons of Claremont high-status white-collar workers participated at a substantial level, just as Claremont high-status white-collar workers did. Like the enlistments of skilled and unskilled workers, sons of skilled and unskilled workers in both towns participated at a high rate.

This high level of participation by Claremont high-status white-collar workers needs to be analyzed, because it differs greatly from what was found in Newport and in Vinovskis's and Rorabaugh's studies. Newport's high-status white-collar workers had a participation rate of 5 percent, whereas in Vinovskis's study of Newburyport and in Rorabaugh's study of Concord a similar percentage for that class was found. This difference in participation between high-status white-collar workers from the two towns can be attributed to the political differences between Claremont and Newport. Claremont was solidly Republican before and during the war, and, as shown in the pages of the two Claremont newspapers, the majority of the high-status white-collar workers were backers of the Republican cause. Newport was more Democratic, and many of its high-status white-collar workers at the time can be identified in the *Argus* as being affiliated with the Democratic Party. Seeing that all high-status white-collar enlistments from the two towns took place within the first two years of the war, when enthusiasm for enlisting was strong, it seems likely that the people who were more enthusiastic about the war at that time (Republicans) participated in the war to a greater extent than the Democrats. My conclusion that a higher percentage of Claremont high-status white-collar workers participated because of political persuasion was reached indirectly: I was prevented from performing a comparison of enlistments of Republicans and Democrats from both towns by the lack of such records. However, this conclusion sheds light on a factor not mentioned in similar studies, which could in fact significantly affect those results.

This high participation level shown in both communities by skilled and unskilled workers can be furthered analyzed by considering wealth. By dividing those aged 18 to 45 years old into three wealth divisions—those having over $1,000 in total census wealth, those having between $100 and $999 in total census wealth, and those having under $100 in total census wealth—a clearer picture of the individuals who were most likely to enlist emerges. Not surprisingly, those with a total wealth of over $1,000 participated at the lowest level in both towns, at a rate of 7 percent in Claremont and 8 percent in Newport. In Claremont, those with wealth between $100 and $999 actually participated at a higher level than those with less than $100, further weakening the concept of a "poor man's war." Even after considering wealth, it is seen that skilled workers and unskilled workers enlisted at a rate near or above the average, in every wealth division and in every age group.

This breakdown by age, class, and wealth clearly shows that there were certain "prime groups" within each community that constituted the bulk of the enlistments. For Claremont, this group consisted of all skilled and unskilled workers, of any age and all levels of wealth; high-status white-collar workers under 29; low-status white-collar workers in the 20 to 24 age group; and 18- and 19-year-olds with no wealth or occupation. In Newport, this prime group consisted of all skilled and unskilled workers of all ages and all levels of wealth, of 18- and 19-year-olds with no wealth or occupation.[82]

These findings refute the idea that the war was a "poor man's war" for these two towns. If the war was fought by the poor, the bulk of the enlistments would have been by poor unskilled workers, which clearly is not the case for Claremont and Newport. Further doubt is cast on the theory when we examine the socioeconomic background of the fathers of those between the ages of 13 and 17 in 1860. The enlistment patterns for the 18 to 45 age group are for the most part mirrored when we look at the wealth and class of the fathers of the 13 to 17 age group. Participation by sons of unskilled and skilled workers also cut across all wealth divisions. Enlistment by farmers' sons from both towns was low, just as it was for adults in both towns. In Claremont, sons of high-status white-collar workers participated at the greatest rate, just as adult Claremont high-status white-collar workers did. The major difference between the enlistments of 13- to 17-year-olds and their adult counterparts was the enlistment of white-collar workers in both towns. Sons of high-status white-collar workers in Newport, and sons of low-status white-collar workers in both towns, participated at a substantial rate, unlike their adult counterparts. When concentrating on wealth alone, it is seen that fathers of soldiers having between $100 and $999 in total census wealth participated at a higher rate in both towns than those whose fathers had more or less money. It is interesting to note that in Claremont, soldiers whose fathers had over $1,000 in total wealth participated at the same rate as those soldiers whose fathers had less than $100.

This high participation rate by both towns' "prime" groups raises

82 Rorabaugh uses the expression "prime military groups" to describe those most likely to enlist. Rorabaugh's prime military group includes propertied small shopkeepers, clerks, and skilled workers in their twenties and thirties. "Who Fought for the North?", 699. Complete tables giving the breakdown by wealth, class, and age for Claremont and Newport are in Kemp, "Community and War," 87–8. Because of space constraints, only the tables containing the age and class breakdown are included here.

questions concerning their motivation to enlist.[83] As Rorabaugh notes, the enlistment of young unemployed workers and propertyless unskilled workers can easily be accounted for, since "throughout history they have constituted the bulk of the world's armies." It is the high participation of skilled workers and others that is of interest.[84] It seems that these workers enlisted for the same underlying reason for which the two towns supported the war effort throughout the war's duration. These workers probably saw in the Union cause a "struggle to preserve a system, in which every man, whatever his station at birth, could achieve social advancement and economic independence." Thus the South was seen as a threat to a system that guaranteed their economic as well as political liberties. With the Constitution intact, skilled workers, young white-collar workers, and unskilled workers believed that they could rapidly advance within society, whereas the "Slave Power" system of government was perceived as the antithesis of the North's vision of "social mobility as the glory of northern society."[85] The emphasis on social mobility in Northern society was very important then—especially given the fear of many workers that economic modernization would "swallow" them up—and "Free Labor" became one of the most appealing ideologies of the Republican Party. It is very possible that these workers believed that they could ensure their personal liberty and their future mobility only by leading the North to victory.[86]

Like the representation of social classes, the ethnicity of participants has also been embroiled in controversy. Many have claimed that the foreign-born were overrepresented within the Union army, but recent studies have suggested that the foreign-born enlisted at a rate equal to or less than that of native-born Americans. In Claremont, the foreign-born were in fact underrepresented, comprising only 8 percent of the soldiers who matched the census, although they comprised over 12 percent of the population. In Newport the foreign-born enlisted at a rate equal to their percentage within the town as a whole. Many historians have felt that the Irish-born were overrepresented in the Union army, but in both towns the Irish-born participated at a lower rate than their proportion within the two communities.[87] If we look at the ethnicity of the soldiers

83 Rorabaugh asks the same question for those most likely to enlist from Concord. "Who Fought for the North," 699.
84 Ibid.
85 Foner, "Causes of the American Civil War," 213–14; Foner, *Free Soil*, 16.
86 Foner, "Causes of the American Civil War," 214; Rorabaugh, "Who Fought for the North," 699–701.
87 Vinovskis, "Social Historians," section entitled "Newburyport and the Civil War"; Rorabaugh, "Who fought for the North," 698–9; Ella Lonn, *Foreigners in the Union Army and Navy* (Baton Rouge, 1951), 441–4.

using the military records, we see that these trends basically repeat themselves. In Claremont, 88.7 percent of the soldiers were born in the United States, a greater rate than that in the town's general population in 1860. In Newport, however, only 91 percent of the soldiers were native-born, as opposed to 96 percent of the town's general population, meaning that the foreign-born may have been slightly overrepresented in Newport.

A completely different picture emerges when we analyze the ethnicity of nonresidents credited to the two towns. Only 40.7 percent of the nonresidents were born in the United States, while nearly 20 percent were born in Ireland and 23 percent were born in Canada. The place of birth of nonresidents was not limited to Canada or Europe, with one nonresident listed as being born in India and another in the West Indies. Although nonresident enlistments only accounted for 20 percent of the total enlistments from these two towns, the fact that out of this 20 percent more than one-half were foreign-born shows that the foreign-born were overrepresented in the total enlistments from both Claremont and Newport. By analyzing all the soldiers who were either residents of Claremont or Newport or nonresidents credited to one of these two towns, 77.4 percent were native-born, compared to 93 percent of the population of New Hampshire as a whole in 1860. Although the sample size does not permit us to make a generalization for the North as a whole concerning participation by the foreign-born, the importance of looking at the ethnicity of nonresidents who served should be remembered when we look at who participated from other Northern communities.[88]

Another important factor is the affect of marriage on enlistment. It is quite conceivable that married men were less likely to enlist than unmarried men, because they needed to care for their families. Looking at those between the ages of 18 and 45 in both towns, we see in Claremont that married men enlisted at a 15 percent rate, while unmarried men enlisted at an 18 percent rate. In Newport, married men participated at a 19 percent rate, compared with a 29 percent rate for unmarried men. When 18- and 19-year-olds (who were mostly unmarried and had the highest rate of participation among any age group) are not counted, Claremont married men had a higher rate of participation than unmarried men, whereas the percentage difference between married men and unmarried was cut in half in Newport. When we look at married men with children, we can determine that married men with children in both towns participated at

88 This should also be the case with other socioeconomic factors concerning nonresidents credited to Northern towns. Even if all of Claremont's and Newport's nonresidents were unskilled workers, by combining the occupations of residents from both Claremont and Newport with those of nonresidents we can conclude that unskilled workers still did not make up the bulk of the enlistments.

the same rate as married men as a whole. This information leads to the conclusion that the motivation to enlist must have been compelling enough so that many put aside family obligations, especially in heavily Republican Claremont.

The last factor investigated was the education of those 17 and under. Out of males aged 13 to 17 in Claremont, 73 percent had attended school in 1860; in Newport, 76 percent of the same-aged population had attended school in that year. Out of those in Claremont who had attended school, 19 percent participated in the war, while 20 percent of those who did not go to school participated. In Newport, 26 percent of those who went to school participated, as did 26 percent of those who did not go to school. Thus it seems that attendance at school did not act as a deterrent to enlistment, as is the case in Vinovskis's study of Newburyport. Looking at illiteracy within the two communities, 17 percent of those who were listed as illiterate in the 1860 census participated, which is 2 percent lower than the overall 19-percent participation rate for the two communities. It therefore seems that literacy and education did not play key roles in determining enlistments within the two towns.

Finally, let us look at the socioeconomic characteristics of the individuals who purposely avoided the war. As discussed in the preceding section, the enrolled men in Claremont, by the time of the third draft, had banded together to avoid the draft. All of the money raised by the enrolled men went to the hiring of substitutes. For that draft and the next, approximately 35 Claremont citizens had paid $175 each to hire substitutes, whereas the rest of the enrolled men in the community had paid only $15 each. In the first two drafts 41 Claremont men had procured substitutes. What type of person would buy himself out of the war by paying a substitute? Out of the 76 Claremont men who procured substitutes, 54 matched the census. In looking at the socioeconomic backgrounds of these men, we find that most of these men were not part of Claremont's prime enlistment group. Thirty-one percent of these men had over $1,000 in total wealth, well over the 7-percent participation rate for that wealth division. The largest group represented here consists of farmers, the same group who were the least likely to serve in Claremont. Out of the 13 men who purchased substitutes and whose occupation was not listed in the census, 10 of these men were sons of farmers, the group of "unknowns" least likely to participate in the war.

What this analysis reveals was that there were two primary enlistment trends within Claremont and Newport: the high rate of participation among skilled and unskilled workers, and the low level of participation by farmers. For skilled and unskilled workers, participation cut across all age and wealth divisions. When analyzing the participation by farmers within the two towns, it is not surprising that they participated at a low rate, because they probably did not see their future mobility at stake, as did skilled and unskilled workers. It was also seen that political affiliation may have had an important affect in determining who participated, with high-status white-collar workers participating at the highest rate in Republican Claremont, and married men over the age of 19 in Claremont participating at a higher rate than unmarried men. Thus for many people, the Union and what it stood for took precedence over family and friends.

The Legacy of the War for Claremont and Newport

We have examined the towns' reactions to the war and determined the demographic profile of the participants. There remains the question of what legacy the war left for Claremont and Newport. Although it is difficult to assess the direct results of the war on these two small towns after more than a century has passed, we can approach the question by pursuing three lines of investigation. First, we can investigate the affect of the war on the lives of those individuals from Claremont and Newport who participated in the Civil War. Second, we can attempt to determine the impact of the war on the communities as a whole by analyzing the effect of the war on their economies and populations. Finally, we can look at Claremont's and Newport's perceptions of the war after it had ended and determine if these perceptions were similar to the perceptions they had had of the war while it continued to rage. Although this will only provide a few clues to the effects of the war on postwar life in the North, these three inquiries represent important aspects of the community Civil War experience that has received scant treatment by historians.

The effect of the Civil War on the individual is difficult to gauge. Every soldier had a unique experience, which could be analyzed by various methods. However, five of the well-documented individual outcomes of military service obviously would have had a significant impact on a person's life: being killed; being wounded; deserting; being discharged because of disability; and being captured by the enemy. From the military records, I determined that 79 men from Claremont died, while 38 men from Newport died. In Claremont this accounted for 23 percent of its total enlisted soldiers; in Newport this number equaled 19 percent. These numbers equaled or exceeded the Union average of 19 percent. The number of Claremont soldiers who died represented 8 percent of the town's male population between the ages of 13 and 45 in 1860, whereas the number of Newport soldiers killed represented 7 percent of the same-aged male population. Of the 117 men who died from the two towns, 44 percent died of disease, which is nearly 10 percent below the national average of 55 percent of soldiers' death being attributed to disease. The diseases picked up in the ranks even followed many soldiers home, as evidenced by the fact that three Claremont men died at home after the war was over of diseases contracted in camp.[89]

Both towns had as many severely wounded men as there were deaths. Eighty-eight Claremont men were wounded, including 1 soldier who was wounded four times, whereas only 30 Newport soldiers were wounded during the war. During the war 115 Claremont men were discharged due to disability, 25 percent of whom were listed in the military records as having been seriously wounded prior to discharge. In Newport, 38 men were discharged due to disability, 26 percent of whom were discharged because of severe wounds. Capture by the enemy also proved dangerous to an individual's life course, with 11 of the 26 Claremont men captured dying shortly thereafter, while 2 of the 8 Newport men captured during the war also died. Finally, 7 percent of Claremont's soldiers deserted, but only 5 percent of Newport's soldiers did.

An analysis of the individuals who had any one of these five experiences reveals that exactly 68.3 percent of Claremont's soldiers had one of these traumatic war experiences. Whereas 48.7 percent of Newport's soldiers also had some combination of these five experiences. These numbers represent 24 percent of Claremont's male population between the ages of 13 and 45 in 1860, and 5.7 percent of the total Claremont population, as compared to 18 percent of Newport's military-aged population and 4.7 percent of the total population. These percentages are significant, because they show that the war directly affected the lives of many people—not only the soldiers themselves but friends and families. Relatives and friends of soldiers had to cope with returning wounded, and, given the relatively high participation rate of married men in the two towns, the number of widows and orphaned children in both communities must have been significant. Although it is possible to count the number of people directly affected by the war, it is of course impossible to determine the extent of the emotional suffering experienced by those people.

Analyzing the numbers of dead and wounded raises the question of whether a soldier's socioeconomic background determined his chance of being killed or wounded in the war. When we examine the records of men from Claremont, it seems that class was the best determinant of whether someone was killed or wounded. Skilled and unskilled work-

89 Vinovskis looks at four experiences: dying, being wounded, deserting, or being discharged as disabled. Vinovskis, "Social Historians," section entitled "Newburyport and the Civil War." National mortality averages are from the section entitled "Characteristics of the Civil War."

ers made up the bulk of the dead and wounded soldiers from Claremont; high-status white-collar workers and farmers were the most likely to escape harm. Wealthier soldiers in Claremont also had the least likelihood of dying or being wounded. More foreign-born soldiers than native-born soldiers died. The age group in Claremont most likely to die or become wounded included those aged 18 to 19. With Newport, the ages most likely to die or become wounded were those aged 13 to 17 in 1860, followed closely by those aged 18 to 19. Skilled and unskilled workers in Newport also died or were wounded at a greater rate than farmers and white-collar workers. Wealth and ethnicity do not factor in determining which Newport soldiers died or were wounded. Looking at the two towns as a whole, the general trend in both communities was that those from the lower classes were more likely to die or be wounded.[90] The best explanation for this high death and wounded rate among skilled and unskilled workers may be that their health was generally poorer and they were therefore more susceptible to disease.[91]

The significance of desertion by a soldier should also be closely looked at, because the stigma attached to desertion could follow a soldier throughout his life. Men returning home wounded or upon the honorable completion of military service were looked upon with respect, but known deserters were typically looked upon as cowards. It is therefore quite understandable that deserters would not want to return to a place where they could be shunned. What makes this point even more interesting is that a considerable number of soldiers deserted throughout the war. Seven percent of Claremont's soldiers deserted during the war, as compared to 5 percent of Newport's soldiers, and 51 percent of the non-residents credited to either of these two towns deserted. Of the surviving 22 soldiers from Claremont who deserted, it seems that only 2 returned to Claremont permanently. The stigma attached to desertion was probably greater if the soldier was of high social standing within the community. A good example was John J. Prentiss, a Claremont soldier who was appointed captain at the mustering in but was later dismissed for desertion. Prentiss was a former speaker of the house of the New Hampshire legislature, but after his dismissal, he eventually moved to Chicago. We can only speculate on whether or not his desertion and dismissal had anything to do with his leaving Claremont, but it is known that most of

90 The concentration of the dead or wounded in the younger age groups in Claremont and Newport is best explained by the fact that most of the unskilled and skilled workers who participated were young.

91 Vinovskis, "Social Historians," section entitled "Newburyport and the Civil War." Vinovskis also investigates this issue and raises the question of whether citizens from lower classes were assigned to units that were given tasks that were "particularly dangerous."

the deserters associated with Claremont or Newport tended not to return, nor are their whereabouts even known by the military records or town historians.[92]

Another factor arising from the Civil War that may have played an important role in a soldier's life after combat was the receipt of a pension. Sixty-three percent of the 112 Claremont soldiers whose addresses were known in 1894 received a pension. Since the average annual pension awarded in 1900 was $139 and the average annual wage for a worker in that year was $375, the impact of a pension on a veteran's life could have been great.[93]

Another factor that could have significantly affected a soldier's life was his place of residence after the war. The Civil War afforded many Claremont and Newport men their first opportunity to leave their rural surroundings and experience other parts of the country, but did the war inspire many to leave their homes after the war? By looking at the post office addresses of Claremont or Newport soldiers in 1895 or the place of death of soldiers before 1895, we can see that a great deal of mobility occurred. Even given the high mobility of American society in general in the post–Civil War years, the fact that most of the soldiers moved away from towns whose citizens had traditionally stayed there generation after generation suggests that the Civil War must have had some impact. Forty-six percent of those Newport soldiers with a known post office address or place of death either lived in Newport in 1895 or died in Newport before 1895, whereas 35 percent of the Claremont soldiers with a known post office address or place of death lived in Claremont in 1895 or died there before 1895. By adding in the soldiers whose whereabouts are unknown, we find that over 75 percent of both communities' soldiers had moved away from Newport or Claremont by 1895. Looking at the Claremont soldiers who were actually born in Claremont, we see that only 40 percent continued to live in Claremont after the war, while 56 percent of the Newport soldiers who were born in Newport lived or had died in Newport by 1895.[94]

As mentioned previously, there are some inherent limitations to the

---

92 One can partially attribute the high rate of desertion of nonresidents to these people not being citizens of those communities and therefore not having to worry about the stigma attached to desertion within those communities. For a discussion of Civil War desertion and two communities, see Judith Lee Hallock, "The Role of the Community in Civil War Desertion," *Civil War History*, 29 (June 1983), 123–34. The number of men returning to Claremont to live after the war was compiled from Waite, *Claremont War History*, 284–302, and military records.

93 Percentage of those receiving a pension compiled from Waite, *Claremont War History*, 284–302; Pension figures for 1900 from Vinovskis, "Social Historians," section entitled "Civil War Pensions and Union Veterans."

94 Post office address statistics, compiled from the military records.

study of this factor. Recently scholars have discussed the general psychological impact of the war, but each individual must have had a unique experience that shaped his life in a certain way. The Civil War reshaped the lives of some but had a less significant impact on others. Nonetheless, a substantial number of Claremont and Newport soldiers clearly had a traumatic war experience that greatly affected their lives and the lives of those close to them. For many, it seems that the manner in which they had faced battle followed them for the rest of their lives.[95] Even thirty years after the war, participation in the war played an important role by affecting veterans' incomes and residency.

We are also somewhat limited in measuring the effect of the Civil War on both towns as a whole, just as we are limited in measuring the effect of the war on veterans from Claremont and Newport. In terms of local finances, the effect of the war was great. Throughout the war both communities constantly had to borrow money to pay for bounties, and both went quickly into debt (see Table 2.1). To pay for this, the rate of taxation in both communities drastically increased. In Claremont in 1862 the rate of taxation on $100 in real estate was $.39; four years later it was $1.58.[96] By the end of the war Claremont was nearly $71,000 in debt, and Newport was $56,000 in debt–both significant figures, even given the high rate of inflation at the time. The result of this debt signaled a necessary shift in both "local fiscal responsibility and sophistication."[97] Both communities had to make long-term commitments to pay off sizable debts and to manage budgets that were at least three times as large as those before the war.

Industry in both communities was also severely affected by the Civil War. The lack of cotton during the war had a great impact on Claremont's and Newport's cotton mills; many cotton mills were forced to change their machinery so that they could manufacture woolen flannel. Claremont's largest cotton mill during the war, the Monadnock Mills, converted in 1864 and did not change back to cotton machinery until 1881. The number of employees of cotton mills in 1860 in Sullivan County was 490; ten years later, this number had dropped to 330.[98] Industry in

---

95 For example, see Hiller B. Zobel, "Enlisted for Life," *American Heritage*, 37 (June / July 1986), 56–64; Linderman, *Embattled Courage;* Marvin R. Cain, "A 'Face of Battle' Needed: An Assessment of Motives and Men in Civil War Historiography," *Civil War History*, 28 (March 1982), 5–27.

96 Claremont Town Proceedings, 1862–6.

97 Harris, "Sons and Soldiers," 170.

98 Waite, *Claremont Town History*, 194–5. The number of employees working at cotton mills was compiled from the Eighth Census of the United States (1860) and the Ninth Census of the United States (1870) for Sullivan County. U.S. Census Bureau, *Eighth Census of the United States, Sullivan County, New Hampshire, 1860:* U.S. Census Bureau, *Ninth Census of the United States, Sullivan County, New Hampshire,*

both communities therefore had to be restructured to face the multiple effects of war. Another example of how the war affected industry was the attrition of many skilled workers who died during the war and needed to be replaced. As noted earlier, most of the soldiers who were either wounded or killed were from the skilled or unskilled laborer class, and restrictions placed on immigration during the war did not immediately allow these losses to be made up. In addition, many young soldiers did not return to Claremont and Newport, which possibly created a drain on labor.

The last legacy of the war to be examined here is the perception of the war that the communities had well after the war had ended. As we have seen, the reactions of the two communities to the war in 1864 was far from what they had felt in 1861, signaling that the communities' views of patriotism and war had changed. Did the two communities feel the same way about the war after it was over as they did when the war was winding down in 1864–5? It appears that the answer is no. Both communities gradually readopted the vision of war that they had had in April 1861 of war as "noble" and "glorious." Claremont and Newport had in essence come full cycle.

This gradual change in the perception of war was evident at the dedication of Claremont's monument to its Civil War soldiers in 1869.[99] The speaker at the dedication did mention the "maddening carnage" of war, but his speech echoed with allusions to the grandeur of war that had marked speeches of the early war years. The probable reason for this gradual reversion to their initial perception of war was that it is human nature to block out the negative aspects of war and highlight any positive qualities found in it. Both towns had suffered a great deal from the war, and it was less painful to think about April 1861 then it was to think about 1864. Waite, in his war history of Claremont published in 1868, writes more about the first month of the war than he does about the last three years of the war. Waite even fails to mention, in his short biography of each Claremont soldier, that Selden S. Chandler was shot for desertion. The embarrassment of having one of his fellow residents do such a despicable thing as deserting was apparently so great that twenty-four

---

1870. The loss of the cotton mills may have been one of the reasons why Claremont's total population only increased by 27 from 1860 to 1870.

99 The monument contains the names of 75 Claremont soldiers. Three of the men were former residents of Claremont, and the monument also gives the names of three who died in Claremont after the war, of diseases contracted in the service. The military records reveal that an additional 10 men who were listed as residents of Claremont died during the war, but their names are not on the monument. Four of these 10 appear in Waite's *Claremont War History,* including Selden S. Chandler, who was shot for desertion.

years later, in his town history of Claremont, Waite mentioned only that Chandler had "died in the service."[100]

Veterans were slower to forget the emotional wounds caused by the war. They seem to have gone into "hibernation" after the war, trying to heal both external and internal wounds.[101] A post of the Grand Army of the Republic (GAR) was formed in Claremont in 1868 but was disbanded a few years later, apparently because of lack of interest. Selective memory was setting in—the "strong psychological propensity to suppress the painful"—and eventually veterans would come to accept the vision of the war to which civilian society had, relatively quickly, reverted. A GAR post was reorganized in Claremont in 1880, and the GAR become one of the dominant institutions in both communities in the 1880s and 1890s. This seems to have been true also of the rest of the nation: "Veterans' organizations in both North and South often enjoyed a social influence commensurate with that of school and church."[102] By that time the pain that the two towns had felt had been forgotten, and the Civil War was fondly looked upon as a glorious and noble adventure, a "test of heroism and virtue." Given the rapid transformation of society occurring at the time, it is not surprising that many glorified the Civil War, perceiving it as a model in which the outcome of complex events could be resolved by simple tests of courage.[103]

This depiction, which survived the nineteenth century, distorts the truth of the Civil War. But given what Claremont and Newport had to endure during the war, it is not surprising that they, like the rest of the nation, wanted to forget its harsh realities. In many town histories of Newport it is claimed that no one deserted during the war. Why would Newport want to be reminded that some of its residents deserted the nation in one of its most perilous hours? The Civil War was a brutal experience for the lives of many Americans, and it seems to have been an equally horrible experience for the soul of America as well.

Conclusion

Like many other communities throughout the nation, Claremont and Newport entered the war with high hopes and great expectations. Participation in the war by the towns' residents reflected these expectations,

100 Waite, *Claremont Town History,* 273–9; Linderman, *Embattled Courage,* 266–97; Waite, *Claremont War History,* 49; ibid., 285.
101 Linderman, *Embattled Courage,* 266–97.
102 Waite, *Claremont Town History,* 368; Linderman, *Embattled Courage,* 267, 276.
103 Daniel Hall, "The Civic Record of New Hampshire in the Civil War," in New Hampshire Historical Society, *Concord Proceedings* (Concord, N.H., 1905), vol. 4, *1899–1905,* 406; Linderman, *Embattled Courage,* 284–97.

seeing the war as a test of courage, a battle to protect the personal liberties guaranteed by the Constitution. Skilled and unskilled workers and sons of white-collar workers in both towns saw their future mobility at stake, and participation by these individuals cut across all divisions of wealth.

The war turned out to be very different from what Claremont and Newport had initially expected. Four years of bloody war had left the two communities dazed, and the war had taken its toll on most of the soldiers who fought in it. Later on, wounds may have healed and loved ones may eventually have forgotten, but psychologically the war left a painful scar that was only gradually healed over with the passage of time, by the same lofty perception of war that both communities had shared in April 1861.

3

The Northern Soldier and His Community

REID MITCHELL

In sorrow and in anger, Lt. George Kies wrote to his wife in Connecticut from Baltimore, where his company was stationed. "I received a letter from som one yesterday purporting to be from you but i cannot think that you would write me such a letter." His wife scolded him for not writing to her, but he had sent her letters. His wife accused him of involvement with another woman with whom he supposedly had had clandestine rendezvous in Philadelphia. She thought he had spent the money they needed to buy gravestones for their dead children on furs for the other woman. These accusations were so detailed that Kies could only conclude somebody was deliberately telling lies to create trouble for him with his wife. "The one who says I hav is a liar and i would tell them so though [they] are as big as Christ himself." Whoever it was, it upset Kies that his wife believed others instead of him. They had told her that he was telling women that his wife was dead and that he was not a married man. "You say that the soldiers say that i did not take your Death very hard. If you will tell me what soldiers told that i will let you know how hard they will take there [own] Death." His wife's economic well-being worried him; he offered to send her all his pay and to steal for his own living. The lieutenant also sent his wife gifts.

But Kies's letters home indicate that derogatory reports from the front and his wife's accusations still continued after she had received his explanations and presents. He protested, "I hav not touched a woman since i was with you not so much as to feel of her Leg." His wife's charges of infidelity particularly bothered him, because he currently suffered from sexual desire: "I do awfuly want to som times and think that i should not care what become of me in the morning if i could sleep with you one night and have as good times as we used to in each others arms." Mrs.

I would like to thank Liza Buurma for her help with this essay.

78

Kies had relented enough to send him her picture; it brought to his mind "so many pleasant recollection[s]."[1]

George Kies's troubled correspondence with his wife should serve us as more than an interesting, even juicy, tidbit of the Civil War era or even a reminder that Victorians had sex lives. Lieutenant Kies's preoccupation with his domestic life in the midst of war warns us of the danger of neglecting the personal when seeking the meaning of the Civil War experience. More specifically, this exchange of letters demonstrates the way in which information, gossip, sentiment, and acrimony passed back and forth between the men in the army and the people at home. This nexus of personal communication was a context in which men experienced the more purely military aspects of the war. Furthermore, it provided much of the motivation that kept men in the service of their country and their homes.

Recently a number of historians have turned their attention to the question of the motivations and experiences of the soldiers and citizens of the Civil War era. People who typically kept few written records left behind a profusion of letters, diaries, and memoirs for the years 1861 to 1865; the so-called inarticulate became voluble. These materials permit students of the war years to examine the attitudes of mid-nineteenth-century Americans, looking for new keys to the bloodiest puzzle in our history. Military historians, particularly those influenced by John Keegan's *Face of Battle,* have also developed a fresh concern with what makes soldiers fight; they too have started to turn to the lavish records of the war years to understand the American soldier.[2]

In this essay, I will consider how ties with home influenced the experience of the Union soldier during the Civil War. Combat, military discipline, ideology, and leadership have all been evaluated as determinants of soldiers' conduct during the war, but community values were equally important. In fact, they were crucial to the way in which Americans made

1 George Kies to wife, April 25, [1863], April 29, [1863], June 10, 1863, in George Kies Papers, Connecticut Historical Society, Hartford, Conn.

2 An outstanding overview of Union soldiers is Bell I. Wiley, *The Life of Billy Yank* (Indianapolis, 1952). Bruce Catton also helped pioneer the study of the soldiers' perspective in his Army of the Potomac trilogy: *Mr. Lincoln's Army* (1931), *Glory Road* (1952), and *A Stillness at Appomattox* (1953). James I. Robertson, *Soldiers Blue and Gray* (Columbia, 1988), continues working in the Bell Wiley tradition. Joseph T. Glatthaar analyzes the soldiers in Sherman's army in *The March to the Sea and Beyond: Sherman's Troops in the Savannah and Carolinas Campaigns* (New York, 1985). A study that focuses on the ideological motivations for the Union war effort is Earl Hess, *Liberty, Virtue, and Progress* (New York, 1988). Randall Jimerson, *The Private Civil War* (Baton Rouge, 1988), and Reid Mitchell, *Civil War Soldiers* (New York, 1988), emphasize the common attitudes and experiences of Union and Confederate soldiers. Gerald F. Linderman, *Embattled Courage* (New York, 1987), considers the experience of combat in detail.

war from 1861 to 1865. Since the war itself can be viewed as a conflict over the meaning of community, this is not surprising. The closeness of the soldier to his community both undercut the traditional arrangements that armies make for discipline and provided a powerful impetus for military service and patriotic tenacity.[3]

In many ways American armies during the Civil War contravened normal military practice. The process by which men are turned into soldiers – one is tempted to say "reduced to soldiers" – involves removing them from the larger society. They wear distinctive dress, distinctive haircuts, submit to unusual drill, discipline, and ritual, are commanded by officers. They are literally regimented. Armies master people by subjecting them to unfamiliar environments; people adapt to this new environment and thus become soldiers. Armies work by setting men apart.[4]

To a large extent, Civil War armies succeeded in doing these things. The volunteers did become soldiers. But the transformation from civilian to soldier was rarely completed. One reason for this is that in some ways the company – the basic military unit – functioned as an extension of the soldier's home community. In most respects, a soldier's company was the army for that soldier. Within that company he received his orders, his supplies, his companionship. Companies and regiments were raised by local leaders in specific towns and counties; the soldier's officers and fellow soldiers were most often men he had known all his life. In the midst of military life, the soldier was constantly reminded of his civilian life. Unlike the French Foreign Legion, the Union army would have been a wretched institution for any man who joined in order "to forget" – unless he joined up away from his home.[5]

It is important to realize that this way of recruiting and organizing soldiers was not simply accidental. Instead, this voluntary organization of small communities into a national army, the amalgamation of civic pride and national patriotism, serves as an example of how the volunteers imagined the Union should function. In 1861, a Union that went to war by creating a centralized army would have been unrecognizable to them. The localistic nature of the companies and regiments faithfully mirrored the body politic at large.

For new recruits, the army should be a terrifying institution; soldiering should be different from anything they have known before. Like all insti-

---

3   The fact that this essay describes the experience of Union soldiers is not meant to imply that Confederate soldiers did not have a similar relationship to the towns and counties from which they came.
4   A particularly good discussion of this is Eric J. Leed, *No Man's Land: Combat and Identity in World War I* (New York, 1979), 1–38.
5   See Paddy Griffith's discussion of the "regimental matrix" in *Battle Tactics of the Civil War* (New Haven, 1989), Chapter 4.

tutions, established armies have traditions of their own. A Scottish recruit coming to a British regiment, or even an American teenager entering the cadet corp at West Point, would find himself bound – and inspired – not only by formal discipline but by the powerful traditions, history, and myths of his new home. These traditions too play their role in transforming civilians into soldiers. But in most cases Civil War regiments had no such traditions. These were new regiments, making up their regimental traditions. The new soldiers themselves were far more intimately involved in the creation of these traditions, in the interpretation of company history, than is ordinarily the case – indeed, than would be the case for conscripts coming to the armies after 1863.

Civil War companies were first and foremost military institutions, but they were not exempt from the culture of the nineteenth-century American volunteerism that produced them. Sometimes soldiers insisted that their company – their new home – serve other functions. They might form societies "for mutual improvement in cultivating the mind" or for debating important questions of the day, such as whether or not "education has more influence over the mind of man than money." Bible classes held in an Indiana regiment paid special attention to the conflicting claims of Calvinism and Arminianism. Soldiers donated money to buy their regiments libraries, organized Christian associations, and held Sunday prayer meetings – all as if they had read Tocqueville. Companies of Union volunteers, then, behaved much as other American fraternal organizations. The average Civil War company began with all the discipline of a lodge of Elks.[6]

Armies deliberately create distance between a soldier and his officers. Generally, officers are of a different class from that of the soldiers – historically, from an aristocratic class. The army feeds, clothes, and arms officers differently, pays them more, educates them to a higher level. Officers are given legal sanction for their authority, authority that they ultimately can back up with the death penalty. In theory, all of these factors combine to legitimate the authority of the officer corp over the rank and file.[7]

6 John R. Hunt Diary, January 22, 1982, Schoff Collection, Clements Library, University of Michigan, Ann Arbor, Mich. Ichabod Frisbie to wife, November 18, 1862, Civil War Miscellany, U.S. Army Military History Institute, Carlisle, Pa. (See *Key West New Era*, April 5, 1862, in William W. Geety Papers, Harrisburg Civil War Round Table Collection, U.S. Army Military History Institute, for notice of a debate to be held on the same subject. Diary, March 14, 21, 22, 23, 25, 25, 1862.) Richard Henry Pratt Papers, Library of Congress. Diary, April 1, 10, 1863, Francis M. Troth Papers, University of Texas, Austin, Tex. George H. Allen Diary, October 19, 1862. University of Texas.

7 The role of officers, inspiration, and discipline in nineteenth-century combat is discussed in John Keegan. *The Face of Battle* (New York, 1976), Chapter 3, "Infantry vs. Infantry" (pp. 162–94 in the Penguin edition).

During the Civil War, however, a soldier's immediate officers hardly came from a hereditary caste. They were generally his fellow townspeople or local men prominent in his county. They sometimes had the prestige of having organized the company, and back home they often had been men of reputation and local power. They were also men that the soldier had probably known all his life and men he had trouble thinking of as his superiors in anything but the incidentals of rank.

Officers rapidly became aware of the problem that the local nature of military units posed for discipline. In 1861 Maj. Charles S. Wainwright noted "how little snap men have generally." His regiment's officers, even though they were well thought of, could not "get fairly wakened up." "Their orders come out slow and drawling, then they wait patiently to see them half-obeyed in a laggard manner, instead of making the men jump to it sharp, as if each word of the order was a prod in their buttocks." He blamed this state of affairs in part on customary small-town indolence; he also blamed the process by which companies were organized – "the officers having raised their own men and known most of them in civil life." "I am every day more and more thankful that I never laid eyes on a soul in the regiment until I joined it." As late as 1864, another New York officer, George Anthony, greeted new recruits for his battery with mixed feelings, when they turned out to be men from his county. "I would never take command of neighbors as soldiers again. And the higher the quality of the men the more such a command is to be dreaded." Even soldiers themselves might identify this as a problem. When mismanagement by the quartermaster led to a shortage of rations in one regiment, one soldier, who a few weeks earlier had complained of strict discipline, attributed the inefficiency to the fact that affairs were run on a volunteer basis: "The officers have no dignity & the men no subordination."[8]

The threat to discipline posed by the community came from others besides the soldiers themselves. Frequently the community kept in close touch with the companies it sent to war. Newspaper articles reported their exploits, homefolk sent and received letters, soldiers returned home on furloughs, and civilians even visited their friends and family members in the army. The reenforcement of local values that this constant communication permitted could run counter to military values. When Capt. John Pierson told his wife that his soldiers were probably writing home that he was a tyrant, he was not alone. Officers usually planned to return

8 Allan Nevins, ed., *A Diary of Battle: The Personal Journals of Colonel Charles S. Wainwright, 1861–1865* (New York, 1962), vii. George Anthony to Ben Anthony, October 14, 1864, George Anthony Letters, Schoff Collection. William H. Bradbury to wife, September 13, 26, October 10, 1862, William H Bradbury Papers, Library of Congress.

to their communities when the war was over. Letters home were not all of the problem, either. Because citizens visited their friends in camp, they could interfere with military values right on the spot. In one Massachusetts regiment the soldiers welcomed their colonel's decision to limit drill: His wife came to visit and told him that he drilled the men too hard. The community never entirely relinquished its power to oversee its men at war.[9]

As unfamiliar as the military experience was to most Union soldiers, the presence of friends and even brothers, uncles, or cousins, the frequent communication with those at home, and the ad hoc nature of the volunteer army served to make it more familiar than is typical of armies. Small-town mores were an impediment to military discipline as classically understood. The constant reminders of home provided men with an alternate set of values and diminished the authority of their officers – men who were equally imbued with civilian values, in any case. Yet at the same time small-town mores reduced the soldier's military efficiency, they also worked as the glue of this citizen army. If community values helped make the Union soldier a difficult one to command, they also helped make him as good a soldier as he turned out to be.

First, soldiers believed that they were fighting for their families and communities. The homefolk had sent them to war. Rallies, public meetings, exhortations from the press and pulpit had encouraged the teenagers and men of the North to enlist; their communities had presented them with homemade American flags, promised always to remember their bravery, and had marched them out of town to the accompaniment of brass bands. The question of why parents and wives seemed so eager to sacrifice their men is a troubling one, but it is clear that their influence helped persuade many men to volunteer. To be a good son, a good brother, a good husband and father, and to be a good citizen meant trying to be a good soldier.[10]

The call of home could, of course, unravel a soldier's morale. Silas W. Browning confessed to his wife, "I have not shad tears but twice since I left Home & that was when I received your letters." One Philadelphia soldier lamented, "I supoze I wont hardly know Phila when I get to see it." He was moody when he wrote, because some homesick new recruits were playing "Home, Sweet Home." "They get in their tents and practice it all day." "I dont like to hear it for it makes me feel queer." A preacher's sermon on "the dear ones at home" could start veterans crying. A New Jersey soldier claimed that in the trenches around Petersburg, soldiers

9   John Pierson to wife, August 15, 1862, John Pierson Letters, Schoff Collection. Albert Wilder to William and Sarah, March 26, 1863, Albert Wilder Letters, Schoff Collection.
10 Mitchell, *Civil War Soldiers*, 11–23.

literally died of homesickness. But as long as soldiers were sure that those they most missed believed in them and the cause for which they fought, their love for home stimulated their support for the Union.[11]

Second, soldiers knew that their behavior while in service was monitored by the folks back home. The army provided little escape from the prying eyes of small-town America. News of a man's conduct, moral and military, was too easily sent home. And home was where the volunteer expected to return when the war was done. The surprising amount of communication between the soldiers and their homes, through both letters and furloughs, kept soldiers informed of the expectations of their loved ones left behind. Soldiers wanted to meet these expectations; they wanted to be able to truthfully write home that they had done their duty.

Furthermore, the soldier himself was not the only one in close communication with his townspeople. His officers and fellow soldiers also wrote their loved ones and went home on furlough. They could report his behavior – or misbehavior – to the folks at home. This communication created powerful constraints on soldiers' conduct. Discipline, bravery, perseverance, and good moral behavior all could represent an attempt to maintain the respect of civilian society as well as adaptation to frontline conditions.

Information and opinions circulated easily among soldiers in camp and people back at home. For example, soldiers read each other's mail. If a soldier's family sent him news from home – or, better still, a newspaper from home – it might circulate throughout his company until the letter or newspaper was all worn out. The men took rumors and hometown opinion seriously. One soldier wrote to his parents that he and "the other boys were amazed that you heard that we were guilty of unworthy conduct." Denying the story, he asked who was spreading it. On the other hand, soldiers were not particularly reluctant to spread rumors themselves. One mother, who warned her son always to speak respectfully of his officers, received a defiant answer: "I intend to write just as I think they deserve and tell the truth and nothing but the truth." The son proceeded to do so: "Our captain is just as good as so much trash." This man was far from being the only Union soldier who told tales on his officers and fellow soldiers.[12]

11 Silas W. Browning to wife, December 10, 1862, Silas W. Browning Papers, Library of Congress. Numa Barned to A. Barned, March 27, 1863, Numa Barned Letters, Schoff Collection. Capt. Robert Goldthwaite Carter, *Four Soldiers in Blue: or Sunshine and Shadows of the War of the Rebellion, a Story of the Great War from Bull Run to Appomattox* (1913; reprint, Austin, 1978), 141. George C. Chandler to uncle, December 19, 1864, Civil War Miscellany, U.S. Army Military History Institute.

12 John Griffith Jones to Parents, March 6, 1863, John Griffith Jones Papers, Library of Congress. Frank Badger to sister Mary, October 28, 1862, Alfred M. Badger Papers,

This reportage influenced soldiers' conduct in all aspects of their lives. For one thing, a man knew that his behavior on the battlefield would be reported to his community. Men oversaw each others' behavior in battle, and they sent home accounts of bravery and cowardice. Bravery was a virtue that would earn a soldier the respect of his community back home, not just his company, and cowardice its contempt. A man who skulked or ran faced not just ridicule among his comrades but a soiled reputation when he returned to civilian life. When one captain dodged battle in 1862, a soldier under him broadcast his conduct. "He contrived to stumble, then gave out he was wounded in the knee, and called for a stretcher, was put on it, and carried a little ways when the carriers rested and the shells falling a little to thick for the Captain, he told them men to hurry up which they did not do, when he jumped and beat the whole to the Hospital, after which we never saw him until we got upon this side of the Rappahannock."[13]

Soldiers demanded courage of their officers in a way they rarely did of their fellow soldiers. Soldiers who had enlisted under their company commanders had a right to feel particularly betrayed if their captains proved cowardly. After all, the officer who had formed a company among his friends and neighbors had promised them, either implicitly or explicitly – usually the latter, and in most grandiloquent fashion – to lead them into battle. James K. Newton wrote home that the reputation of his captain's bravery at Shiloh "was all a hoax." On the contrary, the captain had disappeared when the battle began. "When asked where he was going he replied 'that he was going down to the river to *draw rations* so that the boys could have something to eat as soon as they were done fighting.' " Shortly after the battle, the captain resigned. Newton accused the captain of stealing the company funds, as well as cowardice. Perhaps Newton was wrong. But clearly, an officer who resigned after his company had had its first taste of combat laid himself open to the contempt of his men, contempt so great that Newton was ready to believe that this man was both a swindler and a shirker.[14]

During combat, could men think of their reputations? The answer is probably yes. Men wrote home that they had thought of their loved ones even in the cannon's mouth; men did die with their beloved's name on

Library of Congress. For examples of letters and newspapers circulating throughout a company, see Theodore Preston to Edward Preston, March 10, 1862, Jacob Preston Papers, Michigan Historical Collections, Bentley Library, University of Michigan; Orra B. Bailey to wife, January 1, 1863. Orra B. Bailey Papers, Library of Congress.

13 William Hamilton to mother, December 28, 1862, William Hamilton Papers, Library of Congress.

14 Stephen E. Ambrose, ed., *A Wisconsin Boy in Dixie: The Selected Letters of James K. Newton* (Madison, 1961), 16–20.

their lips. The desire to live up to the expectations of those at home reinforced natural bravery and military discipline and helped to determine men's conduct on the battlefield. Nonetheless, combat has its own compulsions. The good opinion of the folks back home was probably a more important influence on men's decision to continue their service than it was on the battlefield.

Although courage in battle could be inspired by the excitement of the moment, it took considerably more reassurance to stay in the army day after day, year after year. There were military compulsions: Deserters could be shot. Many deserted successfully, however, and the so-called bounty jumpers made a career of enlisting and deserting. The continual reassurance that those back home approved of one's service, a reassurance provided by letters – and painfully missed when letters did not come – was crucial to the soldiers. As long as the communities of the North supported the war effort, there would be Northern soldiers in the ranks of the Union army.

Yet the hunger for a family's respect and admiration, the desire to satisfy those at home that one was a patriot and a hero, could be undercut by other duties that a man held. A man's patriotism had to compete with other equally important values; military service was possible when he believed that things were all right at home; otherwise, the claims of home threatened his devotion to the army.

Pvt. William DeLong, considered one of the best soldiers in his regiment, could not help being affected when a neighbor wrote to him that his wife had been washing clothes four to five days a week to earn money, had become very sick and was "destitute of every Thing for her comfort and With out food or wood." Even though her neighbors had helped her with everything they could, she wanted him to get his pay and come home immediately. DeLong did not want to leave his company, but he did brood about his wife's suffering. He brought the neighbor's letter to George Anthony, his commanding officer, who "assured him that this letter is unreliable" but who also immediately wrote to his brother back home, telling him to find out what Mrs. DeLong needed and buy it for her. The officer attested that DeLong felt "the sufferings of a true man" over the misery of his wife. Here lay the contradiction. A true man fought for the Union, which was indeed a way of fighting for his family. But a true man also sheltered his family. A man was expected to earn a living; a man was expected to protect and support his family. Joining the army was an extension of the duty to protect one's family, but men anticipated that military service would support them as well. If it did not, their morale declined.[15]

15   Uretta A. McWhorter to William Delong, January 15, 1865, and George Anthony to Ben Anthony, January 21, 1865, George Anthony Letters, Schoff Collection.

Sometimes the demoralization reached the point where soldiers would desert; they believed they had to go home and look after those whose claims were more immediate than those of the Union. For example, during the winter of 1863 infrequent paydays caused John E. Lowery to desert and return home, where he did odd jobs – chopping wood and working at a limekiln – to support his family, until he was arrested and returned to his company. But when men felt certain that their families were looked after and that their desertion would shame both them and their families, the force of the community helped keep them in the army. By and large, this was the case for the Union soldier during the Civil War.[16]

Finally, gossip home included reports on men's moral behavior. David Seibert wrote to his father indignantly that he had not been going with disreputable women, no matter what had been written about him. In varying measures of glee and shock, soldiers told of their officers having sex with prostitutes or other women; if these women were black or "yellow" it added additional cause for comment. "Good business for married men," one of them sardonically noted. Another told of his captain's desire to "stick close to a yalow girl after night"; surely the captain "would improve the stock very much." This Presbyterian soldier informed on his captain, because "i said when i left home that i would not write a lie home and i shall not do it."[17]

This is not to claim that Union soldiers always lived up to the dictates of Victorian morality. The army saw its share of gambling, drinking, smoking, and fornication. Even so, our more pungent discussions of these activities come from the letters of moralistic soldiers. Men's behavior coarsened, but they did not lose the sense that there were moral standards by which they were expected to abide.

Gerald Linderman calls courage – which is for him a cluster of values, many of them domestic – "the cement of armies." One could also say that the love of home was "the cement of armies." Small-town mores influenced the behavior of the men at war. Love of home helped keep men fighting for the long years of the war. Concern with reputation supplemented military discipline in camp, on the march, and in battle. The familiarity that so jeopardized discipline initially came from a set of shared values that helped mobilize the teenagers and men of the North, kept them in the army once they were there, and saw that they maintained a

16 John E. Lowery Diary, February, March, April, 1963, Harrisburg Civil War Round Table Collection, U.S. Army Military History Institute.

17 David Seibert to father, August 7, 1863, Seibert Family Papers, Harrisburg Civil War Round Table Collection, U.S. Army Military History Institute. John Crosby to Abby J. Crosby, February 11, 1863, John Crosby Papers, Connecticut Historical Society. Andrew Sproul to Fannie, December 3, 1862, Andrew Sproul Papers, Southern Historical Collection, University of North Carolina.

high standard of behavior. They were an individualistic society's substitute for militarism, a voluntary society's substitute for coercion.

> I guess we all do things away from home we wouldn't do at home.
> And since most of us are never at home we're always doing things
> we would never do.
>   Fardiman, in Malcolm Bradbury's "Composition"

While the constraints that community oversight placed on soldiers were powerful, they were not irresistible. As the war continued, soldiers necessarily became inured to discipline, hardship, and bloodshed. The ties that bound them to their homes rarely broke but often frayed. The distance between a soldier and his home helped encourage drastic changes in his behavior, even to the point of helping him create a new identity more appropriate to the conditions of war than of peace. There is no doubt that soldiers behaved in ways they never would have at home – otherwise they could not have been soldiers.[18]

Even though the tug toward home never lost its power over most soldiers, as the war continued veteran soldiers also felt a psychological distance grow that matched the physical distance between their camps and their homes. Part of the transformation from volunteer to soldier was a tendency to disassociate oneself from both one's former life and one's old community, but the distance also came from the soldiers' growing fear that the community both no longer respected soldiers and no longer deserved a soldier's respect.

The soldiers had marched off hoping to become heroes; as the war went on they began to suspect they were the only set of heroes their hometowns were going to produce. Whatever the difficulties experienced by the civilians of the North, they looked insignificant to the men at the front. As towns scrambled to meet their quotas of soldiers or squabbled over wartime politics, soldiers wondered if most of their communities' patriotism had not left with them. Soldiers saw themselves as better embodying the values of the community than those who selfishly stayed behind; indeed, the center of moral authority shifted from the community at home to the community in arms, from the civilian fathers to the soldier sons.[19]

When soldiers cursed those who paid the commutation fee or fled the draft, they were not referring simply to some general set of cowards. They often had specific individuals in mind – former neighbors, fellow schoolboys, hometown rivals. Henry Carroll asked his mother to tell "the

18 For a fuller discussion, see Mitchell, *Civil War Soldier*, Chapter 3, pp. 56–89.
19 See Thomas R. Kemp, "Community and War: the Civil War Experience of Two New Hampshire Towns," Chapter 2 in this volume.

Gentry" who planned to go to California to avoid the draft that "they had better make their calculation to stay when they go there. The boys say when they get back they dont intend to let any such craven cowards and skulkers come back to enjoy the peace." The soldiers dismissed those who opposed the draft as cowards; those who opposed the war – the Peace Democrats or Copperheads – they called traitors. A Connecticut soldier, hearing that his hometown of New Milford had supported the Democratic candidate for governor, said that he hoped he had no friends among the disloyal. Park H. Fryer, an Ohio soldier, supported the soldier-led mobs that sometimes destroyed the presses of newspapers of Peace Democrats. "I say go in Boys fight while you are at home as well as in the Field if you can find the enemy. . . . I could cock my Enfield at a Rebel at home just as cool as down here in dixy." Another Ohio soldier composed – or at least copied – a rhyming malediction directed at the Copperheads – "Brazen faced Copperheads / White livered Copperheads / False-harted Copperheads" – of his township. Furthermore, in many cases the animosity directed at individuals broadened to include whole communities. Henry C. Bear lambasted Oakley, Illinois, where he imagined citizens advocated resisting conscription. "I suppose they wold talk about resisting a Hurricane in their weakness and blindness, there in that God forsaken place."[20]

Indeed, the constant intercourse with home played its role in creating distance. When away from home, soldiers felt neglected. When home on leave, soldiers felt treated with disdain. The spectacle of life going on without them might be profoundly unsettling. The neglect or contempt, real or imagined, that soldiers felt angered and depressed them. Letters home kept the men in touch with those that they had left behind, but they also revealed the immense distance that grew up between the worlds of civilian and soldier. When soldiers received letters complaining of the high price of black powder or how hard it was to buy silk dresses, they felt little sympathy. The seeming inability of the civilians to compare their lot with that of the soldiers infuriated men. One protested, "These persons do not consider us who are opposed to bullets and steal blades under dangerous hardships." Perhaps partially inspired by the magnificent irrelevance of the gripes from his hometown, this particular soldier

20 Henry S. Carroll to mother, March 29, 1863, Henry S. Carroll Papers, Harrisburg Civil War Round Table Collection, U.S. Army Military History Institute. H. R. Hoyt to brother, April 11, 1863, Civil War Miscellany, U. S. Army Military History Institute. Park H. Fryer to brother, March 20, 1864, Civil War Miscellany, U.S. Army Military History Institute. Diary, 1862, Andrew J. Sproul Papers, Southern Historical Collection, University of North Carolina. Wayne C. Temple, ed., *The Civil War Letters of Henry C. Bear: A Soldier in the 116th Illinois Volunteer Infantry* (Harrogate, Tenn., 1961), 37.

deserted less than a year later. Desertion did not become the norm, but alienation did.[21]

Of course, some soldiers had never liked their hometowns to begin with. Leander Chapin expressed this sentiment when he advised his mother to leave their Connecticut home and move to Springfield, Massachusetts. *"I would not stay in aristocratic gossiping Enfield for an interest in Goshen."* He was glad when he left Enfield, and he "was glad that I do not as a soldier count on the quota of the town." Nor did all soldiers regret leaving their families behind. One soldier assured his father that he was sending him all the money he could spare but told him not to share any of it with "that wife of mine if I must caule her wife."[22]

In general, however, a soldier's alienation reached its limits when it threatened his feelings toward his immediate family. The soldier exempted parents, children, wife, and sisters from his attacks on Northern civilians, and even brothers, uncles, and male cousins usually got the benefit of the doubt when Copperheads and cowards were damned. The strongest claim that home had on a soldier was his family. It was a rare soldier who did not imagine peace as a return to his household.

Soldiers regularly claimed that it was only through leaving their homes and suffering through army life and the violence of war that they had learned domesticity's true value. A soldier in Sherman's army, "heartily sick of this kind of life," longed for "a pleasant retreete from the repulsive scenes of this man slaughtering life" and for "the society of my family in some secluded spot, shut out from the calamities of war." One officer contrasted the "bursting warm hearts love" of a boy who was willing to join the regular army in order to get a furlough home with the "cold amphibious blood" of gentlemen who lounged in their clubs because they "vote home a bore." "This little boy was already a Veteran. . . . But in order once more to get home, to sit once more with his mothers & sisters around the family hearth, this brave little boy was willing to bare his little Body to five years more of Battle and Hardship." The officer asked, "Is there anything that can more strongly than this, point out the great power and influence of Home?" "If I am spared to ever get home again I think I shale know how to appreciate [it]," one soldier wrote his wife and daughter. "I thought I had know it before but a man does not untill he gets in the army." Leaving home, then, was a precondition for knowing home.[23]

21 Patrick McGlenn to John Brislin, February 19, 1862, John Brislin Letters, Harrisburg Civil War Round Table Collection, U.S. Army Military History Institute.
22 Leander Chapin to Mrs. Amelia Chapin, February [probably March] 2, 1864, Albert A. Andrews Papers, Connecticut Historical Society. James R. French to parents, February 22, 1864, Albert Wilder Letters, Schoff Collection.
23 Glatthaar, *March to the Sea*, 43. Paul Oliver to mother, November 12, 1864, Paul

Home looked mighty good compared to the army. A song like "Just before the Battle, Mother" served not only to express soldiers' deepest feelings – their longing for family and home – but to instruct them as to what their feelings should be. Remembering home, dreaming of it, planning for an eventual return to it allowed men to focus on something other than the army and the war and thus to a certain extent retain their prewar identities. In most cases the lure of home was sufficient to prevent the civilian from being permanently submerged in the soldier.

Nonetheless, for the time being the soldier had to predominate. One soldier explained this by saying that he belonged "to Uncle Sam, mentally, morally, and physically." His job, his duty, was to be a soldier. "My virtues and vice must correspond to that of my fellows; I must *lie* to rebels, *steal* from rebels and *kill* rebels." And if a man's duty called upon him to embrace deceit, theft, and murder, is it surprising that he also might fall prey to profanity, tobacco, women, and liquor? Particularly when he was away from home for the first – and perhaps the last – time of his life? Community values reenforced the military regimen to discipline the Union soldier, but even in tandem they were not always successful. So the war to defend their communities led soldiers temporarily away from their community values.[24]

The logic of this war became such that in its last year, some Union soldiers literally made war on the homes of their enemies. Sherman's march was intended to demoralize the Southern people. Sherman said that he proposed to make them "feel that war and individual ruin are synonymous terms." The demoralization would spring from Southern recognition that their government was helpless to protect them from Union soldiers and Union armies. Northern soldiers entered the homes of their Southern counterparts, terrorized their wives, parents, and children, confiscated their food, and sometimes burned down their houses. Deserting Confederate soldiers, whose numbers swelled as their families' helplessness grew, affirmed the effectiveness of this policy. During the Atlanta campaign, one Union officer said of the Southern people whom they had impoverished, "It is but right that these people should feel some of the hardships of war, they will better appreciate peace when it does come." Much like home, the value of peace and the Union could best be learned – by Southerners at least – in their absence.[25]

Sherman's men were a long way from home, in terms of time, distance, and often psychology. Emblematic of this is the perhaps trivial-sounding

Ambrose Oliver Papers, Princeton University. Abram F. Conant to wife and daughter, January 9, 1863, Abram F. Conant Papers, Library of Congress.

24 Mitchell, *Civil War Soldier*, 81.
25 Glatthaar, *March to the Sea*, 6–7, 120.

fact that during the march and the campaign of the Carolinas, Sherman and his men could not receive any messages from home – no letters, no telegrams, no orders. Sherman himself testified to the freedom he felt when he cut the wire from Atlanta to Washington and knew that the authorities could not stop him from undertaking the great march. Rarely had the Northern soldier been so free from supervision as he was during the march to the sea and through the Carolinas. He behaved with corresponding license and gusto. The fact that the countryside he traversed did not look, sound, or smell much like home also encouraged the soldier to treats its inhabitants and their property more harshly than he otherwise might have. The plantations he destroyed were built on slavery, an institution popularly portrayed as antithetical to family and home. The soldier also took revenge for his long absence from home by destroying the homes of Confederate soldiers.[26]

This assault, both symbolic and literal, on the Southern home, provided an oddly fitting end to this war in defense of community values. For, finally, was not the Civil War a war over the meaning of home? It has often been called a fratricidal war, a war over who shall rule the home that was the American nation. Closer to the point, however, is the fact that the dispute between the North and the South was over the different concepts that people had of this American home. Lincoln had warned against "a house divided." When a Northern recruit joined the army to protect American institutions, his idea of those institutions came from his own, usually limited, experience. The institutions, the values for which he fought were those with which he had grown up. Democracy meant the town hall; education meant the schoolhouse; Christianity meant the local church. As for broader concepts – freedom, Constitution, democratic rule – so frequently had they been mediated by local figures that even they might be thought of as community values. In the North, localism aided rather than hindered national patriotism. The Northern soldier fought for home and for Union, for family and for nation. For him, the Civil War experience made sense only in relation to both the domestic and the civic components of his world.[27]

26 See Glatthaar, *March to the Sea*, for a thorough discussion of the Northern soldier during Sherman's march. Without using the specific idea of home, there is a lengthy discussion of the alien appearance of the Southern landscape in Mitchell, *Civil War Soldier*, Chapter 4. For slavery and the family, consider Harriet Beecher Stowe's *Uncle Tom's Cabin*.

27 For a "familial" interpretation of the sectional conflict, see George B. Forgie, *Patricide in the House Divided: A Psychological Interpretation of Lincoln and His Age* (New York, 1979). For the relationship between Northern small towns and American institutions, see William R. Brock, *Conflict and Transformation: The United States, 1844–1877* (Baltimore, 1973), 132–4.

4

Voluntarism in Wartime: Philadelphia's Great Central Fair

J. MATTHEW GALLMAN

In September 1864 Philadelphian John J. Thompson penned a lengthy description of America's "fearful ordeal" to a cousin overseas. Although there had been "gloomy and discouraging periods," as the conflict came to a close the iron manufacturer found cause for pride:

> The progress of our war has of course worked great changes in military and naval matters – but it has also developed an amount of sympathy, active, earnest and working, with suffering sick & wounded soldiers, such as has no parallel in the history of the world – The amount of volunteer labor on the battle fields, and in the Hospitals, has been extraordinary and the voluntary contributions by our citizens through the Sanitary Commissions amount to many millions of dollars in money & hundreds of tons in merchandize etc![1]

This enthusiasm for Civil War voluntarism was especially marked in Philadelphia. Soldiers passing through the City of Brotherly Love repeatedly paid tribute to its particularly benevolent citizenry.[2] As one French traveler reported, "Philadelphia has not lost her religious character; she remains equally faithful to her philanthropic traditions."[3]

Civil War Voluntarism

Thousands of Philadelphians took part in the "peoples' contest" from behind the lines by working at sewing circles, visiting hospitals, staffing

Most of the material in this chapter appears, in a somewhat different form, in J. Matthew Gallman, *Mastering Wartime: A Social History of Philadelphia during the Civil War* (New York: Cambridge University Press, 1990).

1 John J. Thompson to (cousin) John Thompson, September 26, 1864, Society Misc. Collection, Historical Society of Pennsylvania, Philadelphia (hereafter *HSP*).
2 See Emil Rosenblatt, ed., *Anti-Rebel: The Civil War Letters of Wilbur Fisk* (Croton-on-Hudson, N.Y., 1983), 56; Christopher Pennell to "Migonne" [Sabra Snell], July 14, 1864, Christopher Pennell Papers, Frost Library Archives, Amherst College, Amherst, Mass., transcribed by Daniel Cohen.
3 Auguste Laugel, *The United States During the Civil War*, ed. Allan Nevins (1866); reprint, Bloomington, Ind., 1961), 177.

refreshment saloons, or raising money for one of the score of local and national soldiers' aid organizations.[4] Philadelphia supported its own array of voluntary groups, but two national organizations – the United States Sanitary Commission (USSC) and the United States Christian Commission (USCC) – dominated the national scene. In the war's first months a New York group, led by Unitarian minister Henry W. Bellows, organized the USSC to improve health conditions for Union soldiers. Although military authorities initially disapproved of civilians on the battlefield, the Sanitary Commission soon gained official recognition and blossomed into an enormous national organization, bringing clothing and medical supplies to Union field hospitals. While the USSC was strongly conservative and militantly secular, the Y.MCA–sponsored Christian Commission, launched in November 1861, dispensed Bibles and evangelical enthusiasm with their blankets and bandages.[5]

Despite their differences, the two national commissions shared a common structure: Each had a central executive committee, regional branches based in major cities, and hundreds of local affiliates.[6] At the local level, both bodies were dominated by female volunteers.[7] As he closed the first of his four-volume *War for the Union*, Allen Nevins considered Northern society after a year of war and observed that "[a]ll over the map . . . voluntary effort had exhibited a vision and strength which shamed inertia and self-seeking. It was already clear that women could write a lustrous page in public affairs . . . and [the Sanitary Commission's] success was to show that a new era of national organization was opening." Three volumes later Nevins concluded that "[p]robably the greatest single change in American civilization in the war period . . . was the replacement of an organized nation by a highly organized society – organized, that is, on a national scale."[8]

These two interpretive threads – that the Civil War accelerated Amer-

---

4 For a detailed discussion of these varied forms of wartime voluntarism, see J. Matthew Gallman, *Mastering Wartime: A Social History of Philadelphia during the Civil War* (New York, 1990), Chapter 5.

5 See George M. Fredrickson, *The Inner Civil War: Northern Intellectuals and the Crisis of the Union* (New York, 1965), 98–112; Robert H. Bremner, "The Impact of the Civil War on Philanthropy and Social Welfare," *Civil War History*, 12 (September 1966), 293–307; Robert H. Bremner, *The Public Good: Philanthropy and Welfare in the Civil War Era* (New York, 1980), 39–46, 54–62; William Q. Maxwell, *Lincoln's Fifth Wheel: The Sanitary Commission* (New York, 1956); [Linus Pierpont Brockett], *The Philanthropic Results of the War in America* (New York, 1984), 33–76, 96–164.

6 See Bremner, *Public Good*, esp. 58.

7 See Mary Elizabeth Massey, *Bonnet Brigades* (New York, 1966); Agatha Young, *The Women and the Crisis* (New York, 1959); Frank Moore, *Women of the War; Their Heroism and Self-sacrifice* (Hartford, Conn., 1866).

8 Allan Nevins, *The War for the Union*, 4 vols. (New York, 1959–71), 1:416; 4:395. See also 1:v.

ica's evolution toward "a highly organized society" and that the experience of women in the war's voluntary organizations helped thrust them into "public affairs" – are woven, usually independently, through much of the scholarship on American social history. In his analysis of the Sanitary Commission, George Frederickson argued that "[i]ts success and the public acceptance of its policies . . . symbolized this new willingness of Americans to working large, impersonal organizations."[9] Anne Firor Scott has suggested that women's "long apprenticeship in [antebellum] voluntary associations" left them better prepared to orchestrate affairs on the home front than their male counterparts were to fight on the battlefield.[10] This wartime experience, in turn, she claims, aided women in the "process of inventing a public role" in the postwar decades.[11] Nancy Hewitt, in her study of women's activism in Rochester, New York, found that their voluntary experiences "led wartime workers into wider public service when the [Soldier's Aid Society] disbanded."[12]

The Great Central Fair

Organization

Between June 7 and June 28, 1864, Philadelphia held its Great Central Fair, which raised over $1 million to replenish the Sanitary Commission's dwindling funds. This grand event was the product of months of labor by thousands of Philadelphians. Its organization and character are an excellent lens through which to view life on the Philadelphia home front. Moreover, the fair offers an opportunity to examine the centralizing forces underlying wartime voluntarism and to investigate the role of women within the newly fashioned patriotic organizations.

The Sanitary Commission's "fair movement" began in Chicago in late 1863 with a ten-day fund-raising fair for its Northwestern Branch. This event earned nearly $80,000, a figure that was almost doubled one month later in Boston. Soon Cincinnati, Cleveland, Albany, Brooklyn, and St. Louis followed suit. New York's Metropolitan Fair, which cleared

9 Frederickson, *Inner Civil War*, 111.
10 Anne Firor Scott, "On Seeing and Not Seeing: A Case of Historical Invisibility," *Journal of American History*, 71 (June 1984), 12.
11 Anne Firor Scott, "Women's Voluntary Associations in the Forming of American Society," *Making the Invisible Woman Visible* (Urbana, Ill., 1984), 281–2.
12 Nancy A. Hewitt, *Women's Activism and Social Change: Rochester, New York, 1822–1872* (Ithaca, 1984), 201. Mary Ryan, in her study of Utica, New York, found that after their wartime voluntary experiences "it seemed that women were poised to make an assault on the male sphere and were determined to take direct control of municipal services." See Ryan, *Cradle of the Middle Class: The Family in Oneida County, New York, 1790–1865* (New York, 1981), 213.

$1,183,505 in April 1864, was the most successful of these ventures, topping Philadelphia's total by about $150,000.[13] By the end of the war, roughly thirty "sanitary fairs" had been held, earning about $4.4 million. Some raised money for regional branches of the USSC; others collected funds for supplies to be sent to the home troops through Sanitary Commission channels. Over 80 percent of the $2.7 million funneled directly into the USSC's coffers came from the New York and Philadelphia fairs.

The Great Central Fair extended established practices. Antebellum Americans had often turned to fund-raising fairs to support civic charities, and as the Civil War progressed Philadelphians learned to rely on festive affairs to stir the patriotic sentiments of a war-weary citizenry.[14] But the sanitary fairs melded entertainment and benevolence in events that eclipsed anything in America's experience, in both scope and design. Like London's Great Exhibition of 1851, these fairs enticed their visitors with a wide array of manufacturing and artistic exhibits displaying local accomplishments and foreign curiosities. But whereas Prince Albert conceived of the Crystal Palace to showcase the marvels of industrial progress, the sanitary fairs' organizers devoted their ingenuity to creating diverse methods for extracting money from their guests' pockets.[15]

The initial impetus for Philadelphia's fair came from the highly patriotic Union League, which passed a resolution on January 11, 1864, asking the Philadelphia associates of the Sanitary Commission to join the nationwide fair movement. Two weeks later the USSC's local branch voted to put on a fair, under the supervision of an executive committee headed by prominent merchant John Welsh.[16] On February 20 the committee announced the coming fair in the city's newspapers. Its open letter set the tone for the ensuing months:

> We call on every workshop, factory, and mill for a specimen of the
> best thing it can turn out; on every artist, great and small, for one of
> his creations; on all loyal women for the exercise of their taste and
> industry; on farmers, for the products of their fields and dairies. The

13 For good general background information on the fair movement, see William Y. Thompson, "Sanitary Fairs of the Civil War," *Civil War History*, 4 (March 1958), 51–67. Also see Philadelphia's official fair newspaper, *Our Daily Fare* (hereafter ODF).

14 On antebellum fairs, see Bremner, *Public Good*, 20; Catherine Clinton, *The Other Civil War: American Women in the Nineteenth Century* (New York, 1984), 81. For a good account of an 1842 fund-raising fair, see Isaac Mickle, *A Gentleman of Much Promise: The Diary of Isaac Mickle, 1837–1845*, ed. Philip English Mackey, 2 vols. (Philadelphia, 1977), 2:254, 291, 293–5. On wartime fund-raising, see Gallman, *Mastering Wartime*, Chapter 5.

15 Thompson, "Sanitary Fairs of the Civil War," 51–67; R. K. Webb, *Modern England* (New York, 1968), 278. For an excellent study of postwar expositions, see Robert W. Rydell, *All the World's a Fair: Visions of Empire at American International Expositions, 1876–1916* (Chicago, 1984).

16 *ODF*, June 20, 1864.

miner, the naturalist, the man of science, the traveler, can each send something that can at the very least be converted into a blanket that will warm, and may save from death, some one soldier who the government supplies have failed to reach.

The organizers sought to touch everyone by emphasizing that no gift would be too small.[17]

The Philadelphia fair's organizational structure was enormously complex, with over 3,000 volunteers in nearly 100 different committees, ranging from the 5-member Committee on Gas Fixtures to the roughly 330-strong Committee on Schools.[18] Most committees were organized around a particular craft or branch of manufacturing. A member visited each of the city's establishments in search of donations of cash or goods to be sold at the fair. Other committees solicited flowers, fruit, handmade items, or "Relics, Curiosities, and Autographs." Tea merchant L. Montgomery Bond's Committee on Labor, Income, and Revenue adopted a massive advertising campaign encouraging all Philadelphians to donate the proceeds of a day's work to the fair.[19]

Volunteers

One of the first orders of business for the executive committee was to recruit people to chair the various committees. The burden of chairing a committee was large, and more than 40 nominees refused to serve.[20] Nevertheless, the executive committee enlisted many of Philadelphia's business leaders. J. B. Lippincott headed up the Committee on Book Publishers, Booksellers, and Bookbinders; David S. Brown, one of the region's largest textile manufacturers, chaired the Wholesale Dry Goods Committee; William J. Horstmann, the proprietor of the city's foremost military uniform and regalia establishment, led the Committee on Military Goods.[21]

It was up to the chairs to form their own committees;[22] once formed, individual groups adopted quite different structures. The members of the Ladies' Committee on Boots, Shoes and Leather visited stores individ-

17   Furness Scrapbook, Box 1, H. H. Furness Papers, HSP.
18   *List of Committee Members of the Great Central Fair for the U.S. Sanitary Commission Held in Philadelphia* (Philadelphia, 1864). A copy of this pamphlet is in Box 5, F-1, Furness Papers.
19   *ODF*, September 11, 1865. This particular appeal, which netted $247,500, seems to have been a Philadelphia innovation. For a good description of Bond's visit to the Manayunk woolen mills, see *Germantown Telegraph*, June 15, 1864.
20   Box 5, F-2–F-5, Furness Papers.
21   *List of Committee Members*.
22   For a good description of the experiences of a committee chairman, see "Autobiography of William F. Miskey," 58, HSP.

ually, only meeting periodically to report their progress and to discuss plans for decorating their display. The official list includes 26 women on the committee, but the minutes show that only 3 came to all six meetings, one-half came to four or more, and 2 never attended.[23] The minutes of the Women's Committee of the Children's Department of Toys and Small Wares reveal a far more complex infrastructure. Initially, this group of 33 women split into six subcommittees to visit local dealers. Later they formed seven topical subcommittees, which met separately (each keeping its own minutes) for the next month.[24] The all-male Wholesale Dry Goods Committee also had poor attendance at committee meetings, with most of the serious work being accomplished in smaller subcommittees.[25]

As with many peacetime organizations, the fair's committee structure divided men and women into separate but parallel bodies. Although the women's committees enjoyed substantial autonomy, their tasks often reflected different concerns and circumscribed gender roles. The Wholesale Dry Goods Committee voted to leave the designing of a suitable badge to their ladies' committee; the women's committee of the Children's Department of Toys and Small Wares left the construction of a Maypole to their male affiliates. The women's committees generally devoted special attention to determining the appropriate apparel for committee members to wear at the fair.[26]

Despite its enormous scale, the Great Central Fair was a notably decentralized, individualized event. At each level citizens sought to mold the fair to their own desires. Much of recording secretary H. H. Furness's time was devoted to sorting out squabbles among committee heads. These battles reflected the difficulties inherent in forcing independent-minded volunteers into a large cooperative structure.

Mrs. George Plitt, secretary of the Committee of Women and chair of the Women's Committee on Internal Arrangements, peppered the executive committee with notes on a wide range of issues. On March 15 she suggested to Furness that a Miss Blanche Howell should be removed from the published list because she was too young. Later she insisted on re-

---

23 Ladies' Committee on Boots, Shoes and Leather – Account Book and Minutes, Box 1, Furness Papers. Despite this poor attendance record, the committee collected $1,517.15 in cash, twelve morocco skins to be sold at the fair, and a wide assortment of shoes.

24 "Minute Book of the Children's Department of Toys & Small Wares – Great Central Fair, 1864," Minute Book, HSP.

25 Minute Book of the "Wholesale Dry Goods Department – Sanitary Commission Fair," HSP. The minutes of the Newspaper Committee and the Sword Committee reveal similar patterns of procedure, with various tasks being turned over to subcommittees, so that the committee as a whole met less frequently. See Society Misc. Collection, Leland Papers, HSP.

26 "Minute Book of the Children's Department of Toys & Small Wares"; Minute Book of the "Wholesale Dry Goods Department."

moving a woman's name from a chairwomanship because "no lady should be published as [chair] of 2 [committees]." As opening day approached, Mrs. Plitt suggested a Turkish Department to Mr. Welsh, demanded more stamps from Mr. Furness, and continued her efforts at "keeping the names of *sweet young girls* from the public eye" by excluding them from published committee lists.[27]

While Mrs. Plitt sought to have a hand in all of the fair's activities, other committee chairs were directing their groups like well-drilled armies battling for territory. The most violent controversy swirled around S. Montgomery Bond and his Labor, Income and Revenue Committee. This group used extensive newspaper advertising and personal visitation to solicit one day's wages or profits from every Philadelphian. When rival chairmen accused Bond of stealing their thunder, he complained that he was being victimized by "the carpings of others." He maintained that his methods earned more but said that he left certain territories alone when asked.[28]

Bond's usurpations led Alexander R. McHenry, the chairman of the Oil Committee, to dissolve that committee.[29] Soon after, McHenry wrote to the executive committee, this time wearing the hat of chairman of the Receiving Committee, to complain of further indignities. His committee had recently sold a gift of several dozen eggs and placed the receipts in the general funds rather than passing the profits on to the Restaurant Committee. The chair of the Restaurant Committee complained so bitterly about this slight that the executive committee passed a resolution barring similar actions in the future. McHenry became furious at the implication of this decision and wrote, "I will not consent to be placed in an unpleasant position again – I had enough of this in Mr. Bond's case." Although the executive committee rescinded what McHenry termed the "vote of censure," the damage was done. He kept his formal position but refused to reenter the fairgrounds.[30]

These battles suggest that within the fair's hierarchical structure, committees enjoyed a wide latitude and chairpersons acted as individuals, not as cogs in a patriotic machine. Similarly, many Philadelphians who were outside the fair's administrative structure viewed the event as their own. Both executive committee chairman Welsh and receiving secretary Furness regularly received letters from townspeople suggesting ways to improve the fair. One inventive writer argued that the executive committee

27 Box 7, F-1, F-2, Box 8, F-2, Furness Papers.
28 Bond to Furness, April 18, 19, 1864, Box 7, F-2, Furness Papers.
29 McHenry to Furness, April 22, 1864, Box 7, F-2, Furness Papers.
30 McHenry to Welsh, May 7, 9, 1864; Welsh to McHenry, May 9, 1864; McHenry to Furness, May 23, 1864, Box 8, F-2, Furness Papers.

should send a wagon through the city to collect rags, old shoes, and newspapers. He believed that such a venture "would raise $20,000 to $30,000." Another citizen took note of the annual infestation in Logan Square's trees and suggested that "a *committee on worms* is very much wanted." Other correspondents proposed separate committees for soaps and candles, auctions, fireworks, architects, ship owners, and engravers.[31] These people took their fair seriously, and sought to do their part, however small, to make it a success.

In her diary entry for April 4, 1864, Anna Ferris reported the opening of New York's Metropolitan Fair, noting that "every effort will be made to equal it in Phila. & everybody is at work to do what they can for the cause." She added that "the unselfish devotion to a great purpose makes life better."[32] Anna Blanchard shared Ferris's selflessness. As a member of the Restaurant Committee, she worked six-hour shifts and usually stayed late, "always finding there was something to be done."[33] Joseph Harrison, businessman and inventor, chaired the Fine Arts Committee, which put together the fair's Art Gallery. Several weeks before the fair opened, Harrison explained to a neglected business associate that "I have *much* to do in arranging my department of the Fair." A few days before the opening, he could only manage a hurried note to his friend while sitting in the middle of the Art Gallery, surrounded by busy workers. Soon Harrison put aside business entirely, explaining that "my time has been so much taken up with the Sanitary Fair . . . that I [have] little time to think of or do anything else." The results lightened his burden, however, because Harrison found the fair "a great success, particularly the Art Gallery, which has never been equalled in modern times."[34]

Whereas Harrison and Blanchard devoted long hours to the fair, others offered special talents to the cause. Dr. S. M. Landis volunteered to serve as a lecturer on phrenology, and Jonathan M. Thompson made his bookkeeping skills available.[35] Joseph Boggs Beale contributed his artistic talents by drawing an eagle for the Boys' Central High School Display; James Tyndale Mitchell lent his time to the Music Committee and his voice to several fund-raising concerts; Sydney George Fisher penned

31 Unsigned to Furness, April 28, 1864, Box 7, F-2, Furness Papers; Susan R. Barton to Furness, March 23, 1864, Box 7, F-1, Furness Papers; miscellaneous letters, Box 7, Furness Papers.
32 Anna Ferris diary, April 4, 1864, Film Ms-F, Swarthmore College, Swarthmore, Pa.
33 [Anna Blanchard] diary, June 1864, Anna Day Papers, HSP. This diary is not signed and is not identified by HSP. I have been able to attribute it to Anna Blanchard because of her position on the Restaurant Committee.
34 Joseph Harrison to Thomas Luders, May 17 and June 21, 1864, and undated June note, Harrison Letterbook, HSP.
35 S. M. Landis to Furness, undated, Box 5, F-1, Furness Papers; Thompson to Furness, March 16, 1864, Box 7, F-1, Furness Papers.

a poem "on the part woman plays in this war" for a poet's album to be sold at the fair.[36]

Like other wartime relief organizations, the fair relied on donations of money and goods. In some cases the gift entailed only a small sacrifice, but in other instances the offering was – to the giver – quite significant. Individuals flooded the Receiving Department with all manner of heirlooms, trinkets, handicrafts, and farm products. One Union League member donated a deed to a downtown plot of land valued at $500; another man offered to share the proceeds from a holding in Iowa worth $1,500. A Wilmington inventor wanted to raffle off his patent for coal-oil burners (splitting the profits with the Sanitary Commission), and a second inventor hoped to display his new gas stove. If these latter gifts appeared partly self-serving, the same could not be said for the man who sent pieces of wood he had collected at Gettysburg or the New Yorker who contributed 5 gallons of water from the Amazon River.[37]

Perhaps the most interesting assortment of gifts came to the Department of Singing Birds and Pet Animals. One poor woman wrote that since her husband would not give her any money she was sending six kittens. The offerings from the countryside included a pet donkey that purportedly had served in the War of 1812 and two white mice from China. One 10-year-old boy had only his black terrier to offer; the committee chairwoman gratefully accepted the donation, bought it herself, and returned it to its young owner. Finally, the chairwoman reported, there were "thirty-six parrots, well accustomed to low company," with vocabularies befitting their background.[38]

Numerous organizations and labor groups sent contributions to the fair. The employees of John Bromley's carpet factory gave $41.50; the city's policemen donated over $1,000 in wages; the men aboard the steamer *Ladona* offered a day's pay; members of Philadelphia's Anderson Troop collected items in the field; and the officers and crew of the ship of war *Constellation* sent $842.75 all the way from Italy. The fair also enjoyed one day's profits from an all-star baseball game; a traveling circus; the Chestnut Street Theater; several local railways; and Bird's Billiard Saloon.[39] Small businesspeople, such as dressmaker Mrs. E. C. Tilton and

---

36 Joseph Boggs Beale diary, June 3, 1864, HSP; James Tyndale Mitchell diary, 1864, privately owned; Nicholas B. Wainwright, ed., *A Philadelphia Perspective: The Diary of Sydney George Fisher* (Philadelphia, 1967), 471, entry for April 25, 1864.
37 *ODF*, June 11, 1864; unsigned letters, June 22, 1864, Box 8, F-2; May 6, 1864, Box 8, F-2; undated, Box 7, F-2, all Furness Papers; USSC and Fair Papers, Box 1, F-2; Box 1, F-3, HSP.
38 *ODF*, June 11, 1864.
39 *Philadelphia Evening Bulletin*, June 4, 1864 (hereafter *EB*); Furness Scrapbook, Furness Papers; Suzanne Colton Wilson, ed., *Column South with the Fifteenth Pennsyl-*

grocer Joshua Wright, offered part of their revenues; the Great Valley Association for the Detection of Horse Thieves sent $30.[40] The range of donations was limited only by the reach of citizens' imaginations. The Carpenters and Bricklayers helped construct the Logan Square buildings, and representatives of various fire departments agreed to cooperate to protect the fair from fire.[41]

Many businesses used the festivities for publicity. Newspapers reported on a fierce competition between sewing-machine companies, each seeking the title of most generous establishment in the city. The Singer Sewing Machine Company donated $300; three days later the Florence Sewing Machine Company matched that figure. The American Button Hole Machine Company gave two of its machines (valued at $650) and $50 in cash, which the *Bulletin* acknowledged as "the largest contribution of any sewing machine company so far."[42]

Visitors

The 15,000 Philadelphians who attended the fair's opening ceremonies on June 7 viewed a scene that was "possibly the most imposing ever witnessed in Philadelphia." The procession to the speaker's stand consisted of the executive committee (which included many of Philadelphia's most prominent citizens); Mayor Alexander Henry; Bishop Matthew Simpson, of the Methodist Episcopal Church, who represented President Lincoln during the ceremonies; selected clergy; the governors of Pennsylvania, Delaware, and New Jersey; General George Cadwalader and other military officers; members of the city council and several committee chairmen.[43]

The ceremony was marred by the sudden collapse of a hastily installed platform for the choir, but after a few moments of confusion the program continued.[44] In his welcoming speech Mayor Henry applauded the work of both national relief commissions, which, he said, had jointly provided "wide channels through which the oil and wine of soothing kindness and of strengthening cheer may flow." Governor Andrew Curtin added that "the work before this great nation is big enough for all."[45]

The visitor to the fair who made his way to the center of the Logan

    vania Cavalry (Flagstaff, Ariz., 1960), 62; *EB*, June 13, 1864; Philadelphia *Press*, May 25, 30, 1864; Furness Scrapbook.
40 *Press*, May 2, 3, 1864; *EB*, June 13, 1864.
41 *Press*, May 7, 1864; Furness Scrapbook.
42 *Press*, May 28, 31, 1864; *EB*, June 3, 1864.
43 *ODF*, June 8, 1864. The fair was actually less crowded for the inaugural ceremonies than it was on later days, because the admission price had been doubled to $2 for the day.
44 *EB*, June 8, 1864.
45 *ODF*, June 8, 1864.

Square buildings found his senses assaulted by the smells from two large, canvas-domed rotundas housing the restaurant and the Horticultural Department.[46] From that central location, Union Avenue presented a crowded display of tables and flags for half a block in each direction. On the far side of the Horticultural Department stood the 500-foot long Art Gallery, featuring what was repeatedly referred to as the greatest collection of its kind in the nation's history.[47]

If the guest walked down Union Avenue, toward the Eighteenth Street exit, she passed displays of items such as umbrellas, glassware, and shoes; hallways on either side housed the exhibits built by the city's public and private schools, and the popular Arms and Trophies room. At the end of Union Avenue, she could choose between the Delaware display to her right and the New Jersey effort on the left. If she chose to turn around and meander back up Union Avenue, she found some of the most crowded exhibits, including the Pennsylvania Kitchen, the William Penn Parlor, the machinery and shipbuilding display, and a wide assortment of sewing machines.

While enjoying the splendor of the surroundings, the visitor had innumerable opportunities to give to the cause. Ticket sales earned nearly $180,000. Many visitors purchased items on sale at the committees' tables. Others spent $2 to vote on the recipient of one of the elegant gifts donated to the fair. And most took time to sample the restaurant's bill of fare, which ranged from mock turtle soup and lobster salad to an assortment of Hungarian wines.[48]

To do the fair justice required several days, and many Philadelphians returned frequently during the fair's three weeks. The city's newspapers — as well as the official *Our Daily Fair* — provided meticulous coverage of each department and event, seemingly competing to achieve the loftiest heights of hyperbole. The *North American and United States Gazette* promised that "[t]he exhibition will be . . . infinitely superior to all ordinary displays which have taken place in this city." The *Evening Bulletin* praised the "display of baby houses [as] without a parallel in the history of baby architecture."[49]

The evidence of contemporary diaries suggests that nearly every Phil-

46 This description of the fair is from a combination of newspaper and diary accounts, *ODF*, and *Godey's Lady's Book* (August 1864), 179 and (September 1864), 262. A map of the fairgrounds is on the frontispiece of the bound collection of *ODF*, which was printed immediately following the fair.

47 Wainwright, ed., *a Philadelphia Perspective*, 474, entry for June 12, 1864.

48 The gifts to be voted on included a sword valued at $2,500, to be presented to a Union general; a silver trumpet, for the most popular fire company; and a bonnet, for the city's favorite general's wife. *ODF*. For the restaurant menu, see Helena Hubbell, "Civil War Scrapbook," Book 2, HSP.

49 *North American and United States Gazette*, June 3, 1864, *EB*, June 9, 1864. The account went on to refer to the play houses as "palatial juvenile establishments."

adelphian was aware of the fair, that most visited it, and that almost all were strongly enthusiastic. As early as March 10, Anna Blanchard wrote that "the town is in excitement in relation to [the] Great Central for the Sanitary." A month later Henry Benners noted that the fair buildings were progressing rapidly and that workers in his glass factory had each given a day's wage to the cause. And by the time opening day arrived, Anna Ferris reported that it "occupies the thoughts & interests of the public to the exclusion of most other things."[50]

Some were less pleased. George W. Fahnestock, who had already refused to serve as a committee member, complained bitterly of being "beset with circulars begging for everything," claiming – rather ironically – that "of course we need no such reminder of incentive to duty." Later he visited the fair buildings, recording his view that the whole affair seemed like "childs play particularly when the Sanitary Commission do not need the money." After he visited the fair, Fahnestock's litany of dissatisfaction included the crowds, the high prices, the "uncouth dances" of the "savages" at the Indian display, and the quality of the horticultural exhibit. But even this great cynic found himself swept up in the enthusiasm, and four days later he returned for four evening hours.[51] Another naysayer, 75-year-old Jacob Elfreth, Sr., dismissed the whole fair as a "waste of money." But although he never went himself, Elfreth's son and daughter were regular visitors, and he soon admitted that it "appears to be very attractive."[52]

Most Philadelphians needed no convincing. Joseph Boggs Beale visited the fair at least ten times; Susan Trautwine mentioned four visits; James Tyndale Mitchell went almost every day; Mary Dreer often went twice a day. Dr. Lewis Walker found it such a "magnificent display" that he bought season tickets and returned after dark to see the fair by gaslight. Sydney George Fisher called the event a "miracle of American spirit, energy, & beauty." Anna Ferris added that it was "the most wonderful display of everything under the sun." After his first visit, an enthusiastic Jacob Elfreth, Jr., made a lengthy journal entry in which he called the Horticultural Department the "most magnificent I ever saw," the Art Gallery the "largest collection of Pictures I ever saw," and the entire fair "the greatest collection of curiosities that ever was exhibited in this city." It was certainly, as Anna Blanchard put it, "an Exhibition of which [Philadelphia] may well be proud."[53]

---

50 Blanchard diary, March 10, 1864; Benners diary, April 12, 1864; A. Ferris diary, June 8, 1864. For an excellent firsthand account in a published form, see Wilson, ed., *Column South*, 163–4.
51 George W. Fahnestock diary, 1864, HSP.
52 Jacob Elfreth, Sr. diary, June 7, 11, 1864, Haverford College Library, Haverford College.
53 Lewis Walker diary, June 17, 1864, HSP; Wainwright, ed., *a Philadelphia Perspective*,

On June 16 President and Mrs. Abraham Lincoln visited the city. Their short stay brought together public officeholders, civic leaders, and spontaneous crowds in a series of celebrations that reflected the complexity of both the war's rituals and its voluntarism. The Lincolns' carriage rolled down Broad Street toward the Continental Hotel amid cheering throngs, enjoying a general business holiday, massed on both sides.[54] In the afternoon, several Union League members met the city council at the Continental to escort Lincoln to the fair. Sydney George Fisher joined this group and "[w]as much pleased by [Lincoln's] contenance, voice and manner. He is," Fisher continued, "not awkward & uncouth as has been represented." But Jacob Elfreth, Jr. – who viewed the president from outside the hotel – found him "very tall and ungainly looking and not at all showy."[55]

The president pleased the throng waiting at the fair by vowing to fight for three more years, if necessary, and by applauding all the "voluntary contributions, given freely, zealously, and earnestly, on top of all the disturbances of business, the taxation, and burdens [of] the war." That evening Lincoln visited the Union League and the National Union Club, before returning to the Continental around midnight. There he found more crowds, a band, and a fireworks display. Lincoln later recalled that by the end of the day "I was the most used up that I ever remember to have been in my life."[56]

The fair's doors stayed open for a week after Lincoln's visit, but some of the novelty had worn off, and many of the best displays had been picked clean. On June 27 and 28 the committee lowered ticket prices from $1 to $.25, but still the turnout remained low. By the time the fair closed, 253,924 ticket holders had made an estimated 442,658 visits, an average of 29,510 visitors each day.[57]

Over 250,000 people bought tickets to the fair.[58] There were roughly 608,000 Philadelphians in 1864.[59] Even allowing for thousands of visitors from out of town, the fair attracted a large proportion of the city's population. Most accounts of the Great Central Fair stress that all seg-

---

473, entry for June 7, 1864; A. Ferris diary, June 9, 1864; Jacob Elfreth, Jr., diary, June 15, 1864, Haverford; Blanchard diary, June 1864.

54   For descriptions of Lincoln's visit, see *ODF*, June 17, 18, 1864; Maxwell Whiteman, *Gentlemen in Crisis: The First Century of the Union League of Philadelphia, 1862–1962* (Philadelphia, 1975), 71–76; *EB*, June 16–18, 1864; and Kenneth A. Bernard, *Lincoln and the Music of the Civil War* (Caldwell, Idaho, 1966), 216–18.

55   Wainwright, ed., *A Philadelphia Perspective*, 475, entry of June 16, 1864; Jacob Elfreth, Jr. diary, June 18, 1864.

56   *EB*, June 16, 17, 1864; Bernard, *Lincoln and the Music*, 217.

57   *EB*, June 25, 1864; *ODF*, September 11, 1864.

58   *ODF*, September 11, 1864.

59   Roger Lane, *Violent Death in the City: Suicide, Accident and Murder in Nineteenth Century Philadelphia* (Cambridge, Mass., 1979), 11.

ments of Philadelphia society combined to make it a success. Two months before the fair began George Fahnestock wrote, "Everybody is working for it, talking about it, begging for it. The newspapers are full of it – advertising columns and all – and everybody in town, male and female, is on some committee – self appointed or otherwise."[60] The *North American and United States Gazette* marveled at "how thoroughly this Great Fair has worked into the popular sympathy," and the *Bulletin* noted the "thousands of men, women and children" who worked for its success and the further "thousands who contributed money, labor, time, gifts or loans."[61] *Forney's War Press* made the case even more directly: "There is not one man, woman, or child out of a hundred within the limits of the city, who is not directly interested in the Great Central Fair, who has not given it at least one day's labor, and a month's sympathy and earnest aid."[62]

When the rules concerning tickets were first announced, it appeared – mistakenly – that city inhabitants would have to buy season tickets for $5, rather than the $1 single-day tickets that would be available to outsiders. This misunderstanding led a Philadelphia "Workingman" to write an angry letter to the *Press:*

> I had understood that the Great Fair . . . was to be the spontaneous offering of all our citizens, rich and poor, to those brave men who are now engaged in upholding our Government. . . . With this understanding, I and thousands more such as I, gave my mite cheerfully – gave as much as I could to a cause with which I sympathize so fully.

He went on to object to the prohibitive season-ticket prices, which he felt would exclude workingmen like himself.[63]

The committees clearly embraced the ideal of widespread participation. Each group followed the lead of the executive committee's initial announcement in calling on all classes to do their part. Bond's Committee on Labor, Income and Revenue aimed its first circular at "the working men and women of the city," calling on them to give a day's earnings or a day's labor. The flyer distributed by the Committee on Looking Glasses, Picture Frames and Gilt Ornaments was typical in insisting that "no one [should], on account of its apparent triviality, hesitate to send any small article." The Committee on Sewing Women explained that they did not want "to tax heavily those whose livelihood depends upon the needle" but to ensure "that all may be included in this natural ova-

60 Fahnestock diary, April 5, 1864.
61 *North American and United States Gazette,* June 4, 1864; *EB,* 4, June 25, 1864.
62 *Forney's War Press,* June 11, 1864, in Furness Scrapbook.
63 *Press,* May 17, 1864. The decision to reduce the admission fee to $.25 for the last two days was made explicitly to accommodate "the poor" in Philadelphia. See *EB,* June 25, 1864.

tion," for "[in] a moral scale 'the widow's mite' will outweigh a Prince's diadem."[64]

Appeals for contributions usually stressed the twin pulls of patriotism and benevolence. In an editorial on a benefit opera for the fair, the *Ledger* observed that "Patriotism dictates a general attendance." The *Press* argued that "our only tribute to the fallen must be our care for the living." *Our Daily Fare* continually emphasized the good works of the Sanitary Commission and saw the fair as the latest expression of the war's "ongoing tide of benevolence." After the first day, the *Bulletin* concluded that "this scene of wonderful beauty has arisen at the call of the noblest instincts of the human heart – patriotism and humanity."[65]

Beneath the surface patriotism there were other motivations. The committee chairs often used the profit motive to their advantage, reminding businessmen of the goodwill a donation could purchase. A circular aimed at the oil refiners of western Pennsylvania argued that by providing the fair with a good display, "contributors whilst aiding the soldiers of the Union, will at the same time, advertise their respective establishments." The Committee on Labor, Income and Revenue appealed to the pride of the city's shoemakers by announcing that it "had full confidence that the contributions from that branch will be in proportion as liberal as from any source from which it applies."[66] Bond's committee ensured that no benevolent light would be hidden under a bushel by taking out regular newspaper advertisements listing all the latest donations.

Beyond the profits it brought to the Sanitary Commission, the Great Central Fair temporarily freed Philadelphia from the gloom of war. One writer in *Our Daily Fare* argued that even if the fair earned no money at all, it would perform a useful function by spurring the local economy and taking people's minds off the conflict.[67] The fair made Philadelphians proud of themselves and of their city. Much of the pre-fair boosterism challenged the local citizenry to top New York's effort. The *Bulletin* predicted that Philadelphia would outdo New York in size, variety, artwork, and proceeds. This, it said, "affords additional proof that the cause of patriotism is more liberally sustained in money as well as men in the City of Brotherly Love than in any other city in the Union."[68]

64 Circular of the Committee on Labor, Income and Revenue, dated March 28, 1864; Circular of the Committee on Looking Glasses, Picture Frames and Gilt Ornaments, dated March 15, 1864; Circular of the Committee on Sewing Women, undated. All circulars in the Great Sanitary Fair – Misc. File, HSP.
65 *Philadelphia Public Ledger*, May 6, 1864 (hereafter *PL*); *Press*, May 12, 1864; *ODF*, June 8, 1864; *EB*, June 10, 1864. See also *PL*, June 7, 1864, and numerous other newspaper editorials for discussions of patriotism and the fair.
66 Furness Papers; *EB*, June 2, 1864.
67 *ODF*, June 13, 1864.
68 *EB*, June 18, 1864. Also see *PL*, May 14, 1864, and *EB*, June 3, 1864. In a speech to the committee chairmen, the Sanitary Commission's Dr. Henry Bellows challenged

The Significance of the Great Central Fair

The Fair and Philadelphia's Benevolent Traditions

The fair, like the war itself, presented Philadelphia with challenges on a new scale. Mustering committee members and collecting donations, like raising troops, required sophisticated organization and widespread cooperation. But just as the fair itself recast antebellum fund-raising practices on a larger scale, so the organizers relied on Philadelphia's existing organizational forms and associational ties to ensure its success.

Committee memberships suggest the importance of these familiar associational ties. Most committees were organized around particular trades. The 8 men on the Committee on Boots, Shoes and Leather included 2 tanners, 4 leather and skins dealers, and 2 merchants. The 26 members of the associated women's committee were largely relatives of men in the leather trades. All of the Hardware Committee members were hardware dealers, saddlers, or merchants. The Ships and Shipbuilding Committee recognized that it was responsible for collecting from men of varied occupations by forming subcommittees of shipbuilders, joiners, sailmakers, shipsmiths, spar makers, block makers, and riggers.[69]

Those committees that were not organized around trades followed the antebellum pattern of paternalistic benevolence. The 56 men and women on the Restaurant Committee included 9 gentlemen and gentlewomen; 7 manufacturers or wives of manufacturers; 5 attorneys, doctors, and executives or their wives; a major shipper; and the wife of a judge. But the Restaurant Committee was not exclusively the province of elites. It also included several storekeepers, a cashier, a bookkeeper, and a carpenter's wife. The 36-man Executive Committee knew no such diversity. This body was composed of gentlemen, professionals, manufacturers, and leading merchants and traders. Its rolls included prominent attorneys Theodore Cuyler, Charles J. Stillé, and Horace Howard Furness; foundry owner Samuel V. Merrick; manufacturer Joseph Harrison, Jr.; and wealthy gentleman Caleb Cope.

Other committees were formed explicitly around geographic associations. These included the Eighteenth Ward Committee, the West Philadelphia Committee, and the independently run Department of the State of Delaware. The Restaurant Department had special chairwomen for

---

Philadelphians to beat the standard established by other Northern cities. "Miskey Autobiography," 58.

69 *List of Committees*. The occupations are taken from *McElroy's City Directory*. The same pattern holds true for the Bakers Committee and presumably for the other committees organized around trades.

subcommittees representing Germantown, Chestnut Hill, West Chester, Mount Holly, and Roxborough. The extremely large Schools Committee included representatives from the city's various public and private schools, many of which held their own activities to support the fair.

Philadelphia had over seventy benevolent societies on the eve of the war.[70] Many were small, single-gender bodies, but others, such as the Union Benevolent Association (UBA) and the Philadelphia Society for the Employment and Instruction of the Poor (PSEIP), were more ambitious organizations that relied on female volunteers (or "visitors") directed by a male board of managers.[71]

As in the prewar years, many wartime organizations were fairly small bodies staffed exclusively by women.[72] But the larger organizations followed the pattern of the UBA and the PSEIP in using a host of female volunteers, but with men holding the dominant positions. Philadelphia's Citizens' Volunteer Hospital Association, for instance, had 110 "lady members" who visited the hospital at Broad and Washington Streets, and 25 male managers.[73] The members of the executive committees of both the Sanitary and the Christian commissions were all men; most of Philadelphia's rank and file were women.

The fair's organization followed this familiar form. The executive committee was made up of 37 men; the 11-member Committee of Women on Organization served in a subordinate role. Most of the subcommittees listed male members first, followed by a separate "Committee of Women." We have seen that as they prepared for the fair the committees divided duties among men and women according to generally accepted gender roles.

The Fair and Social Change

What can Philadelphia's Great Central Fair tell us about the role of wartime benevolence in social change? We began this account by identifying

70 Isaac Collins and John Powell, *A List of Some of the Benevolent Institutions of the City of Philadelphia* (Philadelphia, 1859); Eudice Glassberg, "Philadelphians in Need: Client Experiences with Two Philadelphia Benevolent Societies, 1830–1880," Ph.D. diss., University of Philadelphia, 1979, 4. For a discussion of the variety of antebellum benevolent societies, see Bremner, *Public Good*, 14–34.

71 *Constitution of the Union Benevolent Association* (Philadelphia, 1831); Union Benevolent Association, 25th–29th *Annual Reports* (Philadelphia, 1856–60). *Constitution of the Philadelphia Society for the Employment and Instruction of the Poor* (Philadelphia, 1847, 1852); Glassberg, "Philadelphians in Need," 147–51, 258, 272–4. See also Gallman, *Mastering Wartime*, Chapter 5. The PSEIP began with a Board of Managers that included both men and women, but soon the female managers became relegated to an auxiliary board.

72 See Gallman, *Mastering Wartime*, Chapter 5.

73 Citizens' Volunteer Hospital Association, *2nd Annual Report* (Philadelphia, 1864).

two common themes: (1) that transition from "the improvised war" to "the organized war" saw an increased centralization of activity;[74] (2) that the wartime experience of female volunteers helped launch women into the public sphere in the postwar years. The fair would seem a logical place to find evidence of each phenomenon.

In his study of Northern intellectuals during the Civil War, George N. Fredrickson argues that the Sanitary Commission's founders embraced a "conservative, basically nonhumanitarian philosophy." These men sought to impose order and discipline in American society by centralizing philanthropy and by ridding it of the sentimental and individualistic aspects that had characterized antebellum charities.[75] The commissioners succeeded in their task in that they directed a large share of the North's benevolent funds toward "suitable" activities. But Philadelphia's experience suggests that these representatives of the nation's elite did not meet their larger goals. Numerous other local and national charities provided the humanitarianism and individualism that the Sanitary Commission rejected. Rather than a highly centralized structure, wartime benevolence took a chaotic form reminiscent of antebellum America.[76]

Moreover, the Sanitary Commission's own fair movement reveals the superficial nature of this centralized control. The impetus for Philadelphia's fair came not from the national commissioners, or even from the local Philadelphia associates, but from a resolution by the independent Union League.[77] The fair was exclusively a local event; moreover, it was essentially a grass-roots effort.[78] Although the executive committee watched over the activities, most of the important work was performed in small subcommittees or by individual volunteers. As we have seen, the papers of the recording secretary are full of letters from interested citizens offering unsolicited counsel on all aspects of the fair's organization, and local diarists repeatedly referred to the fair with a fierce local pride. Such evidence reinforces the conclusion that this was clearly "the people's fair."

What of the wartime experiences of Philadelphia's women? Thousands

74 Allan Nevins used the quoted phrases as the subtitles to his four-volume *War for the Union,* for (respectively) volumes 1 and 2 and volumes 3 and 4.

75 Fredrickson, *Inner Civil War,* 98–112. In her study of benevolent women, Lori Ginzberg accepts Fredrickson's argument that the USSC dominated wartime giving and acted as a force for both efficiency and centralization. "Women and the Work of Benevolence," Ph.D. diss., Yale University, 1984, Chapter 5.

76 Gallman, *Mastering Wartime,* Chapter 5.

77 *ODF,* June 20, 1864. In fact, the local members of the Sanitary Commission had resisted joining the fair movement because they felt that the flow of donations from Philadelphians was already adequate. It is also telling that the histories of the various city fairs reveal a wide range of origins and structures. See *ODF.*

78 The sanitary fair was also an entirely private event. Local politicians participated in the opening ceremonies, but no public monies went to supporting the fair. See Gallman, *Mastering Wartime,* Chapter 6.

of local women served in patriotic organizations, thus giving them valuable experience in organizing. Moreover, these sacrifices did not go unnoticed. Contemporary observers frequently noted the activities of female volunteers, and in the postwar years several publications heralded their contributions to the cause.[79] But what were these contributions, and how were they recognized?

Although women numerically dominated many of the Great Central Fair's committees, the executive committee was entirely male, and where men and women formed parallel subcommittees the men consistently received top billing. In fact, the fair's organizers seemed particularly proud of this structure. As the event came to a close, *Our Daily Fare* looked back on the successful venture and concluded that "[o]ne of the distinguished features of this fair is that its management is more under the control of the gentlemen than any one which had preceded it."[80]

When the doors opened, the relationship between male and female volunteers seemed reminiscent of the gender roles within the Union Benevolent Association. Whereas in the peacetime organization men "managed" and women "visited," during the fair the men managed and the women attended to the selling. Certainly these efforts earned Philadelphia's women substantial notice. *Forney's War Press* applauded the efforts of women, who, "forbidden to fight or to vote for the Union," took this opportunity to aid the cause. "There is scarcely a department of the Fair," the editorial continued," [to] which the hand of woman has not added a charm."[81]

But generally such accolades revealed unflattering gender stereotypes. As opening day approached, the *Press* reported that "[t]he ladies are in a state of excitement about all the little details of the great display."[82] A male committee member wrote, "[W]e have agreed with every female member of our committees on every suggestion that they have made, and when you consider the variety of the suggestions, and their utter inconsistency ... you may imagine the mental strain upon us."[83] *Our Daily*

---

79 See L. P. Brockett and Mary C. Vaughan, *Women's Work in the Civil War: A Record of Heroism, Patriotism, and Patience* (Philadelphia, 1867); Moore, *Women of the War*; [Brockett], *Philanthropic Results*. For a particularly glowing description of the activities of Philadelphia's women, see Septima M. Collis, *A Woman's War Record, 1861–1865* (New York, 1889), 12–13.

80 *ODF*, June 20, 1864. In other cities this was not the case. The Chicago, New York, and Poughkeepsie fairs were all sparked by women. *Our Daily Fare's* Boston correspondent was proud to describe that city's fund-raiser as "a Ladies' Fair." *ODF*, June 9, 13, 15, 16, 1864.

81 *Forney's War Press*, June 11, 1864. Clipping in Furness Papers, Box 2, HSP.

82 *Press*, May 17, 1864. Two weeks later the paper added that "[t]he women are in a state of delightful excitement." *Press*, May 31, 1864.

83 *ODF*, June 9, 1864.

Fare consistently spoke condescendingly of female volunteers, who were "sending palpitations to the masculine heart" while selling their wares, and predicted "extra orders for wedding-cake and white stain, 'when this cruel fare is over.' " One observer described how enthusiastic committee-women ignored all the "formalities of social intercourse" and, on occasion, bullied men like "accomplished overseer[s]."[84] And in response to those who questioned the fair's utility, *Our Daily Fare* pointed out that it had improved young ladies' skills in darning socks, sewing buttons, and writing with a graceful hand.[85]

In private some men appeared even less complimentary. One Philadelphian insisted on turning over his gift to a man, because "[a] woman is a woman" and should not be trusted with "property."[86] L. Montgomery Bond endorsed a proposed mock presidential election for women as an "amusing scheme" that would delight local women by given them "an opportunity for once in their lives to be heard on the great question of the Presidency" while also pleasing "the 'womens rights' people."[87]

As a large, citywide event designed to support a national patriotic organization, Philadelphia's Great Central Fair is a reasonable place to look for evidence of the Civil War's centralizing impulses. The widely recognized role of women in ensuring its success also makes the fair a logical starting point in a search for a widening role for women in the public sphere. But in both cases the signs of change seem outweighed by the evidence of persistent localism and gender divisions. A glance into the following decade emphasizes the point.

The Centennial City

Eight years after Appomattox, the panic of 1873 sent the United States into a crippling depression, and philanthropy-minded Philadelphians faced a challenge reminiscent of 1861. As the city's existing charities did their best to meet the new demands, many Philadelphians followed tradition by forming emergency relief associations. Like their antebellum and wartime counterparts, these groups typically organized at emergency meetings to meet local needs. In most wards male officers and managers directed the local relief association and female visitors distributed relief to the needy. Thus, long after the war these new organizations turned to

---

84 Ibid., June 9, 10, 1864. References to the "attractive" and "charming" saleswomen appear in nearly every issue of the fair's official newspaper.
85 Ibid., June 8, 1864.
86 Ibid., June 11, 1864.
87 Montgomery Bond to Welsh, April 28, 1864, Furness Papers, Box 7.

traditional gender differentiation, as well as to decentralized control, in response to crisis.[88]

But if Philadelphia's benevolent world in 1873 looked much as it had in 1860, the next several years saw signs of change. Although the established organizations did not alter their practices, the annual reports reveal slight shifts in the recognition of women's activities. For instance, in 1874 the PSEIP's report introduced a new page listing the Ladies' Auxiliary Committees and a separate "Report of the Ladies' Board of Managers."[89] The UBA's male managers dispensed with their report in 1874, deferring instead to the ladies' reports. The following year the managers' reports ran a short page and a half, whereas the ladies' report covered thirteen pages.[90]

The PSEIP's lists of managers also indicate continuity through the war decade and then a shift in the mid-1870s. Of 21 lady managers in 1871, 5 had been managers since before the war, 10 had served since at least 1863, and only 1 woman had been a manager for less than four years. Four years later, in 1875, only one of these 21 lady managers remained on the PSEIP's rolls. Among the society's 22 male managers in 1871, 10 had joined the ranks by 1863 and 14 had served for four years or more. But whereas the female membership turned over almost completely between 1871 and 1875, 14 male managers remained by the middle of the decade.[91] Were the PSEIP's new lady managers veterans of Civil War benevolence? None appears among the extensive committee lists for the 1864 sanitary fair. Perhaps they were active among the rank and file but deemed too young to have their names published.[92]

---

88 See *Report of the Tenth Ward Citizens' Association* (Philadelphia, 1874); *Report of the Executive Committee of the Fourteenth Ward Relief Association* (Philadelphia, 1874); *The Germantown Relief Society* (Philadelphia, 1875) (this is a four-page pamphlet describing the society's aims); *Fourth Annual Report of the Board of Managers of the Germantown Relief Society* (Philadelphia, 1877).

89 The society's next two annual reports continued these new features and took particular care to acknowledge the efforts of the Ladies' Branch. PSEIP, *27th Annual Report* (Philadelphia, 1875) and *28th Annual Report* (Philadelphia, 1875); *29th Annual Report* (Philadelphia, 1876).

90 UBA, *43rd Annual Report* (Philadelphia, 1875) and *44th Annual Report* (Philadelphia, 1875). Of course this slight shift in the annual reports does not suggest a movement toward balanced gender roles in the UBA or the PSEIP.

91 PSEIP, 4th–28th *Annual Reports* (1851–75).

92 Seventeen of the PSEIP's 22 lady managers in 1875 were unmarried. Thus, their absence from the sanitary fair committee lists does not merely reflect postwar name changes through marriage. The wartime committee lists did include younger women, but the correspondence suggests that younger girls were sometimes kept off the lists. The membership lists of the all-female Indigent Widows' and Single Womens' Society also suggest strong continuities over the war decade. Twenty of 24 officers and managers in 1859 were still serving in 1866 (2 others were unmarried in 1859 and might have appeared in 1866 under married names). By 1873, 14 of the 1859 officers and

In 1876 Philadelphia hosted the nation's Centennial Exhibition. The exhibition's planning and organization followed some of the patterns set by the 1864 sanitary fair. But the two events were different, suggesting how circumstances had changed in the postwar decade.

In 1870, Philadelphia's Select Council officially resolved to hold an international exhibition to mark the centennial of the Declaration of Independence, and soon afterward the state legislature voted its support of the proposal. In the following year, Congress passed a bill naming Philadelphia the official site of the Centennial Exhibition and providing for the selection of exhibition commissioners from each state. In 1872 Congress authorized the creation of a Centennial Board of Finance to sell stock in the exhibition.

The Board of Finance, which was dominated by the same core of Philadelphia elites who had orchestrated the sanitary fair and Philadelphia's other wartime activities, had to raise $10 million to ensure the exhibition's success. In early 1873, the City Council appropriated $500,000 to the fund; eventually the city donated a total of $1.5 million. The state legislature added $1 million to finance the construction of a permanent Memorial Hall on the exhibition site. Philadelphians held numerous fundraising mass meetings; the city's coal, railroad, and lumber companies made large donations, as did local publishers, fraternal societies, and various other economic and social organizations. But by mid-1874, only $1.5 million in stock had been sold. The federal government resisted requests that it provide financial support for the project, until finally, as the exhibitions opening day approached, Congress lent the Board of Finance $1.5 million to guarantee that the celebration would open.[93]

The Centennial Exhibition, modeled on the world's fairs held in London (1851), Paris (1855 and 1867), New York (1853), and Vienna (1873), featured displays of industrial progress from across the globe, filling more than two hundred buildings that covered 450 acres of Fairmount Park. Between May and November more than 10 million visitors came to Philadelphia to share in the celebration.[94]

managers remained. *42nd Annual Report* (Philadelphia, 1859); *49th Annual Report* (Philadelphia, 1866); *55th Annual Report* (Philadelphia, 1873).

93 Faith K. Pizor, "Preparations for the Centennial Exhibition of 1876," *Pennsylvania Magazine of History and Biography*, 94 (April 1970), 213–19, 223, 228, 231; Whiteman, *Gentlemen in Crisis*, 132; Dorothy Gondos Beers, "The Centennial City, 1865–1876," in *Philadelphia: A 300-Year History*, ed. Russell F. Weigley (New York, 1982), 460–70. John Welsh – who had headed the executive committee of the sanitary fair – served as president of the Board of Finance, which had 15 Philadelphians among its 25 members. Welsh and 7 other board members had been founding members of the Union League. For an excellent description of the exhibition, see James D. McCabe, *The Illustrated History of the Centennial Exhibition* (1876; reprint, Philadelphia, 1975). Rydell's *All the World's a Fair* devotes a chapter to the Centennial Exhibition but does not address the issues discussed here (9–37).

94 Beers, "Centennial City," 213–14. For visitors' descriptions, see William Randel, ed.,

How did the 1876 exhibition compare with the Great Central Fair of 1864? The exhibition's physical design was much like that of its wartime predecessor but on a grander scale. Both fairs featured special horticultural, art, and manufacturing displays. Each had a section reserved for guns and military regalia. Both boasted elaborate restaurants and oddities from around the world. For the visitor, the biggest difference was that the 1876 exhibition was much more ambitious than the earlier fair and included many more international displays. And while the sanitary fair was completely dismantled after a few weeks, the exhibition lasted for half a year, and some of its buildings remained as permanent structures.[95]

Apart from its scale and international aspect, one display in particular set the Centennial Exhibition apart from the wartime fair. In 1876 the Citizens' Centennial Finance Committee formed a women's committee headed by 13 prominent Philadelphia women. This body carried out a grass-roots fund-raising campaign that quickly collected $40,000. When it became evident that the Centennial Exhibition's male organizers had made no plans to display women's work, the women's committee collected an additional $30,000 to finance the construction of a women's building. The Women's Pavilion housed an eclectic assortment of displays, ranging from a 6-horse-power engine to a head carved out of butter, all produced by women. In a fair that heralded the nation's progress, this exhibit – unlike those of its wartime predecessor – explicitly acknowledged women's role in that development.[96]

A further difference between the two fairs was in their organization. Whereas the executive committee of Philadelphia's sanitary fair acted independently of the national Sanitary Commission and without any government aid, the 1876 exhibition received large donations from the city, state, and federal governments as well as financial support from foreign nations.[97] Still, both fairs relied on the direction of a handful of Philadelphia elites, the voluntary efforts of hundreds of local men and women, and the financial support of the city's businesses, fraternal societies, and private citizens.

"John Lewis Reports the Centennial," *Philadelphia Magazine of History and Biography*, 79 (July 1955); 365–74; William H. Crew, ed., "Centennial Notes," *Pennsylvania Magazine of History and Biography*, 100 (July 1976), 410–13.

95 The events also differed in that each part of the Great Central Fair was designed to raise money, while the Centennial Exhibition's organizers sought to celebrate the national anniversary by displaying America's technological progress to the world. Whereas the sanitary fair had been stocked with tables of items for visitors to purchase, the exhibition's displays were not for sale.

96 Beers, "Centennial City," 461; McCabe, *Illustrated History*, 218–20; Randel, ed., "John Lewis Reports the Centennial," 369.

97 Of course the Centennial Exhibition enjoyed such broad support because it was not a local event but a national celebration hosted by Philadelphia.

In 1879 the formation of the Philadelphia Society for Organizing Charitable Relief and Repressing Mendicancy (PSOCR) marked a major milestone in the city's benevolent history. The organization, which had been formed to eliminate the evils of overlapping philanthropies, gave Philadelphia charities the centralized agency that the war years had lacked. The PSOCR's complicated structure included a wide array of subcommittees and an entirely male board of directors, which supervised the activities of affiliated organizations in each ward.[98]

The PSOCR and its ward associations introduced greater efficiency and organization into Philadelphia's benevolent world and also reflected an increased recognition of the role of Philadelphia's charitable women. The original plan followed tradition by placing women in circumscribed roles, attending to visitation and the like, while men served in the highest offices and controlled the funds. But the *2nd Annual Report* included a call for increased "Cooperation of Men and Women Workers" and even indicated that "in some wards women had been placed on the Board of Directors."[99] By 1884 the Eighth Ward Association had 5 male and 5 female directors; in 1888 the combined Thirteenth and Fourteenth Wards Association reported an evenly balanced board of directors and a woman superintendent.[100]

By the end of the 1870s Philadelphia's charities were increasingly centralized and efficient, as well as more open to putting women in positions of authority.[101] Those changes emerged in the postwar years, however. The city that set out to stage a three-week fund-raising fair in 1864 relied on traditional practices rather than recasting familiar ways.

98 Philadelphia Society for Organizing Charitable Relief and Repressing Mendicancy, *1st Annual Report* (Philadelphia, 1879); *Suggested By-Laws for Ward Associations* (Philadelphia, 1878).

99 PSOCR, *2nd Annual Report* (Philadelphia, 1880).

100 Eighth Ward Association of the Philadelphia Society for Organizing Charity, *6th Annual Report* (Philadelphia, 1884); Thirteenth and Fourteenth Wards Association of the Philadelphia Society for Organizing Charity, *8th Annual Report* (Philadelphia, 1888). The evidence is too spotty to detect a shift in the practices of any particular ward association, but in 1881 the Tenth Ward Association reported a more traditional structure, with men serving as officers and directors and women acting as officers of their own "Corps of Visitors," *3rd Annual Report*.

101 But gender differentiation did persist. The women in the Society for Organizing Charitable Relief still did the bulk of the visiting, much as they had for decades in the UBA. In 1881 the ladies of the Indigent Widows' and Single Women's Society reported that extensive repairs to their building had been made, "under the wise direction of an efficient committee of gentlemen." Twenty-eight years before, they had thanked a similar body of gentlemen for almost identical assistance. *64th Annual Report* (Philadelphia, 1881); *36th Annual Report* (Philadelphia 1853).

5

The Civil War and Municipal Government in Chicago

ROBIN L. EINHORN

The Civil War brought machine politics to Chicago. The party realignment that created the Republican Party repoliticized municipal elections that had been nonpartisan for nearly a decade, while the war itself presented emergency situations that forced (or, alternatively, allowed) city officials to tax and spend on an unprecedentedly large scale. By machine politics, of course, I do not mean a Richard J. Daley style concentration of power; that kind of machine would not exist in Chicago until Daley himself built it in the 1950s. Rather, by machine politics I mean a form of city government with two characteristics: first, electoral conflict, consisting of an ongoing battle between "reformers" and "bosses," often waged on the issue of "corruption," and second, municipal finance structured so that the city treasury underwrote what political scientist Raymond E. Wolfinger has delicately called "incentives to political participation."[1] Before the Civil War, Chicago's government had neither of these characteristics.

It did, however, have a third characteristic that historians usually associate with machine politics: It was decentralized.[2] Antebellum Chica-

This essay adapts parts of my "Before the Machine: Municipal Government in Chicago, 1833–1872," Ph.D. diss., University of Chicago, 1988. I want to thank Amy Bridges, Michael Frisch and Philip Ethington for helping me to rethink the version that I presented at the annual meeting of the Organization of American Historians at Reno, Nevada, in March 1988, and the Berkeley Americanists, who dissected a subsequent draft.

1 Raymond E. Wolfinger, "Why Political Machines Have Not Withered Away and Other Revisionist Thoughts," *Journal of Politics*, 34 (1972), 365–98; M. Craig Brown and Charles N. Halaby, "Machine Politics in America, 1870–1945," *Journal of Interdisciplinary History*, 17 (1987), 587–612.
2 The idea that decentralization is the root of machine politics goes back to nineteenth-century elite demands for centralizing "structural reforms." Its leading modern statements have been Robert K. Merton, *Social Theory and Social Structure*, rev. ed. (Glencoe, Ill.: Free Press, 1957), 72–3, which defines machines as hierarchical parties that "organize, centralize and maintain in good working condition 'the scattered fragments of power' which are . . . dispersed through our political organization," and Samuel P.

go's radical administrative decentralization, which I have termed the "segmented system of city government," was destroyed by the Civil War. A system designed to avoid the political redistribution of individual wealth was replaced by one – machine politics – that used its taxing and spending powers to pursue expensive "public interests." Thus, the origin of machine politics lay not in a democratizing decentralization of power but in the addition of centralizing elements to an already decentralized government and, more important, in the political definition of those public interests for which redistribution was appropriate. Chicagoans took their first crack at defining these interests during the Civil War. The results of their efforts, as this chapter will show, suggests a less populist view of the origin of American urban machine politics than historians commonly have portrayed. In particular, the origin of machine politics in Chicago did not, even indirectly, reflect an empowerment of the city's working class.[3]

The Segmented System

In 1866 the Chicago city council debated a request from the city's Grand Eight Hour League to make eight hours the legal day's work for all laborers and mechanics employed by the city. While some aldermen tried to kill the request in committee, others attempted to have the council deny outright its authority "to say what shall or shall not constitute the duration of a days labor." Still others tried to duck responsibility, passing it to the corporation counsel, an appointed officer. The counsel, relying on the "well settled principle" of a strict construction of the city charter, advised aldermen that while they could recommend an eight-hour day to the Board of Public Works, the chief city agency that employed laborers, their recommendation would not be binding on the board. The council, with its agenda thus limited, passed a ringing resolution: Whereas labor should be "performed under such regulations as are consistent with the

Hays, whose articles "The Politics of Reform in Municipal Government in the Progressive Era," *Pacific Northwest Quarterly*, 55 (1964), 157–69, and "The Changing Political Structure of the City in Industrial America," *Journal of Urban History*, 1 (1974), 6–38, have exerted a huge influence. Hays posits a social decentralization that "gave rise" to a decentralized politics, which was democratic precisely because it was decentralized. Hays's machine politics lacks even the centralization that Merton saw in parties. See Terrence J. McDonald, "The Problem of the Political in Recent American History: Liberal Pluralism and the Rise of Functionalism," *Social History*, 10 (1985), 323–45.

3   I am not arguing that the machine was undemocratic *because* it was centralized. Such theoretical identifications do not apply to nineteenth-century American city governments. I am arguing simply that there is no connection between variables that might be conceived as degrees of democratization and centralization.

dignity of a freeman," the Board of Public Works was requested to employ on an eight-hour basis, "so far as practicable," and the legislature was asked to pass an eight-hour law.[4]

This empty resolution did not satisfy the league, especially when the Board of Public Works ignored it. Three months after its passage, the city clerk had not even bothered to forward the legislative request to Springfield. One alderman charged bad faith, a "political design" whereby the council "intended that the resolutions should never take effect, or be enforced." The measure's leading opponents denied any such intention.

> Your [judiciary] committee believe that the members of this Council are in sympathy with all measures which have a tendency to alleviate the sufferings of the working man and dignify labor and that they will do what lies in their power to foster and strengthen the men who constitute our mechanical and agricultural classes, the real wealth and pride of our country.[5]

Very little, however, seemed to lie within their power. When the legislature, early in 1867, passed the nation's first statewide eight-hour law, Chicago's manufacturers refused to obey it, prompting a two-day general strike, during which the city police acted on behalf of the employers who were flouting the law.[6]

While the eight-hour movement failed in Chicago in 1867 – very few trades managed to win the eight-hour day – it illustrated major changes in the nature of the city's government. Aldermen actually debated the eight-hour law. With whatever degree of cynicism, they declared their sympathy for free labor. With whatever misgivings, they acted on behalf of industrial employers. Neither of these interests had anything to do with real estate, the only constituency that had counted a decade earlier, when the city's government had operated through the "segmented system."

The segmented system was a stage in the development of municipal government in nineteenth-century America. It was an intermediate stage between the centralized and elite-ruled "neocorporate" systems of colonial and early nineteenth-century cities and the neighborhood-based machine politics that most cities had developed by the century's end.[7] The

---

4 Chicago City Council Proceedings Files, Illinois State Archives, box 106, documents 1866 / 968, 1866 / 993, 1866 / 1018, box 107: 1866 / 1336, 1866 / 1315, and box 109; 1866 / 254 (hereafter *CP*, with box and document numbers).
5 *CP*, 112:1866 / 840.
6 Richard Schneirov and John B. Jentz, "The 1867 Strike and the Origins of the Chicago Labor Movement," Working Paper, Origins of Chicago's Industrial Working Class Project, Newberry Library, Chicago.
7 On Neocorporate government, see Jon C. Teaford, *The Municipal Revolution in America: The Origins of Modern Urban Government, 1650–1825* (Chicago: University of

segmented system differed from both neocorporate government and machine politics chiefly in its apolitical resolution of public-finance issues. Radically decentralized, the segmented system realized a nineteenth-century ideal of American city government, an ideal that New York City municipal reformer Simon Sterne described as "not a government" so much as "a co-operative organization of property owners for the administration of private property."[8] Controlled directly by the owners of urban real estate, the segmented system enabled a government that was active in the promotion of urban development to act impartially among the financial beneficiaries of that development.

The segmented system was based on the rigorous use of a system of special assessments levied on property owners to pay for physical improvements. In a special assessment, only those property owners whose property benefited directly from a particular public-works project paid for that project. No single property owner, group of owners, or neighborhood received public works as political favors financed from citywide property taxes. In the segmented system, moreover, only those property owners who were likely to be liable for paying a special assessment for any particular project had the right to participate in the decision to build that project. Public-works decisions, therefore, were depoliticized. When an alderman received a petition asking, for example, that a block of street be paved, he followed a simple decision-making procedure. He first determined which properties would be considered liable to assessment for the project and then ascertained whether the owners of a majority of the affected property favored – that is, were willing to pay for – that project. No other considerations were relevant. In the segmented system, localized groups of property owners exerted direct control over the process of physical improvement. Independent decisions by elected officials, whether directed at planning or at other priorities, were described as "corruption."[9]

Chicago Press, 1975); Hendrik Hartog, *Public Property and Private Power: The Corporation of the City of New York in American Law, 1730–1870* (Chapel Hill: University of North Carolina Press, 1983); Richard C. Wade, *The Urban Frontier: Pioneer Life in Early Pittsburgh, Cincinnati, Lexington, Louisville and St. Louis* (Chicago: University of Chicago Press, 1959). On the segmented system, see my "Before the Machine," esp. Chapters 3–4.

8 Quoted in Martin J. Schiesl, *The Politics of Efficiency: Municipal Administration and Reform in America, 1880–1920* (Berkeley and Los Angeles: University of California Press, 1977), 8.

9 Cf. Michael H. Frisch, *Town into City: Springfield, Massachusetts, and the Meaning of Community, 1840–1880* (Cambridge, Mass.: Harvard University Press, 1972), 43; Carl V. Harris, *Political Power in Birmingham, 1871–1921* (Knoxville: University of Tennessee Press, 1977), 177–85.

The segmented system solved for the city the problem of Jacksonian political economy that had surfaced nationally in the internal-improvements debate: How could the government dredge harbors and rivers without redistributing national wealth toward a favored class, party, or section?[10] How, similarly, could a city build a physical infrastructure of streets, bridges, sidewalks, and sewers without redistributing its tax revenues through political formulas? By segmenting decisions related to infrastructure, ensuring that public works were not public goods, Chicagoans launched a street-building boom in the 1850s that was remarkably free of the debate, delay, logrolling, and corruption that tend to accompany the political redistribution of wealth. Physical infrastructure dominated the activity of the city's aldermen. Special-assessment projects generated between one-third and one-half of all of the paperwork passing through the city council from 1853 to 1856 and slightly more than one-half in 1857 and 1858, after which their incidence fell as a result of the panic of 1857.[11]

The system of public finance that Chicagoans established to promote the construction of physical infrastructure had important consequences for the nature of the city's government in the 1850s, and even for the political culture through which Chicagoans viewed their municipal institutions. The segmented system was, first of all, apolitical. Since much of the city's taxing and spending was removed from politics, aldermen exerted little power: They did not decide "who got what, when, and how" from the city. They actively resisted making decisions that could be construed as public policies, ignoring such issues when they could. In an especially clear case, they disguised a decision to use convict labor to crush stone for macadam as solely a matter of reducing the cost of paving material — and even then, only in relation to a single street-paving assessment. They refused for years to formalize this decision in the Bridewell Ordinance, which would have forced them to vote on the notoriously divisive class issue of prison-labor contracting.[12] Similarly, when temperance advocates demanded an end to liquor licensing in Chicago, the alderman not only refused to act but refused even to take a roll-call vote, which would have revealed their positions on this explosive issue. They

10   For the national problem in these terms, see James K. Polk's veto of the 1846 river and harbor bill, in James D. Richardson, comp., *A Compilation of the Messages and Papers of the Presidents, 1789–1897*, 10 vols. (Washington: Government Printing Office, 1896–9), 4:460–6.
11   Computed from Robert E. Bailey et al., *Chicago City Council Proceedings Files, 1833–1871: An Inventory* (Springfield: Illinois State Archives, 1987). The total includes such routine paperwork as oaths and election returns.
12   Cp, 64:1856 / 2023, 1856 / 2127; 66:1856 / 322; 68:1856 / 662.

waited for Know-Nothings and Maine Law advocates to storm the 1855 city election, when an intentionally prohibitive hike in the license fee provoked a riot.[13]

The segmented system also was nonpartisan. Aldermen who made decisions according to the written instructions that property owners delivered by petition had little need of party ideologies to help them to make spending decisions. Neither did voters need party platforms to ensure the conduct of political aspirants who would have little spending authority. From 1848 to 1855, city elections were strictly nonpartisan: The local parties offered no slates; the newspapers made no endorsements; and voter turnout dropped sharply. Aldermanic candidates ran "on their own hooks" in three-, four-, and five-way contests separate from the mayoral race. Partisan printing offices produced ballots "of all kinds and combinations imaginable." Turnout rates that had ranged from 60 to 90 percent from 1837 to 1847 ranged from 30 to 60 percent over the next decade. On one rare occasion, when municipal politics provoked newspaper debate, the subject of that debate was real estate: whether an aldermanic candidate had a sufficiently personal "interest" in the property values of the ward he wanted to represent.[14] Real estate, rather than residence, structured municipal politics.

The segmented system provided a sort of direct equity among property owners. Since each paid for the projects that benefited his own holdings, the system did not redistribute wealth through the public-works process. When Chicago's commodities shippers, represented from 1848 by the Chicago Board of Trade, tried to get the council to use citywide property-tax revenue to dredge the Chicago River, they stressed public benefits that an improved harbor would confer. Increased commerce would raise property values throughout the city, to the benefit of all local owners. Aldermen, however, refused to apply general taxes to a project from which the shippers would benefit "particularly." They levied special assessments on riverfront lots when they dredged the river in the 1850s.[15] The

13   Cp, 26:1850 / 6641; 39:1852 / 1091; Thomas M. Keefe, "Chicago's Flirtation with Political Nativism, 1854–1856," *Records of the American Catholic Historical Society of Philadelphia*, 82 (1971), 131–8; Richard Wilson Renner, "In a Perfect Ferment: Chicago, the Know-Nothings and the Riot for Lager Beer," *Chicago History*, 5 (1976), 161–70.

14   Quotations from Chicago *Democrat*, March 5, 1850, and February 24, February 27, March 4, 1851. Turnout was estimated crudely: I divided the total vote from election returns, Chicago City Clerk papers, by one-fourth of the annual population estimates in Homer Hoyt, *One Hundred Years of Land Values in Chicago*. (Chicago: University of Chicago Press, 1933), 482.

15   Cp, 29:1851 / 326; *John S. Wright et al. v. Chicago*, 20 Ill. 252 (1858); Thomas B. Dwyer to Stephen A. Douglas, February 10, 1853, box 1, folder 26, Stephen A. Douglas papers, University of Chicago Library (hereafter Douglas papers).

shippers, a seemingly dominant interest group in Chicago's antebellum commercial economy, could not identify their interests as the city's "public interest." Simply put, the segmented system recognized no such thing as a "public interest" in either infrastructure or other policy areas. Citywide commerce, temperance, free labor – any issue that could not be segmented – had no place.

The Pull of National Partisanship

Nonpartisanship was the first segmented form to succumb to the pull of Civil War conflict. In the wake of segmentation, the council debated a full range of political issues in addition to the eight-hour day, some very far afield from the old apolitical mandate: In 1868, for example, they staged a full-dress debate on the national currency question.[16] While aldermen had interested themselves in few national issues in the 1850s, slavery had managed to attract their attention. They passed a resolution in 1850 condemning the Fugitive Slave Act and, in an 1857 response to the Dred Scott decision, entertained (without action) a satirical petition asking them to sell "native born Americans of African de[s]cent" to "the highest Democratic bidders" in order to pay off the city debt.[17] While the ability of slavery to distract aldermen from public works in the 1850s may be significant, it is the rarity of the distraction that is crucial. City elections proceeded without reference to ideology or party, and city officers pledged to keep politics out of council debate. Perhaps aldermen could talk about slavery because the institution had few defenders in a city whose state and national electoral behavior followed a free-soil Democratic pattern. Yet the pull of national party conflict over slavery destroyed municipal-level nonpartisanship.

Municipal nonpartisanship began to break down, paradoxically, over the ethnocultural issues (especially liquor) that historians now commonly blame for the destruction of a second-party system that in Chicago was long gone at the municipal level: The Whigs had been moribund locally for ten years. Yet the ethnocultural fight almost instantly yielded to another: the fight over The Kansas-Nebraska Act and the extension of slavery into the territories. Written by Illinois Senator (and nominal Chicago resident) Stephen Douglas and repudiated by the city's entire press until Douglas started his own Chicago *Times*, Kansas-Nebraska repoliticized city elections. Although the 1855 contest, fought on the issues of temperance and nativism, was the first partisan election in nearly a decade, its

16 Cp, 120:1868 / 1243.
17 Cp, 74:1857 / 71; Bessie Louise Pierce, *A History of Chicago*, 3 vols. (Chicago: University of Chicago Press, 1937–57), 2: 195–6.

parties had organized secretly, and the only official ticket – that of the Know-Nothings – was announced only on the morning of the election. The 1856 race, however, marshaled a full range of partisan resources. The Democrats organized ward clubs, held a city convention, and, together with their opponents (an eclectic anti-Nebraska fusion group), declared the election a referendum on Kansas-Nebraska.[18] This election, however, following a year of nativist rule and an explosion known as the "lager beer riot," is best explained as a story of partisan intrigue. At stake was a continued free-soil presence in Stephen Douglas's Illinois Democratic Party.[19]

After a year of liquor debate and a riot in 1855, all Chicago politicians knew that identifiably pro-liquor candidates would win large majorities if there were, as everyone expected, a high turnout of immigrant (especially German) voters in 1856. The task, therefore, was to organize this large turnout to partisan advantage. Since 1854, when Douglas had first introduced Kansas-Nebraska, Chicago's German leaders had repeatedly expressed outrage at his action. German Democrats had worked closely with early movements in Illinois toward the formation of an antislavery party and – because there were few Whigs in Chicago – they were guaranteed an important place in a Republican Party that, by definition, would have to be composed primarily of free-soil Democrats to win elections. Thus, in 1856, anti-Nebraska fusionists (not yet Republicans) tried to woo German voters with a stress on Kansas-Nebraska and silence on liquor. They nominated prominent Democrat Francis C. Sherman for mayor without naming an aldermanic slate that, in some Yankee wards, inevitably would have included candidates vulnerable on temperance. They declared the election a test of Kansas-Nebraska but, in a disingenuous appeal to nonpartisanship, limited the test to the mayoral race, "leaving all other offices to be filled on the individual merits of the different candidates."[20]

18 Keefe, "Flirtation," 140–1; Bruce McKitterick Cole, "The Chicago Press and the Know-Nothings, 1850–56," M.A. thesis, University of Chicago, 1948, 57–60; James W. Sheahan to Douglas, January 29, 1856, box 2, folder 8, Douglas papers.
19 Note that the realignment in Chicago was different from that in cities with viable Whig parties in the 1850s. The road to a Chicago Republican Party was the Democratic-to-Republican road charted in Eric Foner, *Free Soil, Free Labor, Free Men: The Ideology of the Republican Party before the Civil War* (New York: Oxford University Press, 1973), Chapter 5, rather than the Whig-to-Know-Nothing-to-Republican road of the "ethnocultural" historians, whose strongest urban statement is Michael Fitzgibbon Holt, *Forging a Majority: The Formation of the Republican Party in Pittsburgh, 1848–1860* (New Haven: Yale University Press, 1969). See Don E. Fehrenbacher, *Prelude to Greatness: Lincoln in the 1850s* (Stanford: Stanford University Press, 1962); Rima Lunin Schultz, "The Businessman's Role in Western Settlement: The Entrepreneurial Frontier, Chicago, 1833–1872," Ph.D. diss., Boston University, 1984.
20 Chicago *Journal*, February 12, 1856; James Manning Bergquist, "The Political Atti-

The Douglas forces, of course, refused such a limitation of the Kansas-Nebraska test, knowing that it was in the council races that they would win on liquor (it was aldermen who issued liquor licenses). In their ward meetings and convention, they nominated a full slate, led by Thomas Dyer for mayor, and pledged the party to an endorsement of Kansas-Nebraska. Thus, Douglas hoped to use the city election to purge his party's free-soil wing, especially the man who had led the local party since the 1830s: "Long John" Wentworth − four-term congressman, twenty-year editor of the Locofoco (radical anti-bank) Chicago *Democrat* and an Illinois incarnation of New York Barnburner free-soilism. Liquor was the key to Douglas's strategy. By accepting the anti-Nebraska fusionists' challenge, pledging the local party to support Kansas-Nebraska, Douglas forced Wentworth and other free-soil Democrats into opposition, in a contest that their party was bound to win on the liquor issue. It worked. The immigrant vote materialized as expected, in a citywide turnout up 46 percent from 1855 and a vote on the predominantly immigrant north side up 71 percent. Dyer became mayor, and two pro-Nebraska Germans won council seats from the north side. Now actively campaigning for president, Douglas informed the nation of the unlikely result: Chicago had ratified the Kansas-Nebraska Act.[21]

Douglas had purged his party successfully, but the result was a winning Republican coalition that elected Wentworth mayor with heavy German support in 1857. That election, and the next three, hinged on efforts to define a dominant ideological stance for the new party. Not without reason, Wentworth − the only established vote getter in the new local party − expected his positions on economic issues, the basis of his appeal for two decades, to carry great weight. Yet Wentworth now was in coalition with the political and personal enemies of a partisan lifetime. For his part, he demanded that the Republicans adopt his Locofoco economic program (he described bankers as thieves, demanded a homestead bill, and attacked produce speculators, who then were only beginning to build the future Chicago railroad-warehouse oligopoly). His enemies, meanwhile, known collectively as the *"Tribune* clique" of the local Republican Party, included both former Whigs, who had suffered decades

tudes of the German Immigrant in Illinois, 1848–1860," Ph.D. diss., Northwestern University, 1966, 325–51; Bruce Carlan Levine, "Free Soil, Free Labor, and Freimänner: German Chicago in the Civil War Era," in *German Workers in Industrial Chicago, 1850–1910: A comparative Perspective,* ed. Hartmut Keil and John B. Jentz (DeKalb: Northern Illinois University Press, 1983), 163–82.

21 James W. Sheahan to Douglas, January 29, 1856, box 2, folder 8; Sheahan to Douglas, February 19, 1856, box 2, folder 2, Samuel Ashton to Douglas, March 5, 1856, box 2, folder 13, Douglas papers. The vote was computed from election returns in CP. For Wentworth's role, see Don E. Fehrenbacher, *Chicago Giant: A Biography of "Long John" Wentworth* (Madison, Wis.: American History Research Center, 1957).

of editorial abuse and electoral pounding at his hands, and former pro-bank Democrats, who had resented his dominance of their old party and were anxious to purge him from their new one. As state party leader Abraham Lincoln warned the clique, however, they could not yet afford to lose Wentworth's proven popularity at the polls. Only after the 1860 presidential election did they attempt what Douglas had achieved in 1856, purging a troublesome popular ideologue.[22]

Wentworth's "last hurrah" was the 1860 mayoral contest, held several months before the Republican national convention met in Chicago. Lincoln, as a presidential hopeful, played both sides of the Chicago fight and received daily complaints and requests for intervention. In response to Lincoln's seeming encouragement, Wentworth announced his candidacy: The "abuse of the [*Tribune* clique] . . . & other acts of persecution have compelled me to show my strength once more." This he did, but for the last time.[23] Both national parties targeted this city election with campaign swings by their leading speakers. Among the excuses for purging Wentworth, the *Tribune* group soon could add the new mayor's political use of the police force, including embarrassing brothel raids during his own party's convention. Chicago's city elections now were fully integrated into national politics and directly influenced by national events. The Republicans swept into office in the heat of war mobilization in 1861, identifying their municipal fortunes with those of the Union, but were ousted a year later, when Francis C. Sherman (the anti-Nebraska fusionist of 1856) led the Democrats in a campaign fought entirely on national issues related to the war. Democrats kept control of the city until 1865, when Union battle victories brought Republican victory in the city.

The politicization of municipal elections penetrated to the council floor. Local Republicans, following the national party strategy of nonpartisanship under Republican auspices, identified Democratic dissent with disloyalty and made the city council an arena for the effort. Shortly before the 1863 city election, after intense parliamentary maneuvering, Republican aldermen won the midnight passage of resolutions endorsing a Loyal League of Union Citizens, a party intended to supersede "former party names and platforms for the present." Democrats were outraged. Sherman vetoed the resolutions, refusing "to be entrapped by any specious and patriotic disguise" in a scheme to destroy the Democratic Party.

22 Fehrenbacher, *Chicago Giant,* 149, 161–5; Schultz, "Businessman's Role," 160–83.
23 Wentworth to Lincoln, February 19, 22, 27, 1860, all in folder 48, David Davis papers, Chicago Historical Society. "Long John" actually staged one additional political comeback, when his dramatic answer to the Copperhead leader Clement Valladingham on a speaking platform propelled him into Congress in 1864.

His veto message and a debate held after the Democrats swept the 1863 city election – campaigning against the draft, suspensions of habeas corpus, and the Emancipation Proclamation – rehearsed the loyal history of the Democratic Party, chronicled "high-handed" policies of the Lincoln administration that had provoked opposition, and confronted the obvious transformation of the council that this debate represented. Democrats delivered an exhaustive analysis of national politics on the council floor before concluding that "the municipal council of Chicago is not the proper place for the passage of political resolutions."[24]

By 1863, however, the council was indeed a proper place for party politics. As aldermen debated the Loyal League resolutions, the state legislature, also controlled by Democrats, enacted a new city charter that replaced the segmented (real estate–based) ward map with a residentially based Democratic gerrymander that was appropriate for the partisan body that the council had become (hence the 1863 Democratic sweep).[25] The now politically isolated John Wentworth, characteristically, added a twist of his own. Republican (*Tribune* clique) legislators had taken the police away from him in 1861 by creating an independent Board of Police Commissioners. Still a Republican, Wentworth retaliated as a delegate to the "Copperhead" state constitutional convention of 1862. On his urging, the convention mandated Chicago's first home-rule referendum. Chicagoans voted overwhelmingly "for the City of Chicago electing its own officers," but the issue was moot when Illinois voters rejected the constitution itself.[26] The national realignment that led first to the creation of the Republican Party and then to the outbreak of war destroyed segmented nonpartisanship in Chicago.

Military Recruiting and Downward Redistribution of Wealth

Nonpartisan elections had been the least important aspect of the segmented system. Indeed, the council maintained its much more significant segmentation of municipal finance amid six years of tumultuous electoral conflict and a major economic depression, the panic of 1857. Aldermen debated partisan and national issues on the council floor, but they continued to finance public works by the rigorous special-assessment process

---

24 Cp, 95:1863 / 14, 1863 / 62.
25 The segmented ward map, part of the 1847 charter, drew long and narrow wards that cut randomly across neighborhood boundaries that may also have reflected class, ethnic, or partisan boundaries. On the North and South Sides, they ran the city's entire north–south length, a mere two and three blocks apart. For the map and its interpretation, see my "Before the Machine," 110–15.
26 Cp, 92:2862 / 378–98; Fehrenbacher, *Chicago Giant,* 193–6.

and to deny that Chicagoans shared much that could be called a public interest. The Civil War destroyed this fiction – the ideological basis of the segmented system – and replaced it with another, by creating two urgent and extremely "public" interests, both of which implied the need for governmental redistribution of individual wealth. The first of these interests, Union military recruiting, defined a public interest in downward redistribution, while the second, a pollution problem, vastly magnified by wartime stimulation of the local meat-packing industry, defined a public interest in upward redistribution. In the end, city officials rejected the downward and embraced the upward distribution of individual wealth in defining the city's new public interests. These decisions reflected the power structure that created machine politics in Chicago.

The downwardly redistributive public interest resulted from the structure of Union recruiting policy. Both the 1862 Militia Act and the 1863 Enrollment Act delegated the responsibility for recruiting to local communities, reserving the draft as a threat to encourage them to meet federally determined troop quotas with volunteers. As counties, cities, and towns entered into regional bidding wars for recruits, the political effects of this system became plain: Communities throughout the Union acquired a direct, expensive, and public interest in avoiding the implementation of conscription.[27] That this public interest required a downward redistribution of wealth should be obvious. To recruit soldiers, communities had to pay bounties and family stipends intended to supplement low army wages and provide for the families of absent breadwinners. Communities paid these sums to anyone willing to take them, but the payment often occurred in a public patriotic forum where payments to rich men would have been unseemly. More important, after the New York City draft riot of July 1863, the filling of quotas – and the purchase of substitutes for draftees – had an explicit class basis; the wealthy subsidized recruitment efforts, to appease potential rioters from the working class.[28]

The legislative authorization for municipal war spending in Illinois rested on an 1861 statute passed in a special legislative session called for the purpose. The statute allowed counties and cities to add 5 mills ($.50

27 Eugene C. Murdock, *Patriotism Limited, 1862–1865: The Civil War Draft and the Bounty System* (Kent, Ohio: Kent State University Press, 1967), and *One Million Men: The Civil War Draft in the North* (Madison: State Historical Society of Wisconsin, 1971).

28 Adrian Cook, *The Armies of the Streets: The New York City Draft Riots of 1863* (Lexington: University Press of Kentucky, 1974); Iver Bernstein, *The New York City Draft Riots: Their Significance for American Society and Politics in the Age of the Civil War* (New York: Oxford University Press, 1990); James W. Geary, "Civil War Conscription in the North: A Historiographical Review," *Civil War History*, 32 (1986), 208–28.

Table 5.1. *War taxation*

Year	Tax rate (Cents per dollar)		Estimated yield (Dollars)		War tax as percentage of total levy
	Total	War tax	Total	War tax	
1861	1.52	0.200	550,968	72,705	13.2
1862	1.52	0.125	564,038	46,425	8.2
1863	2.00	0.300	853,346	128,002	15.0
1864	2.00	0.000	974,656	0	0.0
Total	7.04	0.625	2,943,008	247,131	8.0

Note: Tax rates were in cents per dollar of *assessed* valuation, an amount that usually was much lower than the actual value of property.
Source: Chicago *Tribune*, August 28, 1861; Chicago *Times*, September 3, 1862, October 6, 1863, October 4, 1864; Chicago, Department of Finance, *Annual Statement, 1877* (Chicago: Hazlitt & Reed, 1878), 172–3.

cents per $100 assessed valuation) to their annual property-tax levies as a "war tax" that they could spend "for the purpose of aiding in the formation and equipment of volunteer companies mustered into the service of the United States or of this state, for the purpose of enforcing the laws, suppressing insurrection or repelling invasion, and to aid in the support of the families of members of such companies, while engaged in such military service."[29] This was a broad grant of power. It allowed localities to raise taxes for bounties, stipends, local defense forces, or almost any other war-related purpose, and the legislature followed it up in 1863 by retroactively authorizing the debts and taxes over 5 mills incurred by eight counties, including Cook County. Chicago's municipal war tax, however, never approached the authorized 5 mills. The council levied 2 mills in 1861, 1.25 in 1862, 3 in 1863 (increased from an original levy of 2 after the New York riot), and no war tax at all in 1864 – meanwhile taxing at the maximum rate allowed by the city charter for all other general spending categories (see Table 5.1).[30]

Aldermen not only practiced restraint in levying the war tax, but they continually reinterpreted the authorization, attempting to define the nature of Chicago's municipal public interest in the Civil War. When Republicans controlled the council early in 1862, they appropriated $10,000

29 Illinois, *Laws, Extraordinary Session, 1861*, 24.
30 Chicago *Tribune*, August 28, 1861; Chicago *Times*, September 3, 1862, October 6, 1863, October 4, 1864; Edmund J. James, ed., *The Charters of the City of Chicago* (Chicago: University of Chicago Press, 1898–9), 156–7; Illinois, *Private Laws, 1863*, 96–7.

of the war fund to the Chicago Sanitary Commission (CSC) for its aid to sick and wounded soldiers at the front, paying $5,000 immediately and promising another $5,000 if necessary. The CSC demanded the second $5,000 within a month, but by this time the Democrats had won control of the council, and, although they had no clear alternative ideas about how to spend the war fund, they definitely wanted to keep it in the city. With an unappropriated fund of $65,000, however, it required ingenuity to avoid the CSC's demands, particularly since recruiting was still quite easy; county and private efforts met Chicago's August 1862 quota on bounties of only $60 per recruit; two years later recruits cost $300. Aldermen reclaimed the CSC's second $5,000 anyway and appropriated the balance to $30,000 for weapons for local defense and $35,000 for stipends for soldiers' families. The Democrats rejected city bounties, approving the county program, but the Republican council minority could not prevent them from linking this approval to the Democratic Party line: support of a war effort that would "restore the Union as it was."[31]

Six months later, Democrats again rebuffed the CSC, this time with a "strict construction" of the war-tax law. The fund, they argued, was intended for "the thousands of families whose natural protectors are away from them," and any use except for stipends was illegal.[32] Democratic aldermen repeated this argument in 1863, earmarking the entire fund for stipends, but changed their minds a month later when New York City exploded, passing an ordinance committing the city to pay bounties, procure substitutes, and pay commutation fees for draftees. The ordinance limited eligibility to those earning less than $800 a year and granted priority to those earning less than $600.[33] The city paid bounties under this ordinance, but because Chicago actually was able to meet this quota and avoid conscription, there was no need to procure substitutes or pay commutations. Late in 1863, with a new, more serious threat of a draft, alderman again supplemented county efforts with stipends and city bounties, but in February 1864, with the war fund exhausted, they resolved that the council had no power to borrow additional money for bounties. They did nothing, and in October Chicago held its first draft lotteries. Observing that "the utmost good humor prevailed," aldermen reinterpreted the 1861 law yet again, resolving that the city had no power to tax for bounties after all.[34]

31 CP, 92:1862 / 319, 1862 / 399; 93:1862 / 99, 1862 / 101, 1862 / 121, 1862 / 139
    (quotation); Weston A. Goodspeed and Daniel D. Healy, ed., *History of Cook County,
    Illinois*, 2 vols. (Chicago: Goodspeed Historical Association, 1909), 1:448–96.
32 CP, 94:1863 / 265; 93:1862 / 152.
33 CP, 96:1863 / 236.
34 *Times*, October 4, 1864; CP, 95:1863 / 31; 97:1863 / 576, 1864 / 582; 99:1864 /
    167, 101:1865 / 451.

Given the partisan atmosphere in which these decisions were made – and the fact that each alderman administered bounty and stipend payments in his own ward – it is astounding that the city failed to tax at the maximum 5-mill rate. Aldermen voluntarily limited their access to a fund that, in retrospect, looks like an ideal source of patronage. Almost any spending level might have been justified in the name of patriotism. Yet Republicans and Democrats both contrived arguments with which to limit the city's role, differing only on the CSC and the proper rhetoric with which to justify spending caution. To put this caution in perspective, Chicago spent a total of $211,000 for recruiting ($120,000 for bounties and $91,000 for stipends). Springfield, Massachusetts, a city one-eighth Chicago's size, meanwhile, spent $175,000. (The figures are not strictly comparable, however, because of the differing legal role of counties in the two states).[35] It was not that Chicagoans spent less overall; Cook County spent $2.6 million on bounties, much of it in Chicago, while for stipends two commercial bodies, the Board of Trade and the Mercantile Association, together spent three times as much as the city. Chicagoans reserved their spending caution for municipal government. Aldermen simply did not see the war fund as an opportunity for or a source of patronage.

In fact, never before in Chicago's history had aldermen had such funds at their disposal. The council had appropriated money for poor relief only once in the 1850s – and the alderman who were delegated to distribute $1,500 worth of food, wood, and coal during the panic of 1857 were far more interested in disqualifying unworthy paupers than in spending their appropriation.[36] Nor, after the war, would the council spend money for poor relief analogous to bounties and stipends. In the late 1860s they pursued something they considered a relief policy, granting free peddler's licenses to disabled veterans, soldiers' widows, and others unable to support themselves because of age or illness, and they took this program seriously enough to detail a policeman to verify applicants' claims of poverty.[37] Even this, however, proved too great an expansion of the purpose of city government. As the only municipal response to the 1870 Illinois constitution's ban on "special legislation" – which had been

35 A. T. Andreas, *History of Chicago*, 3 vols. (Chicago: Andreas, 1884–6). 2: 168; Frisch, *Town into City*, 65. Frisch presents a pioneering analysis of the local politics – and local public interest – of Civil War recruiting.

36 The committee searched applicants' homes thoroughly, finding liquor and food "in plenty under beds and other out-of-the-way places while the cupboard would show a case of extreme want." Their proudest discovery, however, was "the nice sum of $178.45" in silver, gold, and bank bills "ingeniously quilted in strips of cloth and hidden in a chest of clothes" (CP, 73:1857 / 1913).

37 See the hundreds of free peddler's license applications, with council action marked, in the Chicago City Council Proceedings Files for the years 1859–72. Some of them suggest intervention by applicants' aldermen.

aimed at railroad and other corporate abuse – the council stopped its single downwardly redistributive activity. With much of the city still in ashes after the 1871 fire, the corporation counsel delivered his verdict:

> I am aware that the practice of granting free licenses, to individuals
> ... has prevailed for many years, and that some hardships may
> result from the discontinuance of the practice, but it must be also
> considered that special exemptions from the operation of general
> ordinances, and special privileges granted for individual (not the public)
> benefit, lessens the respect of the people for the city ordinances in
> general, and creates a discontent which renders their enforcement
> both difficult and uncertain.[38]

Poor relief, even in the minimal form of free peddler's licenses, was not in Chicago's public interest. The Civil War bounty and stipend programs had provided a unique opportunity for aldermen to define a public interest in the downward redistribution of wealth, but they grasped the opportunity with extreme caution and abandoned it as soon as the perceived emergency of impending riot had passed.

River Pollution and Upward Redistribution of Wealth

Yet in 1865, the council inaugurated two huge public-works projects as subsidies for the city's meat-packing industry. It is probably pointless to compare the $211,000 of war spending with the $5.8 million that the council spent to abate river pollution caused by the packers, though it is another way to put the numbers in perspective. Nor was anyone confused about the redistributive effects of these projects. The two alternatives, stated time and again throughout the war, were clear: The city could either try to force the packers to stop dumping their wastes into the Chicago River, or it could spend citywide tax and bond revenues to clean the river in a way that allowed the packers to keep dumping, thus subsidizing the packers' waste-disposal costs. The council's rejection of downward redistribution of wealth through poor relief was accompanied by a battle, and ultimate victory, for upward redistribution through a subsidy of this powerful industrial interest. Here was the lavish municipal spending that made machine politics possible.

The packers' power, by 1865, resulted directly from the stimulation of the packing industry by the war. A decade before the war's outbreak, the council had debated meat-packing pollution and come to a conclusion opposite to the one they reached in 1865: To solve the public-health problem posed by the industry, aldermen enacted a regulatory ordinance that caused most of the packers to flee to suburban locations in Bridgeport, then part of the town of South Chicago. Chicagoans do not seem to have viewed this as a loss to the city; the sanitary costs of the packing industry far outweighed the economic benefits it conferred. Only the packers themselves complained of the "great pecuniary sacrifice" they made in relocating. They stressed the jobs Chicago would lose, but in 1850 this argument was unconvincing.[39] Although in Bridgeport they were free to dump, the packers had been forced to pay part of the cost of protecting Chicago's public-health. In 1863, the Democrats, who controlled both the city council and Illinois legislature, annexed Bridgeport to Chicago (because Bridgeport's predominantly Irish voters were dependable Democrats). The packers opposed the annexation, but they could not win on a strictly partisan issue.[40] Thus, the packers and their pollution became a municipal problem once again.

The packing industry that Chicago annexed in 1863, however, was very different from the one it had banished in 1850. Although it grew throughout the 1850s, the Chicago-area packing industry tripled in size between 1861 and 1863, as a direct result of (1) Union army contracting; (2) wartime disruption of river transport from antebellum "porkopolis" Cincinnati and from major contender St. Louis; and (3) Chicago's possession of a direct rail route to Western army encampments via the Illinois Central Railroad. A Chicago area industry that had packed 272,000 hogs in its 1860–1 season packed 970,000 in its peak season of 1862–3.[41] Production then dropped but never below 500,000 hogs a year. While in 1858–9 nine Chicago-area firms had packed over 5,000 hogs and none had packed over 50,000, in 1867–8 four firms packed more than 50,000, and one packed over 100,000 hogs in a year. These were huge businesses. The packing industry produced 12 percent of Chicago's total manufacturing output in 1860 and one-fourth in 1868 – and the total output had risen about five and a half times.[42] This increased production translated into increased pollution, because most packers dumped their blood, offal, and other wastes directly into drains mounted on the banks of the Chicago River.

39   CP, 26:1850 / 6673; George Manierre, ed., *The Revised Charter and Ordinances of the City of Chicago* (Chicago: Daily Democrat, 1851), 216; Louise Carroll Wade, *Chicago's Pride; The Stockyards, Packingtown, and Environs in the Nineteenth Century* (Urbana: University of Illinois Press, 1987), 29–30.
40   *Tribune*, December 14, 1862.
41   Wade, *Chicago's Pride*, 32–3; Margaret Walsh, *The Rise of the Midwestern Meat Packing Industry* (Lexington: University Press of Kentucky, 1982), 55–60.
42   Andreas, *History of Chicago*, 2:382; Elias Colbert, *Chicago: Historical and Statistical Sketch of the Garden City, from the Beginning until Now* (Chicago: P. T. Sherlock, 1868), 79; John S. Wright, *Chicago: Past, Present, Future*. (Chicago: Horton & Leonard, 1868), 210.

What made the pollution problem an emergency was the fact that the Chicago River emptied into Lake Michigan near the point at which the city drew its water supply. Not only was the river's odor "so intense that it permeates our dwellings and mingles its nastiness with the air we breathe" but the waterworks pumped this foul mixture into almost every building in the city.[43] Something had to be done. Aldermen tried to force the packers to pay for cleaning the river; they hired a chemist who "proved" that industrial polluters were to blame, and a series of "aldermanic smelling committees" inspected the packing district. In 1861 the council passed a nuisance ordinance almost identical to that of 1850, but the packers responded by founding the Chicago Pork Packers Association and organizing a boycott of the licenses specified by the ordinance.[44] The city's newspapers, consistent champions of the packers, condemned the ordinance as "oppressive to manufacturers," with one, the *Tribune,* actually praising the packers' dumping. If the council tried to curb it "and thereby narrow[ed] the margin for profit," the paper warned, the packers would leave and take "a large percentage of the population of the city along with them."[45] The unimpressive threat of 1850 now was very real.

The packers and newspapers stressed that Chicago had a public interest in cleaning the river. "No tax-payer," said the Democratic *Times,* "will object to furnish his share of the expense for remedying an evil which is so palpable to his senses that he cannot escape it wherever he goes." The city's health was at stake, the Republican *Tribune* exclaimed, and this "is no time to argue who is to blame." It was the council's duty, argued the Board of Trade – whose 1863 president served simultaneously as vice-president of the Pork Packers Association – to provide "immediate relief from the sickening & putrifying waters of the [Chicago] river."[46] Yet, in the midst of this public emergency, aldermen were assembling chemical data and sending "smelling committees" on packinghouse tours. In fact, it mattered very much "who was to blame" for the river's pollution, because, through segmented financial instruments, blame implied financial responsibility in the form of nuisance assessments – special assessments levied on polluters to recover the cost of abating the pollution they caused. At the same time that the council's

43 *Times,* December 30, 1862; Louis P. Cain, *Sanitation Strategy for a Lakefront Metropolis: The Case of Chicago.* (DeKalb: Northern Illinois University Press, 1978); James C. O'Connell, "Technology and Pollution; Chicago's Water Policy, 1833–1930," Ph.D. diss., University of Chicago, 1980.
44 CP, 93:1862 / 120, 1862 / 144; 94:1862 / 237, 1862 / 245; *Times,* December 31, 1862, February 4, 1863.
45 *Tribune,* January 1, 1863.
46 *Times,* December 30, 1862; *Tribune,* July 26, 1862; CP, 93:1862 / 63; Charles H. Taylor, ed., *History of the Board of Trade of the City of Chicago,* 3 vols. (Chicago: Robert O. Law, 1917), 1:297, 303, 310.

informants blamed the packers, the packers and their supporters blamed the municipal sewer system and thus, by extension, the whole city; the river, the *Times* said, was "a great ditch, into which the filth of a whole city flows. Added to this, the offal of packinghouses . . . is but a small item."[47]

This was untrue, of course – even granting some pollution from the sewers, packinghouse offal was hardly "a small item" – yet this was the position that became policy.[48] The city levied no nuisance assessments. Rather, it inaugurated two huge public-works projects in 1865: first, the construction of a two-mile tunnel under Lake Michigan to move the city's water intake away from the mouth of the river (completed in 1867, at a cost of $2.5 million); and second, deepening of the Illinois and Michigan Canal to reverse the river, so that it flowed away from rather than into the lake (completed in 1871 at a cost of $3.3 million). Chicagoans were proud of these projects, both spectacular engineering feats that won international acclaim. European dignitaries visited the world's longest underwater tunnel, while the river reversal is still considered a symbol of Chicago's "go-ahead" spirit of problem-solving ingenuity.[49] As they built these massive projects – especially the river reversal – Chicagoans got their first taste of sustained political conflict over cost overruns, missed contract deadlines, and cronyism in the award of unprecedentedly lucrative contracts. Aldermen and members of the Board of Public Works all played politics with these contracts, some in a manner that clearly can be labeled fraudulent.[50]

More important, however, was the recognition of these public works as municipal public goods. The "share" of each "tax-payer" rested not on his responsibility for polluting the river but on his general property-tax assessment. This was a public interest, at bottom, less in the physical health of Chicago's residents than in the economic health of the city. Chicagoans paid millions to keep the meat-packers in town. Even before the river project was complete, ironically, the largest packers began to leave anyway, though they moved only as far as the new Union Stock

47   *Times*, December 30, 1862.
48   Ellis S. Chesbrough, the engineer who designed the original sewer system in 1855, now was the chief engineer of Chicago's Board of Public Works. He conceded that some sewers did empty into the river – and most historians of this problem fault either him or his cost-conscious employers, the former Board of Sewerage Commissioners, for the poor design – but in no sense was packinghouse waste "a small item" in the pollution of the Chicago River.
49   O'Connell, "Technology and Pollution," 42–7; Cain, *Sanitation Strategy*, 46–57; *The Tunnels and Water System of Chicago* (Chicago: J. M. Wing, 1874).
50   Most of the relevant documents are quoted in full in the official history of the Chicago Sanitary district, G. P. Brown, *Drainage Channel and Waterway* (Chicago: R. R. Donnelly, 1894).

Yards in the adjacent town of Lake. Founded in 1865 by a syndicate of railroad companies to simplify livestock transshipment, the yards soon became a convenient location for meat-packers as well.[51] Perhaps more ironic still, as the city granted these subsidies to the packers, it also tried to force local butchers to use a central slaughterhouse that one of the leading packers operated under a monopoly grant from the council. The Illinois supreme court blocked this, in an 1867 case resembling the New Orleans Slaughterhouse Cases, but the effort illustrates that there was more than one way to finance a public interest in public health.[52] The butchers could not wreck Chicago's economy; the packers could.

The caution with which aldermen met the public interest in military recruiting accompanied a simultaneous embrace of lavish public spending for the public interest in public health. Free peddler's licenses became "special privileges," while industrial subsidies became "public interests." In the segmented system, the Chicago city council had done neither; it provided almost no poor relief, but it also refused to redistribute tax revenue to the powerful. Apolitical, nonpartisan, and largely nonredistributive, it had provided no resources with which politicians could use city money to attract political support. By 1867, Chicago aldermen had begun to look like machine politicians or, in contemporary usage, like "bummers." By 1869, "reform" movements had begun the attempt to "oust the rascals" that would power a machine-reform dynamic still dramatically visible in Chicago.[53] Yet the origin of machine politics, born in Chicago during and over issues raised by the Civil War, was not the populist triumph that elitist reformers condemned and modern historians often praise. It was a triumph for upward rather than downward redistribution. The rascals who emerged from Chicago's Civil War served elite rather than plebeian masters.

Conclusion

The role of the Civil War in expanding the federal government was rendered profoundly ambiguous by the official dismantling of the wartime

---

51 Wade, *Chicago's Pride*, 47–60.
52 CP, 105:1865 / 710, 1865 / 798, 1866 / 836, 1866 / 860; 116:1867 / 422–3; *Chicago v. Rumpff*, case file 15325, Supreme Court of Illinois papers, Illinois State Archives, Springfield.
53 Richard Schneirov, "Class Conflict, Municipal Politics, and Governmental Reform in Gilded Age Chicago, 1871–1875," in *German Workers in Industrial Chicago, 183–205*; Sidney I. Roberts, "Ousting the Bummers, 1874–1876," typescript, Chicago Historical Society; M. L. Ahern, *The Great Revolution; A History of the Rise and Progress of the People's Party in the City of Chicago and the County of Cook* (Chicago: Lakeside Publishing and Printing, 1874); *Addresses and Reports of the Citizens Association of Chicago, 1874–1876* (Chicago: Hazlitt & Reed, 1876).

bureaucracy in the rapid retreat from Reconstruction. What historians used to call "the great barbecue" — that egregious spree of fiscal corruption at the federal level in the 1870s — resulted from the active pursuit of "public interests," chiefly in railroads, by inactive or nonexistent federal bureaucracies.[54] Yet the lack of bureaucracy that historians tend to stress may be less significant than the very pursuit of these public interests. It is hardly surprising that railroad barons wanted a weak government to oversee their use of public subsidies. More decisive were the subsidies themselves — as any Jacksonian would have predicted. In condemning internal improvements, the Jacksonians had argued that a "public interest" was inevitably an elitist interest. Assuming that the wealthy had an automatic advantage in any pluralistic contest to define public interests, they concluded that inaction — no public interest — was the only defense against upward redistribution. In this they differed from Madison, whose tenth Federalist paper had assumed that it was a majority bent on downward redistribution that automatically held the high cards in a pluralist game.

The Jacksonian solution was segmentation. Although much antebellum redistribution occurred through the legal process — in eminent domain and riparian cases, for example — Congress, state legislatures, and city councils strove to avoid public decisions that redistributed wealth.[55] At the urban level, the destruction of segmentation made machine politics possible. In New York, the progressive weakening of special-assessment rules in the 1850s finally enabled Tweed to build a postwar machine that converted public works into patronage, or, in Wolfinger's language (quoted at the beginning of this essay), "incentives to participation."[56] Tweed was far in advance of his Chicago contemporaries, who had not yet experienced any patronage-based city politics, but the new pattern in Chicago also was marked by the decline of segmented finance. Not only did Chicagoans subsidize their packers, but in 1865 the city's three street-railway companies won a comparably valuable grant: They

54 Wallace D. Farnham, " 'The Weakened Spring of Government': A Study in Nineteenth-century American History," *American Historical Review*, 68 (1963), 662–80; Harold M. Hyman, *A More Perfect Union: The Impact of the Civil War and Reconstruction on the Constitution* (New York: Knopf, 1973); Morton Keller, *Affairs of State: Public Life in Late Nineteenth-century America* (Cambridge, Mass.: Harvard University Press, 1977); Stephen Skowronek, *Building a New American State: The Expansion of National Administrative Capacities, 1877–1920* (Cambridge: Cambridge University Press, 1982).

55 Harry N. Scheiber, "Property Law, Expropriation and Resource Allocation by the Government," *Journal of Economic History*, 33 (1973), 232–51; Morton J. Horwitz, *The Transformation of American Law, 1780–1860* (Cambridge, Mass: Harvard University Press, 1977).

56 See esp. Edward Dana Durand, *The Finances of New York City*. (New York: Macmillan, 1898).

bribed state legislators into creating a set of long-term contract rights that the U.S. Supreme Court then interpreted as exemption from special assessment. After 1869, the three property owners most directly "interested" in the condition of Chicago's streets were exempt from the costs of their repair, costs henceforth borne by the "public."[57]

The Civil War did not "cause" machine politics in Chicago, though it sped the developments that did. The war's stimulation of downward redistribution of wealth through the city's recruiting policy, moreover, makes the war in Chicago a perfect test case of a governmental change whose class basis has more often been assumed than explained. The Civil War provided Chicagoans with powerful arguments for both downward and upward redistribution of wealth, since it created emergency situations that justified public interests with both populist and elitist consequences. The war, however, did not dictate the political choice that Chicagoans made among these alternatives; the choices reflected power, pure and simple. Late nineteenth-century Chicago would be the city not only of political scoundrels "Bathhouse John" Coughlin and "Hinky-dink" Kenna but also of robber barons Marshall Field, George Pullman, and the street-railway magnate Charles Tyson Yerkes. Perhaps it was Johnny Powers, Jane Addams's alderman, who described their relationship best: "You can't get elected to the council unless Mr. Yerkes says so."[58]

57 Illinois, *Private Laws, 1865*, 597–8; *Chicago v. Sheldon*, 9 Wall. 50 (1869). See Willard E. Hotchkiss, "Chicago Traction; A Study in Political Evolution," *Annals of the American Academy of Political and Social Science*, 28 (1906), 385–404; John A. Fairlie, "The Street Railway Question in Chicago," *Quarterly Journal of Economics*, 21 (1907), 371–404; my "Before the Machine," 296–311.
58 Ray Ginger, *Altgeld's America: The Lincoln Ideal versus Changing Realities* (Chicago: Quadrangle Books, 1958), 112.

6

Who Joined the Grand Army? Three Case Studies in the Construction of Union Veteranhood, 1866–1900

STUART McCONNELL

For the 2 million veterans of the Union army, the final muster-out in 1865 was a mixed blessing. Obviously these men were happy to be ending what were often long and dangerous periods of service; a few were glad to have lived through short terms of service to collect large bounties. Many more were relieved just to have escaped serious injury. But in "civilian" society, as they now called it, the veterans also would face job competition from men with several years' head start and, in many cases, they had to deal with the additional handicap of wounds or chronic illness. Even more important, they would need to shed their alien wartime world in which the values of "civilian" society had been stood on end. Violence had been justified, social distinctions leveled, individual preference submerged in discipline and order, death a daily occurrence. To noncombatants, the veterans pouring off the trains in the summer of 1865 were familiar, yet remained strangers. "They are, 'tis true, stern looking men, and pass along our streets, with a gloomy melancholy," remarked one country editor in Eau Claire, Wisconsin, "claiming no immunity, asking no applause, and seemingly unconscious of the great service they have rendered."[1]

In these respects, the former Union soldiers differed little from veterans of other American wars. Postwar unemployment has always been a problem (though one could argue that the industrializing economy of the mid-nineteenth century made it worse); by 1865, providing pensions for ill and wounded veterans was already a matter of long-standing public policy. And in the realm of culture, the ambivalence of the soldier's return

[1] *Eau Claire Free Press*, July 13, 1865.

remains one of the oldest themes not only of American literature but of Western culture: Veterans from Odysseus and Cincinnatus to Rambo and the nameless narrator of *Johnny Got His Gun* emerge from the dark passage of war as Others, bearing important messages for "civilian" society even as they remain more or less distanced from it.

To say only this, however, is to miss what is historically specific about the experience of Union Civil War veterans. If every war produces a crisis of veteran reconciliation, each does so in a very different way that often speaks volumes about the postwar period. The tale of Cincinnatus is one of republican virtue upheld; *Johnny*'s message is stridently antiwar; Rambo's is an attempt to avoid grappling with defeat. In each case, veteranhood is something processed through a specific social context, negotiated between the former soldier and the society to which he returns. For Union veterans, this meant striking a bargain between the nation's bloodiest and most divisive conflict and a Gilded Age North, dominated by acquisitiveness, labor unrest, racial reaction, and, in the middle classes at least, sentimental nostalgia.

The Union army version of veteranhood took many forms in the years before 1900 — memoir, parade, war story, monument, pension bill, Memorial Day oration — but at its center was the Grand Army of the Republic (GAR). With hundreds of thousands of members, with a post in every Northern town of any size, with an organized voting strength that made politicians (especially Republicans) tremble, this largest of Union veterans' organizations was also the single most powerful lobby of its age. Beginning in the late 1870s, the GAR was able to pressure Congress and many state legislatures into funding increasingly generous veteran benefits, culminating in the most expensive piece of social-welfare legislation up to that time, the federal Dependent Pension Act of 1890. As early as 1893, military pensions absorbed one federal dollar out of every three. By 1907, the act had cost the government more than $1 billion; annual pension expenditures would continue to rise until 1913.[2]

But to its members, the GAR was more than this. It was a standard Victorian fraternal order, complete with ceremonial ranks and a secret, semireligious ritual. It was an arena for business clientage and deal cutting. It was a provider of local charity in an age without significant public relief. And it was the purveyor of a preservationist, socially conservative version of the war that had ramifications beyond the ranks of veterans.

2 William H. Glasson, *Federal Military Pensions in the United States* (New York, 1918), 243, 246–50, 270, 273; Mary R. Dearing, *Veterans in Politics: The Story of the G.A.R.* (Baton Rouge, 1952). George J. Lankevich, "The Grand Army of the Republic in New York State, 1865–1898," Ph.D. diss., Columbia University, 1967, 196, estimates the eventual cost of the act at $8 billion.

Among members of the GAR, Union veteranhood embraced all of these behaviors, not just the pension lobbying for which the order is usually remembered.

Moreover, even at its height the Grand Army included only a minority of Union veterans: Nationwide, the GAR of 1890 had enrolled only 41 percent (427,981 out of 1,034,073) of the former Union soldiers found by the special census of that year.[3] Nominally this shortfall was the result of an exclusive admissions procedure, which, like that of other fraternal orders of the time, was designed to weed out the "unworthy." To join, a would-be member had to be proposed by someone already in the order, investigated for good character by three other members, and balloted on by the whole post, with a single negative ballot cause for rejection. Yet behind the idea of "worthiness" were assumptions about Grand Army veteranhood that caused a few applicants to be rejected and discouraged many more from applying. Thus, in asking who joined the GAR, we must also ask who was rejected and who was never proposed.

This essay examines the memberships of GAR posts between 1866 and 1900 in three cities: the metropolis of Philadelphia; the industrial town of Brockton, Massachusetts; and the farming and lumber entrepôt of Chippewa Falls, Wisconsin. At points, the analysis is supplemented by data on the occupational structure of other posts in Pennsylvania and Wisconsin.[4] Given the large number of Union veterans who stayed out of the GAR, it is also worthwhile to consider nonmembers in these cities. In Philadelphia, the complexity of the relationship of Post 2 (1,367 ag-

---

3 *Journal of the National Encampment of the Grand Army of the Republic*, 1890 encampment, 79; U.S. Department of Interior, Census Office, *Compendium of the Eleventh Census, 1890*, Pt. 3, 573, 583–6 (Tables 101–2).

4 Information on members of the three posts included in the case study was compiled primarily from internal post records, as indicated in Notes 8 (Philadelphia), 30 (Brockton) and 41 (Chippewa Falls) in the present chapter. This information was entered on a standard computer form, with each category of data (e.g., rank, occupation, duration of membership) indexed by a unique key, and each variation within a category (commissioned officer, noncommissioned officer, private, etc.) by a unique subkey. Lists of members sharing a particular characteristic (all former commissioned officers, for example) then were pulled out of the data base by using the subkeys. Correlations described in this essay (among, for instance, all former commissioned officers who ever held office in a post) were made by pulling lists from the data base by using more than one subkey. Comparisons with the occupational structures of other Pennsylvania posts are from the thirty-nine Descriptive Books of other posts, in MG 60, Pennsylvania Historical and Museum Commission Collections, Harrisburg, Pennnsylvania; similar comparisons for other Wisconsin posts are made from the forty Descriptive Books in the Wisconsin Local Post Records Collection, GAR Memorial Hall Museum, Madison. Full tabulations for these posts are available in Stuart McConnell, "A Social History of the Grand Army of the Republic," Ph.D. diss., Johns Hopkins University, 1987, 570–4, 577–87. Because information on some early members (especially in Brockton) is incomplete, all figures in text and tables are expressed as percentages of those members for whom a given characteristic is known.

gregate members, 1866–1900) to the city's other thirty-five posts rules out meaningful comparison of its membership with the pool of potential members who did not join. However, such comparisons will be made for Brockton's Fletcher Webster Post 13 (540 aggregate members) and Chippewa Falls's James Comerford Post 68 (312 members), using post records and the special 1890 federal census of surviving Union veterans.[5] Finally, although a full picture of GAR veteranhood would require more explication of day-to-day life in the order than is possible here, some of its main features will be suggested by way of conclusion.

For the first decade or so after the GAR's founding in 1866, it seemed unlikely that there would ever be much interest in remembering the war, much less in a Union veterans' organization. Fewer war novels were published in the 1870s than in any other decade, magazines rarely ran articles about it, and the few wartime newspapers catering specifically to veterans (such as the *Soldier's Friend* of New York and the *Great Republic* of Washington, D.C.) quickly disappeared. The regular army was allowed to shrink to a fraction of its former size. Former soldiers' organizations on both sides of the Mason-Dixon line languished or fell apart; the GAR, after a promising beginning, saw membership plunge to an all-time low of 26,899 in 1876. It was, as Gerald Linderman puts it, a decade of "hibernation."[6]

In the late 1870s, however, former soldier and "civilian" alike began to rediscover the war. In literature, Ambrose Bierce, Henry James, and other writers spun stories with war themes. Noted generals were commissioned to write memoirs for analyses of particular battles, with Grant's *Personal Memoirs* quickly becoming a staple of parlor tables across the North (more than three hundred thousand sets were ordered before the first printing). In public architecture, the period saw monuments ranging in size from modest markers in small-town cemeteries to mammoth me-

5 The difficulty in comparing members to nonmembers in Philadelphia is that, unlike the posts in Brockton and Chippewa Falls, Post 2 shared its "recruiting area" with a number of other city posts. Thus it is not possible to separate the potential members of Post 2 from, for example, the potential members of Posts 5, 363, or 400, all of which recruited citywide. Overall, the posts examined in this essay did only slightly better than the national average: Brockton's Post 13 had enrolled 48 percent of those eligible in 1890; Chippewa Falls's Post 68, 42 percent; and the 36 posts of Philadelphia collectively had mustered 43 percent of the city's Union veterans.

6 On the reduction of the army, see Samuel P. Huntington, *The Soldier and the State* (Cambridge, Mass., 1957), 226–30. On the decline of the 1870s, see McConnell, "A Social History of the GAR," 49–53, 164–9; Dearing, *Veterans in Politics*, 185–218; Gaines M. Foster, *Ghosts of the Confederacy: Defeat, the Lost Cause and the Emergence of the New South, 1865 to 1913* (New York, 1987), 47–62; and Gerald Linderman, *Embattled Courage: The Experience of Combat in the American Civil War* (New York, 1987), 266–75.

morials such as the arch in Brooklyn's Grand Army Plaza and the 265-foot Soldiers' and Sailors' Monument in Indianapolis. And among veterans of both armies, remembrance bloomed: The United Confederate Veterans organized in 1889, while a revitalized GAR gained strength rapidly through the 1880s, peaking just after the passage of the Dependent Pension Act in 1890.[7]

Among the first posts formed in 1866 was Philadelphia's Post 2, which survived the membership drought of the 1870s to become one of the most prestigious posts in the order in the 1880s and 1890s.[8] While not quite as exclusive as George Washington Post 103 of New York City (which admitted only members of the Army and Navy Club of New York and held its monthly meetings at Delmonico's) or Columbia Post 706 of Chicago (which limited its membership to 100 and required members to dress in expensive uniforms), Post 2 drew its membership largely from the commercial and professional upper-middle class of Philadelphia. Among its charter members in 1866 were Robert Beath, then a clerk, soon to be an insurance executive; physician Samuel B. Wylie Mitchell; lawyer Joshua T. Owen; insurance agent Robert Bodine; banker Louis Wagner; and merchant Frank Crawford. While much of its membership was drawn from men in middling clerical and sales occupations, the post always contained an equally large complement of merchants and professional men. On parade in the cities they visited during annual GAR "encampments," the Post 2 members struck out-of-town editors as "apparently men of affairs" or "the wealthiest and most influential citizens of Philadelphia."[9]

As in other large cities, the Philadelphia posts tended to segregate by neighborhood, occupation, branch of previous service, or ethnicity. Post 6 was based in Germantown, Post 55 in Frankford; Post 363 admitted only former cavalrymen, while Post 400 admitted only former sailors;

7 Linderman, *Embattled Courage*, 275–97; John Tebbel, *A History of Book Publishing in America*, 3 vols. (New York, 1972–81), 3: 524–6; William S. McFeeley, *Grant* (New York, 1981); Edmund Wilson, *Patriotic Gore: Studies in the Literature of the American Civil War* (New York, 1962); Daniel Aaron, *The Unwritten War: American Writers and the Civil War* (New York, 1973); Foster, *Ghosts of the Confederacy*, 104–14.
8 For Post 2 the main sources of information are the post Descriptive Books, 1866–1900, supplemented by the Post 2 Business Directory, 1886, and Roster, 1896; information on offices held and committee assignments is taken from the Post 2 Minutes, 1866–7 and 1870–1900. All of these documents are housed in the Sons of Union Veterans Philadelphia Camp Collection, GAR Memorial Hall, Philadelphia.
9 Lankevich, "The GAR in New York State," 114; Worcester, Mass., *Veteran*, September 1891, p. 10; Post 2 Descriptive Book and Roster, Sons of Union Veterans Collection; Springfield *Republican*, June 5, 1878, and Providence *Morning Star*, June 28, 1877, in Post 2 Scrapbooks, Sons of Union Veterans Collection.

Table 6.1. *Birthplace of members, GAR Posts 2, 13, and 68, 1867–1900*

Birthplace	Post 2 Philadelphia (N = 1,367)	Post 13 Brockton (N = 540)	Post 68 Chippewa Falls (N = 312)
Local	585 (43%)	36 (9%)	1 (0.4%)
Elsewhere in state	293 (22)	228 (57)	18 (8)
U.S., out of state	265 (19)	86 (22)	134 (59)
Outside U.S.	219 (16)	48 (12)	76 (33)
Unknown	5	142	89

Note: All percentages are expressed as a percentage of members whose birthplace is known. For Post 2, a "local" birthplace is defined as one within the city of Philadelphia. For Post. 13, it is defined as a birthplace in greater Brockton (Brockton, Brockton Heights, North Bridgewater, Montello, Campello). For Post 68, it is defined as a birthplace within the city of Chippewa Falls.
Source: For sources of the tabulations of birthplaces, occupations, terms of service, ranks, and suspensions, see footnotes 8 (Post 2, Philadelphia), 30 (Post 13, Brockton), and 41 (Post 68, Chippewa Falls), this chapter.

Posts 27, 80, and 103 were all black, while others were predominantly German.[10] Although Post 2 had a citywide geographic base, its membership was 84 percent American-born and entirely white; of the 16 percent born outside the United States, most were from Germany or Ireland. The absence of black members is not surprising; throughout the GAR, and indeed in most Gilded Age fraternal orders, segregated local chapters were the rule.[11] The proportion of foreign-born members, while slightly higher than in Brockton, was well below the figure for Chippewa Falls and probably somewhat low for the order as a whole (see Table 6.1). Grant Post 5, for instance, was founded in Philadelphia at the same time as Post 2 but counted 28 percent of its membership as foreign-born, again mostly German and Irish immigrants.[12]

Of the 1,143 Post 2 members born in the United States, more than one-half (51 percent) had been born in the city of Philadelphia, while

10 Cavalry Post 363 Descriptive Book, box 7, MG 60, Pennsylvania Historical and Museum Commission Collections. Black posts in Philadelphia were listed in the *Washington National Tribune*, February 10, 1887, p. 6. New York also had a number of posts limited to members of one ethnic group or one profession: See Lankevich, "The GAR in New York State," 113–14.
11 The issue of black veterans in the GAR was a heated one from 1887 well into the 1890s. See Wallace E. Davies, "The Problem of Race Segregation in the Grand Army of the Republic," *Journal of Southern History*, 13 (August 1947), 354–72; McConnell, "Social History of the GAR," 539–46.
12 Post 5 Descriptive Book, box 5, MG 60, Pennsylvania Historical and Museum Commission Collections.

another 26 percent had been born in Pennsylvania. Almost all post members (94 percent) lived within the city limits; of those living outside the city, more than two-thirds lived in suburbs in Pennsylvania and New Jersey. The few who did not, however, are revealing. These were men such as clay-pipe salesman Frank Lynch of Waterbury, Connecticut, pension attorney Frank Butts of Washington, D.C., and Easton lawyers Frank and Howard J. Reeder. With businesses or professional practices that were more than local, they benefited from the extensive and informal business contacts that a large urban post offered and could use membership in Post 2 as a prestigious calling card at posts in other cities when on business there.

Such men might switch posts several times, as they found it expedient or as they moved from one locality to another. Both Reeders, for instance, transferred into Post 2 from the post at Easton, where they lived. Lawyer Moses Veale transferred out when he left Philadelphia in 1880 and 1890, only to transfer back in 1882 and 1894. Insurance executive Robert Beath, having helped found Post 2, moved on to become commander of Post 5 and then to Post 23 in Pottsville. The total number of transfers, however, was small – in an average year, three joined while five withdrew – and high-status individuals were not significantly more likely to transfer than clerks or manual workers. On the whole, Post 2 was made up of men who had been born in or near Philadelphia, still lived in the city, and were unlikely to leave it.

Occupationally, the post contained a large number of proprietors and professional men (see Table 6.2). High-status, white-collar individuals made up 19 percent of the membership of Post 2 – more than double the proportion in the posts in Brockton and Chippewa Falls and well above that of most other posts in Pennsylvania.[13] This group included manufacturers, judges, stockbrokers, clergymen, physicians, hotelkeepers, and lawyers. Like clubs and voluntary associations in other cities, leading GAR posts undoubtedly facilitated the integration of urban elites to some degree.[14]

The GAR's broad eligibility criteria, however, made it less exclusive and peremptory than other fraternal orders. Even though would-be

13 Among the thirty-nine posts whose Descriptive Books are preserved in the Pennsylvania Historical and Museum Commission collections, only one – Post 76 of Reading, with 19 percent – matched Post 2's contingent of high-status members.

14 On clubs and elite integration in Pennsylvania, see Edward J. Davies, "Class and Power in the Anthracite Region: The Control of Political Leadership in Wilkes-Barre, Pa., 1845–1885," *Journal of Urban History*, 9 (May 1983), 291–334; E. Digby Baltzell, *Philadelphia Gentlemen* (New York, 1958); and John Ingham, *The Iron Barons* (Westport, Ct., 1978). On middle-class fraternalism, see Lynn Dumenil, *Freemasonry and American Culture, 1880–1930* (Princeton, 1984), and John S. Gilkeson, Jr., *Middle-class Providence, 1820–1940* (Princeton, 1986), 136–74.

Table 6.2. *Occupation of members, GAR Posts 2, 13, 68,*
1867–1900

Occupation	Post 2 Philadelphia (N = 1,367)	Post 13 Brockton (N = 540)	Post 68 Chippewa Falls (N = 312)
High-status white collar	250 (19%)	38 (9%)	26 (9%)
Proprietors	223 (17)	45 (11)	25 (9)
Low-status white collar, semiprofessional	428 (32)	35 (8)	24 (9)
Skilled workers	344 (26)	95 (23)	37 (13)
Semiskilled and service workers	52 (4)	174 (42)	14 (5)
Unskilled and menial laborers	6 (0.4)	10 (2)	65 (23)
Active-duty military	25 (2)	0 (0)	1 (0.4)
Farmers	11 (0.8)	18 (4)	89 (32)
Unknown	28	125	7

Note: All percentages expressed as a percentage of members whose occupation is known. Occupations are classified following the scheme of Stephen Thernstrom in *The Other Bostonians* (Cambridge, Mass., 1973), 240–72, with the addition of separate categories for proprietors, farmers, active-duty military men, and those who were retired or listed no occupation. The latter three categories are self-explanatory. The category of "proprietor" consisted of men listing themselves under one of the following occupations: apothecary, bookseller, brewer, butcher, caterer, clothier, confectioner, dealer (all varieties), druggist, eating-house keeper, express-service owner, florist, grocer, laundry owner, merchant (all varieties), peddler, pharmacist, plumbers' supplier, printer, restaurant owner or restaurateur, saloonkeeper, stationer, storekeeper, tobacconist, undertaker, victualler, water purveyor. The great majority of proprietors listed themselves as "dealers" or "merchants."
Source: For sources of the tabulations of birthplaces, occupations, terms of service, ranks, and suspensions, see footnotes 8 (Post 2, Philadelphia), 30 (Post 13, Brockton), and 41 (Post 68, Chippewa Falls), this chapter.

members required sponsors and were balloted for secretly, a member who wanted to blackball an applicant first had to get around the fact that the latter was an honorably discharged veteran. In Post 2, less than 3 percent of all applicants were rejected between 1866 and 1900; evidence from other posts in the state suggest that the rejection rate was almost never above 5 percent. And, at least in their occupations, the rejectees differed little from the members. The 37 men blackballed by Post 2 included four clerks, two painters, and a park guard but also four physicians, three manufacturers, and nine merchants.[15]

15 Post 2 rejectees are identified from references in Post 2 Minutes, 1866–1900, Sons of Union Veterans Collection; rejection rates for other Pennsylvania posts can be estimated from the number of rejectees whose names were published in General Orders,

In addition, well-off members in Philadelphia do not seem to have been significantly more conscientious about keeping up GAR membership or filling offices in the post than those of lower social status. High-status individuals in Post 2 were only slightly less likely to be suspended or dropped for nonpayment of dues (72 percent were never suspended, compared with 65 percent of the membership as a whole) and actually were slightly less likely to become long-term members (60 percent were members for more than 10 years, as opposed to 63 percent of the total membership, though the average duration of membership was 13.4 years among elites and 12.2 in the post as a whole).[16] Even in the holding of post offices and major committee positions, high-status individuals were not significantly more active than the rest of the membership. Between 1866 and 1900, members of this class, representing 19 percent of the post membership, made up 24 percent of those holding elective offices and 20 percent of those in major committee positions.[17] Of the 30 men who commanded Post 2 in this period, only five (17 percent) held high-status jobs in civilian life. The only office dominated by elite members was that of trustee – the three members who oversaw the financial affairs of the post. Six of the 11 trustees of Post 2 before 1900 can be classed as high-status, and two others may have been.[18] Thus, although profession-

1875–1895, ibid. Accurate estimates of rejection in other posts, however, also would require close analysis of their meeting minutes, since reporting of rejectees to the state headquarters in Philadelphia was incomplete, and since between 1869 and 1875 GAR rules did not require the publication of rejectees' names.

16 For several reasons, the tabulation of members who persisted for ten years after joining is a more useful measure of longevity in the GAR than is average duration of membership. In the first place, membership tended to be an either/or decision: Many remained in the order for long periods (some for thirty or forty years), while others dropped out after three or four years; the middle ground of the statistical mean in this case is largely fictional. Second, the intermittent nature of GAR membership – some members joined, transferred, and were dropped as many as five times – makes "duration" of membership difficult to define. Third, statistics on average duration of membership exaggerate the importance of joining early: A member in 1900 who had joined in 1870 and stayed thirty years was not necessarily more attached to the order or less prone to suspension than a member who had joined in 1885 and stayed fifteen years, even though the former's term, by 1900, had been twice as long. Fourth, losses of ten-year members were almost always to death, rather than to voluntary causes such as dues arrears; a measure of longevity in the GAR beyond the ten-year point is mostly a measure of longevity on the planet. Finally, rule changes in the 1890s – including the remission of indigent members' dues – kept many on the rolls who in earlier years would have been routinely dropped, and in fact spurred some who had been dropped to rejoin.

17 For all posts, offices included in this tabulation are post commander, senior vice-commander, junior vice-commander, quartermaster, surgeon, chaplain, officer of the day, officer of the guard, adjutant, sergeant major, quartermaster sergeant, and department encampment delegate. For Post 2, major committees are the standing committees for charity, entertainment, hall upkeep, soldiers' orphans, and Post 2 Guard, and the committees in charge of excursions to the annual national encampments.

18 One of the two trustees in question is Abram G. Rapp, who was listed as a bookkeeper

als and high-status white-collar individuals made up a larger than usual part of the membership, they did not stay members longer or hold office more frequently than their numbers in the post warranted.

Merchants and proprietors fared only slightly better. For the most part these were small businessmen – druggists, grocers, clothiers, butchers, lumber dealers, tobacconists – though some of those listed as "merchants" in the post records undoubtedly were quite well off.[19] As a group, proprietors and merchants made up 17 percent of the membership; they accounted for 20 percent of the elected officers, 19 percent of the committee members, and 30 percent (nine of 30) of the post commanders. Two of the five trustees who were not manufacturers or lawyers were merchants. Yet these achievements – with the exception of the high number of post commanders who were merchants – do not greatly exceed what one would expect form the proportion of merchants in the membership. What is remarkable about both the high-status white-collar and merchant / proprietor segments of Post 2 is not that they held a great many offices but that together they made up such a large part (more than one-third) of the post in the first place.

Despite a $10 initiation ("muster") fee, higher than that of any other post in the state, Post 2 also included large numbers of low-status white-collar and semiprofessional workers. With 32 percent of the membership, this was the single largest group in Post 2, consisting mostly of salesmen, clerks, and bookkeepers.[20] These middling workers were

at the time of his application in 1874. In addition to his unusually long fourteen-year trusteeship, however, he held fifteen other committee posts; the only other trustees who approached that feat were both merchants. He was also once post chaplain, a position usually reserved for a veteran of high status. Finally, he was elected delegate to the department encampment six times between 1884 and 1899; since this duty involved an extended trip out of town, it was not generally conferred on wage workers who could not take the time away from work. The other is Oliver C. Bosbyshell, who, though listed as a clerk in the Descriptive Book, is referred to in the post business directory of 1886 as working in the city controller's office and seems to have been employed even later as an official of the U.S. Mint. This would be consistent with his GAR career: He was elected department commander, attended several national encampments, and proposed several men for membership, all activities more characteristic of businessmen than of clerks.

19 The lack of property data in post records makes it impossible to distinguish between petty and large proprietors, a problem Dumenil acknowledges in using the same category (*Freemasonry and American Culture*, 227–8). Some wealthy individuals probably are included among the proprietors, just as some minor contractors probably are among the major ones included in the high-status category and some small business owners among the skilled workers.

20 The number of members of this class probably was somewhat smaller than indicated by the membership data, because clerk and bookkeeper positions were typical first jobs for young men who later became managers, proprietors, or executives. Especially between 1866 and 1880, when more than one-half of those listed as low-status, white-collar employees in Post 2 joined the order, the "clerks" could have been men just

somewhat less likely to transfer than those in the upper occupational strata, and they tended to be suspended more often (39 percent were suspended at least once, compared with 35.5 percent of the membership as a whole and 28 percent of the high-status white-collar group). They held offices and major committee posts about as often as their numbers would lead one to expect (29 percent of all officeholders) and provided 10 of the 30 post commanders (33 percent). They served on committees more frequently (36 percent of all major committee members), though they tended to serve once or twice, rather than year after year as some of the more prominent members did. Only three were ever elected trustees, one of whom – Oliver C. Bosbyshell – almost certainly was a clerk who later became a businessman. Overall, however, the low-status white-collar group was well represented in the power structure of the post.

The high price of membership acted as a greater barrier to skilled laborers. Skilled blue-collar workers made up 26 percent of the post membership, concentrated in the building trades: carpenters, plumbers, painters, plasterers, paperhangers, roofers, masons, stonecutters. While more numerous than in the posts at Brockton and Chippewa Falls (for reasons to be discussed presently), they were heavily underrepresented compared with other urban posts in Pennsylvania and even in Philadelphia. Post 23 at Pottsville, for example, counted 40 percent of its members in this category; Post 76 at Reading, 35 percent. In Philadelphia, the number of skilled workers ranged from 38 percent of Post 21 to 55 percent of Post 94. Relative to total membership, no post in Philadelphia had as few skilled workers as Post 2.[21] Skilled workers were only slightly less likely than white-collar members to hold office (23 percent of all officeholders) or committee posts (22 percent of major posts). Rarely, however, were they elected trustee or post commander. Only one trustee between 1866 and 1900 was a skilled worker, and he served for only one year soon after the post was formed; five post commanders were skilled workers.

For merchants, salesmen, clerks, and skilled workers, the chief attraction of GAR membership may well have been its fraternal aspect. A merchant who sponsored his clerks for membership, or a salesman who sponsored his customers, developed a clientage relationship that might

entering the workplace (most were in their thirties) who later attained more prestigious white-collar jobs. On the other hand, Post 2 continued to draw large numbers of low-status white-collar workers even in the 1880s and 1890s – 100 in the 1880s and 83 in the 1890s, compared with 245 between 1866 and 1880. By then, most applicants were over 40 – too old to be considered clerks just starting out. Although not conclusive, these later data seem to indicate that many of the applicants of the early years who were listed as "clerks" and "bookkeepers" actually remained clerks and bookkeepers.

21 Posts 21, 22, 23, and 76 Descriptive Books, box 5, MG 60, Pennsylvania Historical and Museum Commission Collection; Post 94 Descriptive Books, boxes 5–6, ibid.

be useful to him in his business relations. For clerks, clientage was at least a gesture in the direction of job security; some large urban posts, including Post 2, also encouraged employer members to give preference to unemployed members in hiring.[22] Post 2 published a business directory and maintained a rack for its members' cards. Its businessmen also were leading recruiters, proposing more than 40 percent of all applicants for membership between 1877 and 1887 (the only years for which such records were kept); by far the leading proposers of new members were salesman Frank Lynch (21 clients) and hardware merchant Matthew Hall (20 clients). Similarly, post membership offered building tradesmen the opportunity to make informal, personal contacts in a business heavily reliant on them: Suppliers and laborers had to be lined up, different projects needed coordination, and above all the market had to be watched for opportunities, since when one job was finished, another needed to be located.[23]

Partly for the same reasons, almost no semiskilled or unskilled laborers belonged to Post 2; together they accounted for only 4.4 percent of post membership. To day laborers, the business associations of post membership were relatively unimportant and the muster fee was a serious expense. A laborer could get the social and entertainment benefits of GAR membership at a much lower price by joining one of the other posts in the city. The scarcity of semiskilled and unskilled workers in Post 2 was quite unusual: Other Pennsylvania posts generally had between 20 and 25 percent of their members in these categories, while in Brockton 42 percent of Post 13's members were semiskilled workers and in Chippewa Falls 23 percent of Post 68's members were unskilled laborers.[24]

On average, the veterans who joined Post 2 had served longer in the Union army, attained higher rank, and been wounded more frequently than members of the Brockton and Chippewa Falls posts (see Table 6.3). More than 80 percent had served terms of more than a year, and of these three out of every four had served for three years or more. By compari-

22 Post 2 Minutes, September 1, September 15, and November 3, 1870, June 8, 1871, December 13, 1877, and October 2, 1884, Sons of Union Veterans Collection; Post 2 Employment Book, 1894, *ibid.*; Lankevich, "The GAR in New York State," 116; Post 13 Minutes, January 23 and July 24, 1889, in private hands; Post 68 Minutes, January 21, 1891, Wisconsin Local Post Records Collection.

23 The list of proposers in Post 2 was compiled from Post 2 Minutes, 1877, Sons of Union Veterans Collection, and Post 2 Orders, 1878–87, ibid. The leading sponsor overall was teacher John H. R. Storey, but 15 of the 26 men he proposed were dropped members seeking reinstatement. Of the other 11 members who sponsored more than ten applicants, six were merchants, one a real-estate broker, one a salesman, one a machinist, and two clerks.

24 Of the seven other Philadelphia posts whose Descriptive Books are preserved in boxes 5–7, MG 60, Pennsylvania Historical and Museum Commission Collections, all have higher proportions of semiskilled and unskilled workers, ranging from 12 percent of Post 363 to 28 percent of Post 18.

Table 6.3. *Military term of service and rank of members, GAR Posts 2, 13, and 68, 1867–1900*

	Post 2 Philadelphia (N = 1,367)	Post 13 Brockton (N = 540)	Post 68 Chippewa Falls (N = 312)
Term of service			
More than 1 year	1,088 (81%)	298 (64%)	197 (71%)
90 days to 1 year	201 (15)	149 (32)	75 (27)
30–90 days	47 (3)	14 (3)	3 (1)
Less than 30 days	11 (0.8)	2 (0.4)	1 (0.4)
Unknown	20	77	42
Rank			
Commissioned officer	193 (14%)	9 (2%)	12 (4%)
Noncommissioned officer	465 (34)	77 (16)	55 (17)
Surgeon or chaplain	28 (2)	1 (0.2)	4 (1)
Private or seaman	541 (40)	352 (75)	238 (76)
Support role (adjt., cook, etc.)	124 (9)	31 (7)	6 (2)
Unknown	16	70	3

Note: All percentages are expressed as a percentage of members whose rank or term of service is known. For all posts, commissioned officers include generals, colonels, majors, and captains. Noncommissioned officers in the army are comprised of lieutenants, sergeants, and corporals, and, in the navy, of engineers, ensigns, and mates. The category "privates" includes naval seamen and landsmen. Separate classifications are made for surgeons and chaplains and for those who served in noncombat roles (cooks, quartermasters, teamsters, adjutants, musicians).
Source: For sources of the tabulations of birthplaces, occupations, terms of service, rank, and suspensions, see footnotes 8 (Post 2, Philadelphia), 30 (Post 13, Brockton), and 41 (Post 68, Chippewa Falls), this chapter.

son, only 64 percent of the Brockton members whose terms of service are known and 71 percent of those in Chippewa Falls had served more than a year. This was because for a number of years Post 2 had an unstated practice of rejecting men who had served short terms. Of the 17 rejectees from the post whose terms of service are know, 13 had served less than one year, and 10 had served for less than six months. The post included only 11 men who had served terms of less than ninety days, all of whom joined late in the century and none of whom was ever prominent in post affairs.[25]

By the same token, the post had an exceptionally high number of for-

25 The best instance of this was in the summer of 1885, when each of three "100 days men" who applied together was rejected three times – Post 2 Minutes, June 25, September 3, and September 24, 1885, Sons of Union Veterans Collection.

mer commissioned officers (14 percent of the membership, compared with 2 percent in Brockton and 4 percent in Chippewa Falls) and noncommissioned officers (34 percent of Post 2, 16 percent in Brockton, 17 percent in Chippewa Falls) and relatively few privates (40 percent of Post 2, 75 percent in Brockton, 76 percent in Chippewa Falls). In part, the glut of officers occurred because military rank and social rank went together. Many regiments of volunteers for the war had been raised by local politicians or businessmen, who expected in return to be named as officers; still others were formed from already existing volunteer militia companies, in which social rank always had played a large part.[26] Any post that recruited a large number of high-status individuals was bound to recruit a large number of officers. Thus in Post 2, of those in high-status white-collar occupations, 20 percent once had been commissioned officers, compared with 14 percent of the low-status white-collar employees and 9 percent of the skilled workers. Most of the former noncommissioned officers (58 percent) were skilled workers and low-status white-collar employees, whereas former privates were distributed among all occupational categories – somewhat more heavily in the lower-status occupations. The correlation between high military rank and civilian status also meant that those chosen as post officers or trustees, many of whom were of high social rank, were former military officers as well. Twenty-five of the 30 post commanders had held a rank higher than private; 13 had held a rank higher than captain.

Post 2 also had more than its share of soldiers who had been wounded in action. Twenty-six percent of the membership reported having been wounded or discharged for disability; about two-thirds of these listed wounds. This was more than double the rate of the Brockton and Chippewa Falls posts and almost double the average for the Union army. Wounds played an important part in the hagiography of the GAR, and veterans who had been seriously wounded were frequently selected for state and national office, several – Lucius Fairchild and James Tanner, for instance – making national political careers from their support among veterans.[27] The large number of wounded members in Post 2, like its

26 Marcus Cunliffe, *Soldiers and Civilians: The Martial Spirit in America, 1775–1865* (Boston, 1968), 215–54; Michael Frisch, *Town into City: Springfield, Massachusetts, and the Meaning of Community, 1840–1880* (Cambridge, Mass., 1972), 56–7; on the continuation of the militia tradition into the era of the Spanish-American War, see Gerald F. Linderman, *The Mirror of War: American Society and the Spanish-American War* (Ann Arbor, 1974), 60–90.

27 The distinction between disability and wounds is this: A veteran might list actual wounds on his application, but he also might indicate only that he had been discharged on a surgeon's certificate of disability. "Disability" often meant wounds, but it also might mean illness or injury suffered in camp. The distinction is made in the case of Post 2 because its adjutants seem to have been more diligent in making it themselves.

blackballing of short-service men, is evidence of the members' determination to admit those who had been involved in the fighting in a substantial way, not simply anyone mustered for any term of service.

The picture of Post 2 that emerges from the membership data is that of an organization of clerks and small shopkeepers, plus some manual workers — but only those well above the status of day laborer — presided over by an aristocracy of business and professional men. Concentrated in white-collar occupations, relatively homogeneous in ethnicity and race, most of these veterans also were local men who had fought in Pennsylvania regiments, many as officers. When they chose leaders, they tended to pick people who had held important ranks in the army and, to a lesser degree, prominent civilians. But never did they choose men, no matter what their social status, who had served short military terms; indeed, some effort was made to keep such men from joining.

Socially, it was a post that featured many of the accoutrements of middle-class urban life: it had a library, held formal dances, had an orchestra, and made elaborate excursions to the annual GAR "national encampments." Its members were punctilious about the performance of the semi-sacred GAR initiation ritual; at the national encampments of 1875, 1876, and 1878 they were singled out to demonstrate the ritual's oaths, symbolic theater, and homilies on "fraternity," "charity," and "loyalty" to delegates from other parts of the country. Indeed, Post 2 seems to have been more prickly than most GAR posts about rules and forms generally. Members were known to spend whole meetings debating such fine points of GAR "law" as how to reconstitute themselves formally after they arrived at Springfield, the national encampment.[28]

Beyond a core of active members, however, Post 2 membership was an occasional thing. Almost nine in 10 members never held any office, and eight in 10 never sat on a major committee. More than one-third were so inactive as to be suspended from membership for non-payment of dues; of these, only a minority bothered to rejoin. Those who were not suspended rarely made it to post meetings regularly unless they held office, and even then there was no guarantee that a merchant who was frequently out of town would be on hand regularly enough to discharge his

In Post 13, only six of the 61 veterans discharged for disability listed wounds — certainly not an accurate reflection of the number of wounded in the post. In Post 68, 11 of the 33 men discharged for disability listed wounds. The best estimate for the Union Army is 277,401 wounded out of approximately 2 million who served (14 percent), though all figures, as noted above, depend on what one considers "wounded." See E. B. Long, comp., *The Civil War Day by Day* (Garden City, N.Y., 1971), 710–11.

28 *Proceedings of the National Encampment*, 1875 encampment, 372; *ibid.*, 1877 encampment, 483–4; ibid., 1878 encampment, 569; Robert B. Beath, *History of the Grand Army of the Republic* (New York, 1888), 165, 192; Post 2 Minutes, May 30, 1878, Sons of Union Veterans Collection.

duties; average attendance at a given meeting generally hovered around 20 percent of the membership.[29] For the ordinary member of Post 2, Grand Army membership meant a costly badge, a meeting every month or two, and Memorial Day services.

Fletcher Webster Post 13 of Brockton, Massachusetts, was a different sort of post from Post 2, located in a different sort of city.[30] Known before the war as North Bridgewater, the city 23 miles south of Boston had changed its name to Brockton in 1881, as the last stage of its passage from a small hamlet on a small river to a heavily industrialized city of 13,608 in 1880. Brockton in the late nineteenth century existed for the making of shoes. It was the site of a dozen major shoe factories and twice as many smaller concerns, as well as every conceivable business supplementary to the shoe trade: It turned out shoe tools, shoe boxes, shoe counters, shoe trees, shoe polish, and a blizzard of other products. It was also, by the early twentieth century, one of the most highly unionized and contentious cities in Massachusetts.[31]

The Brockton shoe industry drew workers from all over the state. Thus, while the majority (64 percent) of Post 13 members had served in Massachusetts volunteer units, only 9 percent of the members of Post 13 with a known birthplace had been born in North Bridgewater. Most had come from other parts of the state (57 percent) or from other states (22 percent). Only 12 percent of Post 13's members had been born outside the United States, a lower figure even than that for Post 2. Of the foreign-born members, half came from Ireland, the rest mostly from Canada,

29 Of the years for which attendance figures are available, the high year was 1879, when 27 percent of the membership attended an average meeting; the low year was 1898, when attendance averaged only 14 percent of membership. See McConnell, "Social History of the Grand Army of the Republic," 574 (Table B.1).

30 For Fletcher Webster Post 13 of Brockton, the primary documents are the Post 13 Quarterly Reports, 1873–1900, Massachusetts Post Record Collection, GAR Room, Massachusetts State House, Boston. These were checked against three other sources: a Post 13 roster published in the Boston *Grand Army Record*, April 1886, p. 6; the manuscript special census of surviving Union veterans and widows, 1890, Plymouth County enumeration districts 694–706, M 123, National Archives, Washington, D.C.; and – for officers, trustees, and charter members only – Brockton city directories for the years 1869–70, 1876–7, 1882, 1889, 1894–5, and 1900, Local History Room, Brockton Public Library. Information on officers and committees is from the Post 13 Minutes, which are in private hands; they were made available to me by Mr. Ken Oakley of Randolph, Massachusetts, and Mr. Dean Sargent of Rockland, Massachusetts. For Post 13, major committees are the same as for Post 2 except that members of the standing committee on applications have been added in lieu of the encampment committees.

31 Bradford Kingman, *History of Brockton, 1656–1894* (Syracuse, N.Y., 1895); Brockton Board of Trade *Manual* (Providence, 1899); "Brockton, a City of Enterprise," *New England Magazine* (September 1911), 67–80; Roy Rosenzweig, *Eight Hours for What We will: Workers and Leisure in an Industrial City, 1870–1920* (Cambridge, Mass., 1983), 22–23 (Tables 1–2).

Sweden, and England. Unlike Post 2, Post 13 did have one black member, Lenuel Ashport, though he acted as drum major for the post's marching unit.

It is doubtful that the lack of black members in Post 13 was the result of segregation such as that practiced by the Philadelphia posts, since there were few black veterans in Brockton: The federal census of 1890 found only three.[32] Nor, despite the small number of foreign-born veterans in Post 13, is there conclusive evidence that the post excluded them; in the two southern and eastern wards of the city, where the concentration of foreign-born (mostly Irish) veterans was highest, the post claimed 45 percent of the eligible men as members, compared with an overall rate of 48 percent. It is more likely that in Brockton, as in Philadelphia, the large proportion of the native-born reflects their predominance in the antebellum population (and, as some preliminary research on the subject suggests, especially in the Union army).[33] From an army mostly native-born and white, in other words, came a veterans' organization that was mostly native-born and white.

Although few of Post 13's members had been born in Brockton, all but 19 of the members with a known residence lived there. In the first ward, the commercial district, about one-half of the eligible veterans (52 percent) were members; in the four working-class wards south and east of it, 44 percent; in the two middle-class residential wards north of it, 56 percent. Despite the recruiting emphasis on the "better" sections of the city, however, manufacturers and businessmen were a distinct minority in the post.[34] High-status white-collar individuals made up only 9 percent of the post, proprietors and merchants only 11 percent. Of 38 members in the high-status white-collar group, 17 were manufacturers (at least 12 of them in the shoe industry), and nine were medical practition-

32 *Compendium of the Eleventh Census, 1890,* 583–586 (Tables 101–2).
33 Marcus Cunliffe argues that immigrants were as numerous as the native born in volunteer units (*Soldiers and Civilians,* 114–20). On the other hand, the work of W. J. Rorabaugh indicates that Irish immigrants were underrepresented in the Union army: See Rorabaugh, "Who Fought for the North in the Civil War? Concord, Massachusetts, Enlistments," *Journal of American History,* 73 (December 1986), 697. Thomas Kemp's study of Claremont and Newport, New Hampshire (this volume, Chapter 2), suggests a third possibility: that immigrants were underrepresented among local volunteers but overrepresented among men recruited by towns through the use of bounties.
34 Manuscript special census of surviving Union veterans and widows, 1890 (enumeration district 694 is Ward 1, the commercial district; districts 695–702 are Wards 2–5; districts 703–6 are Wards 6 and 7). It is something of a problem in this period to distinguish between "shoemakers" and "shoe manufacturers." The post, however, seems to have been aware of the distinction in recording occupations. A check through the city directories reveals that all of those listed in the post records as "shoe manufacturers" also are listed in the directories as heads of manufacturing establishments. None of those listed as "shoemakers" is so listed.

ers (five physicians, four dentists). Most of the merchants, like those in Post 2, were small businessmen. Overall, the high-status and merchant groups were small compared with those of Post 2.

Similarly underrepresented were low-status white-collar workers, who constituted only 8 percent of the membership. Most of these again were clerks, bookkeepers, and salesmen, though they also included a few factory foremen. Fewer white-collar workers might be expected among young men in an industrial city such as Brockton, where entry-level jobs tended to be factory rather than clerical positions. But even as the potential applicant population aged, the occupational pattern of the membership remained relatively constant. This was nowhere as true as among the low-status white-collar recruits, who numbered 10 percent of those mustered before 1870, 8 percent in the 1880s, and 7 percent in the 1890s. Even in the years when most veterans were young, then, Post 13 had few clerks or bookkeepers – certainly nowhere near the number in Post 2.

What the Brockton post did have in abundance were skilled blue-collar workers, especially semiskilled shoe-factory workers.[35] Of the 10 charter members of the post whose occupations are known, four were shoe workers and two were skilled workers, one of them a maker of shoe tools. The predominance of blue-collar workers continued in later years, when skilled workers made up 23 percent of the membership and semiskilled and service workers made up 42 percent. Of the latter, shoe workers were the overwhelming majority – only 16 of the 174 men in this class worked at anything else. Between them, skilled and semiskilled blue-collar workers constituted almost two-thirds of the members whose occupations are identifiable.

Such a membership was not disposed to support a high muster fee or dues, and these were low compared with those of Post 2: $3.50 and $3.00, respectively, in 1881.[36] But even this amount worked a hardship on the shoemakers in the post, resulting in a high number of suspensions (see Table 6.4). Although the number of individuals suspended or dropped at least once was only slightly higher than for Post 2 (39 percent, compared with 36 percent), the incidence of suspension was considerably more frequent. This was because the same members tended to fall into arrears over and over again, periodically lapsing and settling up. An extreme case of this practice was shoe stitcher George Sturtevant, who was suspended six times between 1877 and 1893 before finally being dropped

35 Distinguishing shoe-factory operatives, who are classed as semiskilled workers, from skilled shoemakers also is a difficulty. Although not a perfect solution, those listed as "shoemakers" in post records were classed as semiskilled unless the city directories listed them as proprietors of small shoe shops or as shoe repairmen.
36 Post 13 Minutes, March 4, 1880, and May 19, 1881 (in private hands).

Table 6.4. *Suspensions of members, GAR Posts 2, 13, and 68,*
1867–1900

	Post 2 Philadelphia (N = 1,367)	Post 13 Brockton (N = 540)	Post 68 Chippewa Falls (N = 312)
Never suspended or dropped	881 (65%)	330 (61%)	154 (48%)
Dropped or suspended once; reinstated	99 (7)	77 (14)	24 (8)
Dropped or suspended more than once; reinstated	3 (0.2)	28 (5)	0 (0)
Dropped or suspended once; not reinstated	352 (26)	79 (15)	132 (42)
Dropped or suspended more than once; not reinstated	32 (2)	28 (5)	8 (3)

Note: Because the accounts of dues delinquents often were allowed to slide for a quarter or two before serious action was taken, "suspension" here is defined as suspension *for one year or more*—a length of time sufficient to indicate long-term lack of interest in post affairs. In all categories, those who died while members—some after ten years in a post, some after two weeks—have been excluded from the tabulations.
Source: For sources of the tabulations of birthplaces, occupations, terms of service, ranks, and suspensions, see footnotes 8 (Post 2, Philadelphia), 30 (Post 13, Brockton), and 41 (Post 38, Chippewa Falls), this chapter.

from membership in 1894. Another shoemaker, George Handy, was suspended and reinstated four times in four years before being dropped in 1880. The number suspended more than once from Post 13 amounted to 10 percent; from Post 2, less than 1 percent. Yet even those who had chronic problems keeping up their dues made more of an effort to pay up in Post 13 than in Post 2. In Post 13, about one-half of the first-time suspendees settled their arrearages; in Post 2, less than one-third did so.

The Brockton shoe workers, like the Philadelphia clerks, tended to choose high-status individuals for offices and major committees but not without filling a significant number of positions themselves. High-status white-collar members, 9 percent of the membership, filled 16 percent of the offices and 12 percent of the committee slots between 1876 and 1893. Semiskilled and service workers, conversely, represented 42 percent of the membership while filling 34 percent of the offices and 41 percent of the committee jobs. Other occupational groups held office roughly in proportion to their numbers, with the exception of the low-status white-collar group, which had slightly more of the offices (14 percent) than its portion of the membership (8 percent) warranted, largely because a clerk usually was appointed "adjutant" (the GAR term for "secretary").

While filling somewhat less than their share of offices, then, the shoe workers still accounted for more than one-third of the total. More important, the positions in which they served were not minor. Seven of the 18 commanders of Post 13 were from the semiskilled group, as were two of the seven trustees. In fact, the post was commanded by a shoe worker more often than by a merchant or a professional man. While many of the high-status officers were clergymen who served as post chaplain or physicians who served as post surgeon, thee working-class members tended to fill the secondary leadership positions that eventually led to the commander's chair: senior vice-commander and junior vice-commander. The pattern of leadership thus was the reverse of that in Post 2: Instead of a merchant commander with a staff of clerks, Post 13 usually found itself with a blue-collar commander and a staff of business and professional men.

The service records of Post 13's members fall into the same working-class pattern (see Table 6.5). Whereas Post 2 contained a large complement of former officers, 75 percent of those in Post 13 whose military ranks are known had served as privates. Almost all of the rest had been noncommissioned officers; only nine of the 540 men in the post between 1873 and 1900 had held a rank as high as captain. This was not because the post had an aversion to high-ranking officers; it mustered four of the five Brockton veterans above the rank of captain found by the 1890 census and a majority of the available noncommissioned officers. Rather, like the preponderance of shoe workers among members, the large number of privates reflected the working-class population of the city; the relevant comparison is not with Post 2 but with nonmember veterans living in Brockton. And in this comparison, Post 13 members actually were of marginally higher rank: Only 75 percent of them had been privates, compared with 78 percent of nonmembers found in Brockton by the 1890 census.

Similarly, while Post 13 members were less likely than Post 2 members to have served long military terms, they were slightly more likely to have done so than were non-GAR members in Brockton. In the aggregate membership of Post 13 between 1873 and 1900, 64 percent had served terms of more than one year, compared with 61 percent of nonmembers found by the 1890 census; only 3 percent had served terms of three months or less, compared with 8 percent of nonmembers. Moreover, slightly fewer members (21 percent) than nonmembers (26 percent) had joined the Union forces in the last year of the war – often the mark of a draftee or substitute. Such small differences between members and nonmembers, how-

Table 6.5. *Military term of service and rank of*
Brockton veterans

	Members (N = 311)	Nonmembers (N = 334)
Term of service		
More than 1 year	199 (65%)	180 (61%)
90 days to 1 year	98 (32)	94 (32)
30–90 days	9 (3)	21 (7)
Less than 30 days	1 (0.3)	2 (0.7)
Unknown	4	37
Rank		
Commissioned officer	4 (1)	1 (0.3%)
Noncommissioned officer	57 (18)	50 (16)
Surgeon or chaplain	0 (0)	0 (0)
Private or seaman	228 (74)	249 (78)
Support role (adjt., cook, etc.)	20 (6)	20 (6)
Unknown	2	14

Note: Among members, all percentages are expressed as a percentage of members whose term of service or rank is known. Among nonmembers, all percentages are expressed as a percentage of nonmembers whose term of service or rank is known.

Source: Manuscript special census of surviving Union veterans and widows, 1890, Plymouth County, enumeration districts 694–706, M 123, roll 11, National Archives, Washington, D.C.

ever, hardly indicate the sort of mass blackballing of short-service men practiced in Philadelphia, an impression supported by the record of rejections: Of 14 Post 13 rejectees with known service records, 12 had served more than one year.[37]

With so few officers from whom to choose, it would have been difficult to elect very many post officers, and the members did not even try. Only one former commissioned officer served in an office or on a committee (and then only briefly), whereas only 12 of the 73 post officers and 15 of the 64 committee members whose former rank is known had been noncommissioned officers in the army. Nor were the Brockton veterans hesitant about electing men whose military service had been in noncombat positions: Three post commanders had served in such capacities, two as musicians and one as a private in the quartermaster's department. By and

37 Information on rejectees is tabulated from Post 13 Quarterly Reports, 1873–1900, Massachusetts Post Record Collection, and from the 1890 manuscript census of surviving veterans and widows.

large, Post 13 was an organization of former privates, commanded by former privates.

Despite its working-class makeup, however, the post had little to say on the public questions of labor, unions, or strikes. During a period that saw the formation of a powerful Boot and Shoe Workers' Union local in Brockton (leading, eventually, to the election of a socialist mayor in 1899), the sixteen surviving years of Post 13 minutes (1877–93) make only two passing references to labor.[38] It may be that the Brockton members subscribed to the harmony-of-interest rhetoric espoused by national GAR leaders, who regularly called for "justice and equal rights" or "the dignity of labor," at the same time demanding "law and order" and the suppression of "anarchy." In any case, their egalitarianism was limited to leveling actions within the order – removing the risers from under the chairs of their officers, agitating for the so-called service pension (a measure even more generous than the act of 1890 but viewed with suspicion by conservative members of the order), and struggling to reduce the power of appointed national GAR officers, whom they sarcastically dubbed "the House of Lords."[39]

Overall, then, the Brockton post was an organization of veterans of humble status. The typical member was a worker in a shoe factory, to whom the quarterly dues were a significant expense but to whom the post's frequent social events (such as "campfires," at which the veterans ate army meals, smoked clay pipes, and sang war songs) probably were a major form of entertainment and the promise of post charity or an impressive fraternal funeral significant benefits.[40] He was likely to have been born in a small town in eastern Massachusetts and to have served a term – sometimes a short one – as a private in a Massachusetts regiment. After the war he migrated to Brockton, found a day-wage job in the shoe industry, and joined the local GAR post. While he found it difficult to pay the required dues and might be suspended occasionally in months when he was short of money, he usually managed to pay up before being dropped.

Like his counterpart in Philadelphia, the Brockton GAR member held office infrequently (more than 80 percent of the members never held an office or sat on a major committee) and attended meetings irregularly. None of the men in his post were from very far away, and in terms of

38 Henry F. Bedford, *Socialism and the Workers in Massachusetts, 1886–1912* (Amherst, Mass., 1966), 107–36.
39 Post 13 Minutes, December 30, 1885, and August 18, 1886; on the GAR's attitude toward labor and on the House of Lords case, see McConnell, "Social History of the GAR," 520–4, 181–7.
40 On the importance of fraternal funerals, see Dumenil, *Freemasonry and American Culture*, 40–1.

ethnicity, occupation, and previous military rank, they were even less diverse than the members in Philadelphia. Most of his comrades were native whites and former privates like himself, and most of them also were manual laborers, some of whom worked alongside him in the factory. For the Brockton veteran, membership in Post 13 meant entertainment, the promise of an impressive funeral, and, if he was an officer, a chance to exercise authority denied him in everyday life.

James Comerford Post 68, located in the northwestern Wisconsin city of Chippewa Falls, was not quite agricultural enough to qualify as what editors of GAR periodicals called a "country post," but it was hardly as urban as the Philadelphia and Brockton organizations.[41] It drew its members not only from the city of 8,670 residents (in 1890) but from farm and sawmill hamlets such as LaFayette, Anson, Eagle Point, Bloomer, and Cadott. It was only after the war that the exploitation of the area's dense forests turned the river town of Chippewa Falls into a major lumber entrepôt: Thus only two members of Post 68 had been born in Chippewa County and only 19 had even been born in Wisconsin. Most of the rest had migrated to the county after the war from New York, Pennsylvania, or New England.[42]

Formed in 1883, much later than the Philadelphia and Brockton posts, by 1890 Comerford Post 68 had enrolled 43 percent of the eligible veterans in the county and 68 percent of those in Chippewa Falls.[43] Not much is known about the 50 charter members of the post, a number of whom dropped from view shortly after its formation; some may have

41 For James Comerford Post 68 of Chippewa Falls, the main sources are Post 68 Quarterly Reports, 1883–97; the Minutes of the post, 1883–1900; applications for membership in the post, 1883–1900; and a Post 68 roster of 1889, all in series 1, boxes 10–13, Wisconsin Local Post Records Collection. Residential and service data for members on whom no other information was available were compiled from the manuscript special census of surviving Union veterans and widows, 1890, Chippewa County enumeration districts 51–79. Occupational and residential information on some members was quarried from local gazetteers and histories: Bella French, *Chippewa Falls, Wisconsin* (La Crosse, 1874); George Forrester, ed., *History and Biographical Album of the Chippewa Valley* (Chicago, 1891–2); *History of Northern Wisconsin* (Chicago, 1881); *Golden Jubilee Album of Notre Dame Church* (n.p., 1906); and *Diamond Jubilee Album of Notre Dame Church* (n.p., 1931). Information on other members came from city directories for 1883, 1885, 1893–4, and 1894–5, at the Chippewa County Historical Society, Chippewa Falls; 1887–8 and 1889–90, at the Area Research Center, University of Wisconsin at Eau Claire, Wisconsin; and 1907, at the Library of Congress. For Post 68, major committees are the standing charity, finance, and entertainment committees and the annual Memorial Day committee.

42 French, *Chippewa Falls, Wisconsin*, 137–41; Forrester, ed. *History and Biographical Album of the Chippewa Valley*, 103.

43 Because Post 68 drew members from all parts of the county, the county as a whole represents the post's potential membership base more accurately than does the city alone. The county figure, however, is artificially low because of the presence of small posts at Bloomer and Cadott in some years of the period under study.

helped form a small post at Bloomer, whose records are now lost. But the characteristics of the officers elected at the initial meeting are clear enough: They were the elite of the town. Post Commander William Hoyt was a lawyer, soon to be a county judge; Senior Vice-commander John J. Jenkins was a judge, soon to be a state representative; Junior Vice-commander W. S. Munroe was a manufacturer. Among the lesser officers, Surgeon Alex McBean was a doctor; Officer of the Day Joseph Hesketh ran a hardware store; Officer of the Guard William W. Crandall was county registrar of deeds; Adjutant Thomas J. Kiley was principal of a school; and Sergeant Major Frank Clough ran a general store. With the possible exception of Crandall, these were local worthies. They ran the post at its inception; they, and others like them, would continue to run it most of the time afterward.

The line of post commanders tells the story simply. Hoyt himself was post commander four times between 1883 and 1899; William H. Howieson, a prosperous builder of sawmills, headed the post four other years. The other nine members who served one term each in the commander's chair included a merchant, an editor, a pension attorney, a bookkeeper, a lumber inspector, a painter, a lumberman, a deputy sheriff, and one man whose occupation is not known. Of the eight members who served at least five times in lesser offices, one was a banker and real-estate dealer, one a hotelkeeper, three merchants, one the publisher of the *Chippewa Herald,* one a lumber clerk, one a carpenter. The picture among the trustees and committee members is virtually identical, since the most active committee members also were the most frequent officeholders. In sum, Post 68 leadership was very tightly held among a small group of members, predominantly professionals and shopkeepers, over a period of seventeen years. With a membership that spanned the county, it was run from the town.

Most of the post's members were not proprietors or lawyers: They were farmers or men who worked in the lumber camps. The farmers, 32 percent of the members, were scattered from one end of the county to the other. Only occasionally able to make it to town for meetings, they were not usually among the most prominent of post members. The unskilled workers, almost all lumbermen, accounted for 23 percent of the membership. These outdwelling farmers and transient lumbermen made up the bulk of the membership of a post in which suspensions were common, despite a fairly low muster fee and low dues ($2 to join, $2 a year in dues, in 1883). Some of those dropped for arrears had simply moved on; three members were dropped in 1888, for example, "having left the country."[44] Yet they were no more prone to suspension than the town-

---

44   Post 68 Minutes, April 4, 1883, Wisconsin Local Post Records Collection (muster fee); Post 68 Quarterly Reports, 1888, ibid. ("having left the country").

dwelling members: Of the members ever suspended or dropped, 30 percent were farmers, and 23 percent were loggers – about what one would expect, given their numbers. It was the unsettled nature of the territory as a whole, rather than something specific to farming or logging, that produced suspensions from Post 68.

The high level of transience in Chippewa Falls is most evident in a frenzied pattern of joining and leaving the post, not seen in the urban posts of the East. After the founding of the post in 1883, there was a rush of new members: 71 percent of the total membership joined between 1883 and 1890. The post experienced its peak membership of 215 members in 1884, only a year after it was founded.[45] But almost at once the new recruits began falling away. Some (8 percent) did not last two years; substantially more (37 percent) did not last five. Although new members continued to sign up, membership went down almost without interruption for the rest of the century. This was because so many of the members were in arrears or had been dropped from the rolls. More than one-half of the membership (52 percent) was suspended or dropped at one time or another, and of these, very few (about one in seven) were ever reinstated – a steep rate of loss that more than balanced the extraordinary gain in the first few years. Post 68 was an organization with a high rate of turnover, probably one reason the core of active members was so small and concentrated in the mercantile and professional class of the town. In this respect the post simply mirrored the community in which it was situated, and probably those in other Western towns as well. Studies of other frontier communities in the nineteenth century have found similar situations: small and stable local elites floating atop large and transient populations.[46]

For all their influence, the high-status white-collar individuals and proprietors in Chippewa Falls were not much more numerous in the membership than were the same groups in Brockton. The high-status white-collar group (in Post 68, mostly lawyers and doctors) and the merchants each represented 9 percent of those with known occupations. Given their small numbers, most members of these classes were bound to hold offices in the post or sit on committees if they remained members long enough;

45 Post 68 Quarterly Reports, 1884, Wisconsin Local Post Records Collection.
46 Don Harrison Doyle, *The Social Order of a Frontier Community: Jacksonville, Illinois, 1825–1870* (Urbana, 1978), 92–118; Richard S. Alcorn, "Leadership and Stability in Mid-Nineteenth Century America: A Case Study," *Journal of American History*, 61 (December 1974), 685–702; Merle Curti, *The Making of an American Community: A Case Study of Democracy in a Frontier County* (Stanford, 1982); Hal S. Barron, *Those Who Stayed Behind. Rural Society in Nineteenth century New England* (New York, 1984); Michael B. Katz, Michael J. Doucet, and Mark S. Stern, "Migration and the Social Order in Erie County, New York: 1855," *Journal of Interdisciplinary History*, 8 (Spring 1978), 669–701; Kathleen Underwood, *Town Building on the Colorado Frontier* (Albuquerque, 1987).

32 of 51 did so. The rest of the membership was made up of low-status white-collar employees (clerks and bookkeepers plus a few lumber inspectors, representing 8 percent of those with known occupations); semi-skilled and service workers (5 percent); and skilled workers (13 percent), mostly, as in Philadelphia, in the building trades.[47] The clientage possibilities in a post so full of loggers and farmers were not large, and the usual practice in Chippewa Falls was for the post secretary ("adjutant") simply to sign as "proposer" on most applications for membership. As in Philadelphia, however, the leading proposers, aside from the adjutants, were mostly businessmen: hardware merchant Joseph Hesketh and Judge Hoyt (28 clients each), builder Howieson (19), merchant Frank Clough (11), and hotelkeeper Barney Himmelsbach (7).[48]

Ethnically, the post was more diverse than the Brockton and Philadelphia posts. Although the birthplace of a large number of members (29 percent) is not known, one-third of the rest had been born outside the United States. Two-thirds of these were either Germans – largely represented among the farmers – or French Canadians, who worked for the most part in the sawmills and lumber camps. Of the rest, the Irish were the largest group, but the post also contained veterans from Switzerland, France, Norway, England, and Scotland. This mixture meant the post probably had a larger number of Catholics than either of the Eastern posts. Data on religious background are not given on membership applications, but the post maintained a plot in the local Catholic cemetery, and 16 of the 39 veterans buried there were members. The post also sometimes attended the local Catholic church on holidays (something neither Post 2 nor Post 13 ever did) and elected its pastor, Father Oliver Goldsmith, an honorary member.[49]

Distinguished military service and high rank do not seem to have played a large part in the selection of Comerford Post leaders, and in any case the post was made up, like Brockton's, primarily (75 percent) of former

47 The most common occupations among skilled workers in Post 68 were carpenter, blacksmith, painter, and mason. As befits Chippewa Falls's status as a half-grown city, their numbers are low compared with other small cities in Wisconsin: Compare the posts at Neenah, where skilled workers were 19 percent of members, Fon du Lac (20 percent), Whitewater (22 percent), or Marinette (27 percent) – but high compared with "country" posts in places like Prairie du Sac (4 percent) or Kendall (5 percent). See Descriptive Books, Post 129, Neenah (box 42); Post 130, Fon du Lac (box 24); Post 34, Whitewater (box 6); Post 207, Marinette (box 32); Post 35, Prairie du Sac (box 6); Post 88, Kendall (box 17); all series 1, Wisconsin Local Post Records Collection.

48 Proposers in Post 68 were tabulated from the collection of applications for membership and from Post 68 Minutes, 1883–1900, Wisconsin Local Post Records Collection.

49 Burial list appended to Post 68 Minutes, 1893, Wisconsin Local Post Records Collection; ibid., November 22, 1887.

Table 6.6. *Military term of service and rank of Chippewa County veterans*

	Members (N = 203)	Nonmembers (N = 275)
Term of service		
More than one year	146 (73%)	159 (66%)
90 days to one year	52 (26)	70 (29)
30–90 days	2 (1)	11 (5)
Less than 30 days	0 (0)	0 (0)
Unknown	3	35
Rank		
Commissioned officer	7 (4%)	0 (0)
Noncommissioned officer	41 (21)	33 (13)
Surgeon or chaplain	1 (0.5)	1 (0.4)
Private or seaman	142 (72)	222 (86)
Support role (adjt., cook, etc.)	5 (3)	1 (0.4)
Unknown	7	18

Note: Among members, all percentages are expressed as a percentage of members whose term of service or rank is known. Among nonmembers, all percentages are expressed as a percentage of nonmembers whose term of service or rank is known.

Source: Manuscript special census of surviving Union veterans and widows, 1890, Chippewa County, Wis., enumeration districts 51–79, M 123, roll 116, National Archives, Washington, D.C.

privates (see Table 6.6). Only 12 of the members (4 percent) had been commissioned officers. Of these, only four sat even once on a major committee, and although one – colonel and newspaper publisher George Ginty – was a trustee and an active member, none of the others held office at all. As in Brockton, however, members still had slightly more distinguished service records than non-GAR members in Chippewa County. More nonmembers had been privates (86 percent of those found by the 1890 census, compared with 75 percent of the aggregate membership, 1883 – 1900) and fewer had served military terms of more than one year (66 percent, compared with 71 percent of the aggregate membership). And, as in Philadelphia, the post worried about short-service men: Of eight rejected applicants, five had served terms of less than one year in the Union army.[50]

50 Of the other three Chippewa Falls rejectees, the service term of one, John LaFane, is not known, while the other two are clearly special cases: Charles Chase was odious because of his family connection with a celebrated local murder, while Chauncey Merrill was elected on a second ballot several months after his rejection.

The local notables who ran the post had only average service records. Although all of the post commanders had served at least one year, the highest rank achieved by any of them was first lieutenant, by William Hoyt. Three of the other 10 post commanders had been sergeants, one a corporal, five had been privates, and one was a hospital steward. The post contained several wounded veterans (11 percent of the membership), but none was elected commander, only one a trustee, and only six to any office or committee post over seventeen years. The impression one takes away from the data is that military rank was not irrelevant to the members of Post 68, but it was not something about which they worried very much. It was more important for a would-be leader of the post to be a respected local citizen – the type not likely to leave the county in a year or two – than it was for him to have compiled a sparkling military record.

In short, Post 68 closely resembles a small-town businessmen's club. Its active members, like the top leaders of Post 2, were men with a real stake in the local social order. Unlike Post 2, however, the scope of Post 68 was distinctly limited. In Philadelphia, Post 2 quickly grew too large to function solely as an arena for the city's elite; one reason it kept raising its already high muster fee in the 1880s and 1890s was to keep the size of the membership down. Post 68, on the other hand, was small enough to provide a meeting place for prominent men who, for the most part, had only recently arrived in the Chippewa Valley from all over the country and from other nations. Virtually the only things they had in common were a current address in the county and service in the Union army. The active members had one other important thing in common: They stayed put. Although the membership as a whole was turbulent, with 13 members joining and 16 departing or dying in an average year, the core of the post remained essentially stable. In fact, there were really two posts: the mass of hastily recruited loggers and farmers who made up the bulk of the membership at any given point, and the smaller group of longtime residents who led it. For the average member of Post 68, the GAR meant a trip to town, a chance to hobnob with local worthies, and commemoration of the shared experience of war in meetings of men with whom he shared little else.

The differences among the memberships of these three posts give some idea of the diversity of the GAR; it will not do simply to say that its members were mostly former privates, or mostly businessmen, or mostly Protestants. Yet at least four general conclusions seem warranted. First, although previous military rank and duration of service were only marginally important in deciding who could join the Grand Army, they usually meant a good deal when it came to the election of leaders. In both a working-class post such as Post 13 of Brockton and an elite post such as Post 2 of Philadelphia, a former commissioned officer was likely to be called on to serve as an officer. Although social considerations might intrude, as they did in Post 68, former rank was always a strong recommendation at the local level of the GAR as much as at the department and national levels, where former captains, colonels, majors, and generals abounded. Length of military service also was a prime consideration, both in the selection of officers and in the screening of applicants for membership. Though not formally barred from joining, short-term soldiers tended to be excluded by the formal or informal blackballing of post members; the resulting posts tended to be made up mostly of men who had served more than one year. The members were inclined to elect as officers those for whom the war had been central and to reject as members those for whom it had been only a fleeting experience.

A second characteristic of the GAR was the predominance of native-born white men. Compared with the population as a whole, all of the posts studied here included relatively small numbers of immigrants, while only one black veteran can be found among their 2,225 members. The segregation of black veterans was intentional and obvious, part of the routine racism that marked American life in the late nineteenth century. The relative paucity of foreign-born veterans is perhaps more surprising; this, however, does not necessarily indicate active discrimination on the part of the GAR. Rather, it may reflect the ethnic makeup of the nation at the outbreak of the war. By the 1890s the United States was drawing a larger number of immigrants from nations only slightly represented in the population of 1860. The GAR limited its membership to Union Civil War veterans, unlike the earlier Society of the Cincinnati or the later American Legion and Veterans of Foreign Wars, which were opened to veterans of other conflicts: Thus the order functioned as a kind of passive nativist organization. It did not openly bar nonwhite, nonnative non-males: Like the contemporaneous Daughters and Sons of the American Revolution, it simply drew the line of qualification for membership around participation in a historical event that had occurred too early for the latecomers. As the number of immigrants in the population began to swell in the late 1890s, the ethnic narrowness of GAR veteranhood would become increasingly anomalous.

Third, no matter what the social composition of a post's membership, it tended to serve as a forum for high-status professionals and businessmen. To be sure, others filled the ranks, just as they had in the army. Industrial workers predominated in posts like the one at Brockton; members of country posts in places such as Lime Ridge and Dallas, in Wisconsin, were virtually all farmers. But even in Brockton the local notables held more than their share of the post offices, and in other industrial cities, such as Neenah, Wisconsin, and Reading, Pennsylvania, most of the charter members were high-status individuals, despite the fact that most of the later recruits were blue-collar workers.[51] Both Post 2 and Post 68 were usually commanded by merchants, lawyers, or manufacturers and served as centers of business clientage; Posts 13 and 68 mustered more members from the commercial districts than from working-class city wards. The concentration of GAR leadership in the hands of the prominent shows even more clearly in a tabulation of national officers' occupations made by Robert Beath in his *History* of 1888 (a list that incidentally testifies to the predominance of former colonels and generals in the national leadership): Save the 17 for whom no occupation is listed, every one of the 117 national officers between 1866 and 1888 was either a businessman, a manufacturer, or a professional.[52] The national leadership was the local leadership writ large: Local notables selected state notables, who in turn selected national notables.

Finally, despite the penchant for elite leadership, the striking thing about GAR membership as a whole is its tendency to cut across class boundaries. In this finding there is much support for Mary Clawson's thesis that nineteenth-century fraternal orders, far from being pegged to particular social classes, were substitutes for class-based organizations.[53] In each of the cases studied here, the composition of an individual post followed the occupational and ethnic contours of the town in which it was located. Industrial Brockton's post was filled with shoe workers, rural Chippewa Falls's post with farmers and lumberjacks. In Philadelphia a large veteran population divided into separate posts on the basis of occupation, as well as race, ethnicity, type of military service, and even geography. Taken as a whole, however, the class and ethnic bases of the Grand Army were fairly broad. Just as the Union army had subsumed a welter of local militias by absorbing them within its structure, the Grand Army offered a national version of veteranhood that superseded more particularistic attachments within it.

The national GAR, however, had its own peculiarities. The cosmology of veteranhood that bound together the wide variety of local post expe-

51 Descriptive Book, Post 129, Neenah, Wisconsin Local Post Records Collection; Descriptive Book, Post 78, Reading, Pennsylvania Historical and Museum Commission Collections.

52 Robert B. Beath, *History of the Grand Army of the Republic* (New York, 1888), 68–378.

53 Mary Ann Clawson, "Fraternal Orders and Class Formation in the Nineteenth-century United States," *Comparative Studies in Society and History*, 27 (October 1985), 672–95.

riences was a sort of white bourgeois paradise: leadership by business-men; voluntary (but also quasi-military) orderliness; dampened ethnic and class identification; pro forma black equality, safely relegated to the other side of town. Day-to-day life in the average post reinforced this picture at every turn. The highly formal arrangement of space in the GAR post room emphasized order and submission to discipline. At the meet-ings that took place within it, lack of self-control – particularly intem-perance, the leading cause of expulsion or "court martial" – was an un-pardonable sin. At GAR "campfires," the war itself was remembered in sentimental terms as a time when brothers in arms "drank from the same canteen." Meanwhile, developments that threatened public order outside the post room invariably struck the veterans as ominous. In 1877, the clerks of Post 2 organized to fight alongside the Pennsylvania state militia in putting down the great railroad strike; in the 1890s, members worried by the new flood of immigrants launched campaigns for schoolhouse flags and schoolboy military drill. And throughout the postwar period, GAR leaders continued to hope that Southern racial violence would simply go away.[54] The domestication of the war in the Grand Army post room was the cultural component of the order's well-known stalwart Republican-ism: conservative, backward-looking, orderly. In the GAR telling, the war had been a struggle to preserve an already perfect Union, not an event that implied major social or personal change.[55]

Lost underneath this complacent view of veteranhood were other ver-sions that struggled in vain for a hearing. Frederick Douglass, for one, spent the rest of his life urging Northerners not to forget the emancipa-tory message of the war or the Reconstruction laws that followed it. Dissident Grand Army members such as Oliver Wilson complained about "the sentiment of the lodgeroom" and "the morbid, 'goody goody' in the Order," while literary realists such as Ambrose Bierce and Stephen Crane would have to wait until the 1890s to undomesticate the war in fiction. Finally, one suspects that the *frontideologie* so prevalent among veterans of other wars – alienation and loathing, verging on hatred, for "civil-ians" and their institutions – was not entirely absent among the Union veterans, even though the sentimental fraternalism of the GAR gave them nowhere to express it. Among the thousands of nonmembers, surely there must have been real-life counterparts to Sherwood Anderson's fictional

---

54 On the patriotic campaigns and racial struggles of the 1890s, see Dearing, *Veterans in Politics*, 402–99; McConnell, "Social History of the Grand Army of the Republic," 500–60.

55 It also may represent the postwar persistence of the same domestic values for which so many soldiers fought: See Reid Mitchell "The Northern Soldier and His Commu-nity," this volume, Chapter 3.

Union veterans, men who retold war stories until "a something snapped in their brains and they fell to chattering and shouting their vain boastings to all as they looked about hungrily for believing eyes."[56]

Instead, the GAR offered veterans a way to fit the war back into their civilian lives with minimal disruption. The process of becoming a Union veteran was a process of domesticating one's military experience, of translating military rank into business clientage, Union into transethnic classlessness, and the uncompromising evangelicalism of the war years into the complacency and passive nativism of the 1890s. In the Grand Army, former soldiers had created a fraternal refuge from a nation increasingly unlike the one they had saved in 1865. They had come back, in the words of GAR founder and Union general John Alexander Logan, to "that place of heaven called home."[57]

56 David W. Blight, "For Something beyond the Battlefield: Frederick Douglass and the Struggle for the Memory of the Civil War," *Journal of American History,* 75 (March 1989), 1156–78; Oliver M. Wilson, *The Grand Army of the Republic under Its first Constitution and Ritual* (Kansas City, Mo., 1905), 68, 157; Sherwood Anderson, *Windy McPherson's Son* (1916), cited in Aaron, *Unwritten War,* 340. On Civil War literature's forgetfulness, see Aaron; Thomas C. Leonard, *Above The Battle: War-Making in America from Appomattox to Versailles* (New York, 1978), 20–4; and Wilson, *Patriotic Gore,* 617–34, 669–742, 684, 701.

57 *Proceedings of the National Encampment of the Grand Army of the Republic,* 1869 encampment, 34.

7

"Such Is the Price We Pay": American Widows and the Civil War Pension System

AMY E. HOLMES

> What eye, save that which comprehends immensity, can measure a nation's grief, as, like the foot-worn soldier, she bows over the graves of her fallen sons, and from the depth of her anguish, cries out, "Such is the price we pay for human freedom"?[1]

If we know little about the soldiers and sailors who fought and died in the Civil War, we know even less about those they left behind. Not only did the Civil War produce far more military deaths than any other American war; it left more families without husbands, fathers, and sons.[2] This chapter explores the impact of the federal Civil War pension upon widows. How many women were widowed by the war, and how were widows' lives changed by receiving pension payments? To get some answers to these questions, this study focuses on the household arrangements of widows who received pensions in Kent County, Michigan, and in Essex County, Massachusetts.

The Federal Military Pension System

In the summer of 1862, Congress passed, and President Lincoln approved, pension legislation that became the blueprint for all subsequent

An earlier version of this paper was presented at the 66th Annual Meeting of the Southwestern Social Science Association in Houston, Texas, March 1988, as "Remembering the Noble Ladies: American Widows and the Civil War Pension System." I wish to thank Maris Vinovskis, who suggested studying Civil War widows and pensions and gave helpful comments and guidance. I am indebted to Victoria Getis and Nancy Horn, who read and commented on earlier drafts of this essay.

1   Charlotte E. McKay, quoted in Frank Moore, *Women of the War: Their Heroism and Self-sacrifice* (Hartford, 1866), 229.
2   Maris Vinovskis, "Have Social Historians Lost the Civil War? Some Preliminary Demographic Speculations," Chapter 1 in this volume.

pension legislation until 1890 and that instituted unprecedented expenditures by the federal government on military pensions. In addition to providing benefits for injured and disabled veterans, the law provided pensions for widows, children, and other dependent relatives of soldiers who either had died in service or who had died of causes that could be directly traced to military service. From the founding of the federal government to the beginning of the Civil War, the federal government spent a total of about $90 million on military pensions.[3] In the fifty years that followed the Civil War, it spent almost sixty times that amount – about $5 billion.[4] More than forty percent of the federal budget in 1893 was taken up by payments to former Union soldiers and their dependents.[5] Widows comprised a substantial portion of the pension recipients. In 1883, one in six on the pension rolls was a widow, and over one-half of them had children under 16 years of age.[6]

In order to receive a pension, a widow had to prove that her husband had died from a service-related disease or wound. For this the widow received the same pension that would have been allowed for the totally disabled soldier, anywhere from $8 to $30 a month. If the woman remarried, pension payments were terminated. She could, however, still receive the sum that had been due her before she remarried, even if she applied for the money after her remarriage. She also could apply to be restored to the rolls if she became widowed again. Minor children who lived with widowed mothers were provided for in 1868. Widows receiving the private's $8 monthly rate received $2 a month extra for each child under the age of 16. In 1886, Congress passed a pension increase from $8 to $12 a month for widows and dependent relatives of privates.[7] Twelve dollars a month represented a significant amount: $144 a year, compared with average annual earnings of $438 for all workers in 1890, or about one-third of what the average worker earned.[8] A widow receiving an $8 monthly pension payment benefited more than a former soldier receiving the same amount, because these payments represented a larger proportion of the wages that she could otherwise earn. In 1885, women could expect to earn only about three-fifths of the wages of an adult man.[9]

Not only did widows receive substantial monthly pension payments;

3   William H. Glasson *Federal Military Pensions in the United States* (New York, 1918), 123.
4   Ibid., 273.
5   Vinovskis, "Social Historians."
6   William Henry Glasson, *History of Military Pension Legislation in the United States* (New York, 1900), 86, Glasson, *Federal Military Pensions,* 273.
7   Glasson, *Federal Military Pensions,* 125, 139.
8   U.S. Census Bureau, *Historical Statistics of the United States, Colonial Times to 1957* (Washington, D.C., 1960), Series D-603.
9   Clarence D. Long, *Wages and Earnings in the United States, 1860–1890* (New York, 1975), 104.

they could receive lump-sum payments as well. According to an 1868 act, widows were entitled to payment of the pension from the date of death of the soldier, provided they filed within five years of his death. In 1879, Congress changed that policy, and payment could be had from the date of death of the husband, no matter when the claim was filed.[10] In some cases, arrears were quite large. In 1881, the average first payment to army widows, minor children, and dependent relatives of soldiers was $1,022, more than twice the average yearly earnings of all workers.[11]

Large pension payments to remarried widows generated concern in the government. In 1898, the commissioner of pensions cited an exceptional case in his report:

> In 1871 this captain [an infantry volunteer] died. He was not a pensioner, and had never filed a claim for pension. His widow remained a widow until March 30, 1887, when she remarried, having filed no claim, and, having remarried, had no pensionable status. In 1892, five years after the act of June 7, 1888, had passed, six years after her remarriage, and twenty-two years after the death of her soldier husband, she files her claim for pension as a widow from the date of the death of her soldier husband, in 1871, to the date of her remarriage in 1887 – sixteen years – and gets nearly $4,000, practically for the use and benefit of the second husband.[12]

Even under the 1868 law, widows could receive substantial lump-sum payments. The widow of a private could conceivably apply five years after her husband's death and, at the monthly rate of $8, receive a lump sum of $480, plus her future monthly pension.

Because widows had to prove that their husbands' deaths were service related, the pension system inaugurated by the law of 1862 had limited impact. On June 27, 1890, however, Congress considerably widened in scope the number of persons eligible to receive a pension. After 1890, a widow of an honorably discharged Union soldier or sailor who had served ninety days or more was entitled to a pension of $8 a month, regardless of the cause of the soldier's death, provided she had married the soldier before June 27, 1890.[13] Congress had passed what amounted to an old-age pension, for veterans' widows that affected not only those women who had been married during the Civil War but women who had married Union veterans up to twenty-five years after the war had ended.[14]

10 Glasson, *Federal Military Pensions,* 152, 163–4.
11 Ibid., 175.
12 Ibid., 201.
13 Ibid., 235. Widows with minor children received $2 for each child (of the soldier) as well. Note that widows under the old system, who married soldiers before march 19, 1886, still received $12 a month.
14 See Vinovskis, "Social Historians," section 1 entitled "Civil War Pensions and Union Veterans." The function of the federal Civil War pension as an old-age pension has

These women received significant sums of money over a long period of time. How many American women in the late nineteenth century were likely to have reaped the benefits of the pension system? Although a very crude method, at best, one way to estimate the number of soldiers' wives widowed during the war is to look at the number of men killed in the war. If the Civil War was the bloodiest war in our history, with deaths exceeding those of World War II by over 50 percent, then it is likely that the war left more widows than other American wars as well.[15] An esti- mated 618,000 soldiers, Union and Confederate, died in the war; of these, approximately 360,000 were Union soldiers.[16] If we estimate that 30 percent of those soldiers and sailors were married, then 108,000 women could have been widowed by the war itself.[17] Many soldiers who sur- vived were wounded, and many almost certainly died later of those wounds or of illnesses contracted in the service. In 1883, almost twenty years after the end of the war, about 52,000 widows or one-half the estimated number of war widows, were on the pension rolls.[18] Census enumerators in 1890 counted 145,359 widows of Union soldiers and sailors.[19] After 1890, when the pension system expanded considerably, most of those women were probably eligible to receive the pension.

The federal pension undoubtedly had a significant impact on the lives of Union widows of the Civil War. The effects of federal pension pay-

been noted in the literature on aging. See Michel R. Dahlin, "From Poorhouse to Pension: The Changing View of Old Age in America, 1890–1929," Ph. D. diss., Stan- ford University, 1982, 166, and Carole Haber, *Beyond Sixty-five: The Dilemma of Old Age in America's Past* (New York, 1983, 111–3.

15   Vinovskis, "Social Historians," Figure 1.2.

16   Claudia Goldin, "War," in *Encyclopedia of Economic History,* ed. Glen Porter (New York, 1980), 3:948.

17   This estimate was arrived at by looking at the age breakdown of soldiers and sailors in the 1890 census. Seventy percent of the Union survivors of the war listed were age 55 years or less. In 1861, these men would have been age 25 years or less. The first census to break down the population by marital status was taken in 1890. To get a general idea of the percentage of men who might have been married, the percentage of men between the ages of 15 and 25 who were married was calculated from the proportion of married men in 1890. The proportion of men age 25 and above was calculated as well. These percentages were then multiplied by the number of soldiers and sailors surviving in 1890 who would have been in each of the two age groups (below 25 or 25 and above) in 1860, to give a weighted estimate of the percentage of soldiers and sailors who might have been married: 30 percent. That 30 percent of the soldiers were married may be a reasonable estimate. A study of enlistment in Deerfield, Massachusetts, found that an average of 32 percent of the soldiers who enlisted throughout the war were married. See Emily J. Harris, "Sons and Soldiers: Deerfield, Massachusetts and the Civil War," *Civil War History,* 30 (June 1984), 168. The actual number may be lower, if married men were less likely to be killed than single men.

18   Calculated from Glasson, *History of Military Pension Legislation,* p. 213.

19   Department of the Interior, U.S. Census Office, *Report on the Population of the United States at the Eleventh Census: 1890* (Washington, D.C., 1895), 2 vols, 1, Pt. 2, Table 123.

Figure 7.1. Union widows as a percentage of all widows, by state, 1890. *Source:* Data derived from Department of the Interior, Census Office, *Report on the Population of the United States at the Eleventh Census: 1890.* Vol. 1: Pt. 1, Table 81, and Pt. 2, Table 123.

ments become even more interesting when we look at how those payments were concentrated. First, Civil War pensions were mostly paid to women in the North. The map in Figure 7.1 shows the proportion of all widows in each state that were Union widows. Union widows in most of the Northern states made up between 6 and 11 percent of all widows; in Oklahoma, Kansas, and Indiana they made up 12 to 17 percent of all widows. Pension payments constituted a substantial rerouting of federal money to individuals in Northern states.

Second, payments were concentrated by age group. Pensions were paid to the women whose husbands had been of military age during the war. Table 7.1 shows Union and Confederate widows in 1890 as a proportion of all U.S. widows by age cohort. These figures must be approached with caution. In 1890, the Census Office was ordered to take a special census of Union veterans and widows; the office began the task by drawing up a list of pensioners. Persons not receiving pensions may therefore be underrepresented, and Confederate widows are almost certainly underrepresented, since no special effort was made to seek them out, and the numbers given for them in the special census are unusually small. Nevertheless, almost one in every six American widows between the ages of 45

Table 7.1. *Civil War widows as percentage of all U.S. widows in 1890, by age cohort*

Age cohort (years)	Union (%)	Confederate (%)	Civil War total	
			%	N
All U.S. widows	7	3	10	205,564
Selected age cohorts:				
35–44	10	3	13	39,656
45–54	12	5	17	74,812
55–64	8	4	12	56,222
Over 65	3	1	4	29,048

Source: Department of the Interior, U.S. Census Office, *Report on the Population of the United States at the Eleventh Census: 1890,* vol 1: Pt. 1, Table 82 and Pt. 2, Table 126.

and 54 was a Civil War widow, and about one in eight widows between the ages of 45 and 54 was a widow of a Union soldier or sailor.[20] The 1890 pension law made most of these women eligible for the pension. The youngest women may conceivably have received a pension for decades, carrying the effect of the pension system well into the twentieth century.

Most Civil War widows were between the ages of 35 and 55 in 1890 and lived in the North, concentrating the impact of war widowhood and pension payments by both cohort and region. We will explore that impact by studying widows in the early 1880s on a community level, using pension records and the federal manuscript census of 1880.

Widows and Federal Military Pensions in Kent County, Michigan, and Essex County, Massachusetts

> Each man drew forth the irresistible daguerrotype, and held it for me to look at, full of pride and affection. There were aged mothers and sober matrons, bright-eyed maidens and laughing cherubs, all carried next to these brave hearts, and cherished as life itself.[21]

Like the daguerrotypes carried by the soldiers and sailors of the Civil War, this brief glance at their wives and mothers, using information from the census, is a snapshot of general characteristics. From this snapshot, however, we can learn about them and about other widows. Using infor-

20 Ibid., vol 1, Pt. 1 Table 82, and Pt. 2, Table 126.
21 A. H. Hoge, quoted in Moore, *Women of the War*, 369.

mation from pension lists published in 1883 and from the 1880 manuscript census, I compared 182 pensioned widows from urban Grand Rapids, Michigan, and rural Kent County, Michigan, and from urban Salem, Massachusetts, and nonurban Essex County, Massachusetts, with a one-in-five sample off all widows from the same communities consisting of 759 widows.[22]

The death of a spouse confronts an individual with many problems, including coping with grief, with new household, financial, and family responsibilities, and possibly the loss of an independent household.[23] The way widows experience these changes is shaped by age, ethnicity, family situation, community of residence, and sources of both emotional and financial support, the latter of which could include a pension.[24] I will focus upon several aspects of widows' lives that may be examined from information in the 1880 census, including age; whether they were American-born or foreign-born; presence of minor and adult children in the household; relationship to the head of household; employment; and other means of financial support. Looking at these measures should give us an idea of how much pension payments changed the lives of widows in the late nineteenth century.

In 1890, 9 percent of Michigan widows and 7 percent of Massachusetts widows were widows of Union soldiers.[25] Michigan and Massachusetts were typical of many other Northern states in this respect: In 1890, between 6 and 11 percent of all widows were Union widows (see Figure 7.1). But while Michigan and Massachusetts had similar proportions of Civil War widows, the two states differed demographically and economically in important and interesting ways. Michigan had more men for every woman than Massachusetts did. There were 114 men for every 100 women over age 10 in Michigan in 1880, and only 91 men for every 100 women in Massachusetts.[26] Amount and type of employment differed dramatically as well. In 1880, 23 percent of Massachusetts women were gainfully employed, compared to only 10 percent of Michigan women.[27] In Michigan, 72 percent of employed women worked in a profession or in personal service, and 23 percent worked in manufacturing and mining,

22 The nonpensioned sample is a one-in-five systematic sample of widowed women in Salem, Grand Rapids, and nonurban communities chosen in Kent and Essex counties.
23 Arlene Scadron, "Introduction," in Scadron, ed., *On Their Own: Widows and Widowhood in the American Southwest, 1848–1939* (Urbana, Ill., 1988), 1–13.
24 Ibid.
25 U.S. Census Office, *Report on the Population: 1890*, vol. 1: Pt. 1, Table 81, and Pt. 2, Table 123.
26 Department of the Interior, U.S. Census Office, *Compendium of the Tenth Census: June 1, 1880:* Pt. 1, *Population* (Washington, D.C., 1883), Table 101, 1356–7.
27 Ibid.

while in Massachusetts 40 percent worked in a profession or in personal service and 56 percent worked in manufacturing and mining.[28] The states differed also in numbers of women who were native- or foreign-born. In 1890, fewer white Michigan widows were foreign-born: about 21 percent, compared with Massachusetts's 29 percent.[29] In Grand Rapids, 79 percent of white widows had been born in the United States; 68 percent of white Salem widows were native-born.[30] Finally, a higher percentage of women were widows in Massachusetts, and those widows were older than widows in Michigan.[31] These differences between Massachusetts and Michigan have important implications for how widows lived their lives, influencing their chances of remarriage, employment, and employment of family. They defined the context in which the effects of pension payments played themselves out.

Kent County, situated in the western-central part of Michigan, was chosen for this study because rural and urban widows could easily be compared and primary sources – newspapers and manuscript censuses – were readily available for study. Late nineteenth-century Kent County boasted a well-populated city, Grand Rapids (pop. 32,106 in 1880), surrounded by rural townships. Grand Rapids's claim to commercial fame was the manufacture of furniture, although the city also had a fair number of other factories.[32] Farming and timber production dominated the rest of the county.

Communities in Essex county, Massachusetts, were chosen for this study to provide a regional contrast to Michigan. Essex county contained communities that were similar socially, demographically, and economically to other communities in the Northeast.[33] Salem (pop. 27,563 in 1880), situated in the southeastern part of the county, had an economy based upon a combination of industrial and commercial concerns, a population that grew modestly between 1850 and 1885, and a higher concentration of younger people than outlying towns.[34] Ten smaller communities in

28 Ibid.
29 Ibid.
30 Ibid.
31 U.S. Census Office, *Report on the Population: 1890*, vol. 1: Pt. 1, Tables 82–4, 829, 831, 951–2.
32 *History of Kent County, Michigan: together with sketches of its cities, villages, and townships ... biographies of representative citizens* (C. C. Chapman, 1881). Micropublished as publication no. 143 on reel 47 of *County Histories of the Old Northwest, Series V: Michigan* (New Haven: Research Publications, 1973).
33 John Modell and Howard P. Chudacoff, "The Setting: The Essex County Context," in *Transitions: The Family and the Life Course in Historical Perspective*, ed. Tamara K. Hareven (New York, 1978), 99–112.
34 The population figure comes from U.S. Census Office, *Compendium: 1880:* Pt. 1, *Population* Table 19, p. 123. On Salem's economy, see Modell and Chudacoff, "Essex County Context," 100.

central and southern Essex County were chosen as the nonurban sample: Boxford, Essex, Georgetown, Hamilton, Lynnfield, Middleton, Rowley, Saugus, Topsfield, and Wenham. Boxford, Hamilton, Lynnfield, and Wenham generally declined in population between 1850 and 1880; none of the ten communities contained more than 2,700 people in 1880, and none was truly rural. People in these communities mostly supported themselves through a mixture of farming, boot and shoe manufacturing, cotton and linen manufacturing, transportation, trade, and domestic service.[35]

This study uses a list of pensioners published by the Bureau of the Census in 1883.[36] The bureau divided pensioners by state and county and listed the name of each person, along with the certificate number, post-office address, reason why pension was granted, monthly rate received, and date of the original granting of the pension. I have included all widows from the pension list, not excluding widows of the War of 1812 and dependent mothers of dead Union soldiers, who received pensions as a result of the Civil War legislation. Since the pensions affected this second group of widows, they also were included in this study.

Names of widows from the 1883 pension lists were matched with names of widows from the 1880 manuscript census. The Michigan urban sample consists of women living in the city of Grand Rapids. Seventy-six women in Grand Rapids received pensions in 1883: 50 Civil War widows, 16 dependent mothers, and 10 widows of the War of 1812. Of these 76 women, 43 were found in the 1880 census: 62 percent of Union widows, and 46 percent of mothers of Union soldiers or widows of the War of 1812, were found. The urban sample in Salem, Massachusetts, showed linkage rates similar to those in Grand Rapids. Of 113 women who received pensions, 50 were found: 62 percent of Civil War widows, and 45 percent of Civil War mothers and 1812 widows. The nonurban samples in Kent and Essex counties had similar linkage rates too. For the Michigan rural sample, 34 of 54 widows from fourteen rural townships were matched with the census: 72 percent of Union widows, and 50 percent of Civil War mothers and 1812 widows.[37] Seventy-six percent of Essex County nonurban Civil War widows listed, and 59 percent of Civil War mothers and 1812 widows listed, were found: of 65 listed pensioned

35   Cyrus Mason Tracy, *Standard History of Essex County, Massachusetts* (Boston, 1878), 79, 115, 121, 161, 262, 301, 355, 398, 410–11, 416; Modell and Chudacoff, "Essex County Context," 103–8.

36   U.S. Bureau of the Pension, *List of Pensioners on the Roll, January 1, 1883* (Washington, D.C., 1883).

37   The rural townships in Kent County are as follows: Solon, Nelson, Sparta, Algoma, Courtland, Oakfield, Alpine, Plainfield, Cannon, Grattan, Ada, Byron, Gaines, and Caledonia.

widows, 45 were found in the census. Overall, 57 percent of the female pensioners in Grand Rapids, 53 percent of those in Salem, 63 percent of Kent County rural widows, and 69 percent of Essex County nonurban widows were linked to the 1880 census.[38]

Although the proportion of widows linked may seem low, this is not surprising, considering that the pension lists used were made three years after the census. The oldest group of widows – dependent mothers and 1812 widows – and city dwellers were harder to find than younger widows or those in more rural communities. Census takers perhaps missed some of the oldest. These women, if living with daughters, might have been listed under a son-in-law's surname, and one may speculate that some families avoided reporting the woman's death to the pension bureau as well. Censuses often miss the very poor, and city-dwelling women may have been missed because they were more likely to live in densely populated housing or because they were more mobile. Although the sample may show some bias with respect to age and may undercount those who did not head their own households, we have no reason to believe that the sample is biased in other respects.

Most of the widows on the pension list in 1883 received the $8.00-a-month private's pension.[39] Only one widow received less that $8.00; she received the $2.00 a month. Maximum pensions paid out were higher in urban areas, where the highest pensions were $25.00 and $30.00, while the highest pension paid to widows outside the cities, in Essex and Kent counties, was $20.00 a month. Mean pension payments were highest in Grand Rapids, where the average was about $9.50 a month. Mean pensions in Salem, rural Kent County, and Essex County were about $8.75, $8.70, and $8.35, respectively.

The data in Table 7.2 show the age distribution of pensioned and non-pensioned widows in relation to pension origin and community of residence. Mothers of Civil War soldiers and widows of the War of 1812 are treated as separate categories in this table, so that the characteristics of Civil War widows can be more easily discussed. Widows in the Michigan sample were younger than Massachusetts widows, and widows in urban communities were younger than those in nonurban communities, a pattern that appears even among Civil War widows and mothers and 1812

38 In Salem, 33 of 53 Civil War widows, and 27 of 60 mothers and 1812 widows, were found. In Grand Rapids, 31 of 50 Civil War widows, and 12 of 26 mothers and 1812 widows, were linked. In rural Kent County, 23 of 32 Civil War widows, and 11 of 22 mothers and 1812 widows, were found, and in the nonurban sample for Essex County 29 of 38 Civil war widows, and 16 of 27 mothers and 1812 widows, were found.

39 Although monthly pension rates are listed for these women, the lists do not tell us whether women receiving more than $8 a month were receiving extra money for their children or because they were officers' widows.

Table 7.2. *Age, pension origin, and community of residence of war widows and mothers, 1880*

Community of residence	Age group (years)						Total	
	Under 35	35–44	45–54	55–64	65–74	Over 75	%[a]	N
Kent County								
Grand Rapids								
Civil War widows	0	39	23	23	13	3	101	31
Mothers; widows, 1812[b]	0	0	8	8	50	33	99	12
Nonpensioned	14	13	27	21	16	9	100	199
Nonurban								
Civil War widows	4	30	22	39	4	0	99	23
Mothers; widows, 1812	0	0	9	9	45	36	99	11
Nonpensioned	2	12	18	27	25	16	100	121
Essex County								
Salem								
Civil War widows	6	12	36	36	6	3	99	33
Mothers; widows, 1812	0	4	0	27	19	50	100	26
Nonpensioned	4	13	20	26	23	14	100	303
Nonurban								
Civil War widows	3	10	41	35	0	10	99	29
Mothers; widows, 1812	0	0	0	0	50	50	100	16
Nonpensioned	4	9	14	20	24	29	100	133

[a] Total percentages do not add exactly to 100.0, because of rounding.
[b] The "Mothers; widows, 1812" category refers to dependent mothers of Civil War soldiers, and widows of the War of 1812.

widows. Civil War widows were mostly between the ages of 35 and 64, clearly demarcating the impact of war deaths on women of marriageable age at the time of the war. Civil War widows in Massachusetts were older than those in Michigan; they were mostly between 45 and 64 years old. These women would have been 30 to 49 years old at the end of the war. Possible explanations for the age gap are a younger population in Michigan, selective migration of younger persons to the West, and a younger age at marriage in Michigan. A younger age at marriage in Kent County is supported by different sex ratios in Essex and Kent counties. From 1860 to 1880, the sex ratio in Kent County varied between 106 and 108 men for every 100 women, while in Essex County the sex ratio was be-

Table 7.3. *Nativity, pension status, and community of residence of war widows, 1880*

Community of residence	Native-born widows			Foreign-born widows (%)	Total	
	Parents born in U.S.A. (%)	Parents foreign-born (%)	Unknown (%)		%	N
Kent County						
Grand Rapids						
Pensioned	56	16	2	26	100	43
Nonpensioned	45	8	2	45	100	199
Nonurban						
Pensioned	82	12	3	3	100	34
Nonpensioned	61	7	5	27	100	121
Essex County						
Salem						
Pensioned	63	7	0	30	100	60
Nonpensioned	54	7	1	38	100	305
Nonurban						
Pensioned	91	0	2	7	100	45
Nonpensioned	84	4	2	10	100	134

tween 91 and 93 men for every 100 women.[40] Women of 20 undergo a transition from marriage to widowhood very differently from women of 40. The lifetime experiences of Civil War widows in Michigan communities were very unlike those of Massachusetts widows, simply as a result of their collective ages. Their experiences differed from those of other widows in their communities as well.

Although the pensioned widows of Kent and Essex counties differed in age, the relative proportions of foreign-born and native-born among them do not differ greatly. Table 7.3 shows generation in the United States by pension status. Most widows receiving pensions were born in the United States – in nonurban communities, overwhelmingly so. In both counties, foreign-born widows were concentrated in the cities, probably because there were more opportunities for employment of women and the foreign born in the cities. Even in the population as a whole, the proportion of foreign born was higher in the cities: 27 percent of Salem's population and 31 percent of Grand Rapids' were foreign-born in 1880.[41]

40 U.S. Census Office, *Population of the United States in 1860: Compiled from the Original Returns of the Eighth Census* (Washington, D.C., 1864), 218–19, 230–1; U.S. Census Office, *A Compendium of the Ninth Census (June 1, 1870)* (Washington, D.C. 1872); 571. U.S. Census Office, *Compendium: 1880*, 580–1.
41 U.S. Census Office, *Compendium:1880*, 426, 457.

Pensioned widows in Michigan who were born in the United States were more often of foreign parentage than both nonpensioned widows in Michigan and widows in Massachusetts. Even when mothers of Union soldiers and widows of the War of 1812 are excluded, this difference persists. This finding suggests that second-generation Michigan men may have either served or died in greater proportions in the war than first-generation Americans, or that their widows may have more often applied for pensions. Vinovskis, in a study of Newburyport in Essex County, Massachusetts, found that second-generation men were more likely to serve and that foreign-born and second-generation men were more likely to die in service.[42] If that pattern was typical of the rest of Essex County, widows of second-generation soldiers either remarried, migrated, or did not receive pensions.

Pensioned widows differed significantly from nonpensioned widows in Kent County, Michigan. In Grand Rapids and outlying communities, many more widows not receiving pensions were foreign-born. In Essex County the two groups did not differ markedly from one another. The difference in generation between pensioned and nonpensioned Kent County widows is puzzling. Overall, the proportion of the population that was foreign-born grew 5.4 percent in Essex County between 1860 and 1880, while it only grew about 2.6 percent in Kent County.[43] Since there was little rise in the proportion of foreign-born in both counties, we would expect little difference in generation between widows in both counties. The difference in the percentage of foreign-born cannot be attributed to a higher level of foreign immigration to Kent County.

Several plausible explanations can be offered for the difference. First, Grand Rapids nearly quadrupled in size during this period, while Salem only experienced a modest 20-percent increase in population.[44] The foreign-born probably were better established in Essex County, where the population remained relatively stable, than in Kent County, where the population grew rapidly between 1860 and 1880. Newly arrived foreign-born women, whose families had had little time to accumulate assets, may have been more needy after their husbands' deaths, and less attractive candidates for remarriage. Foreign-born women who received a pension had more financial stability as a result, and perhaps remarried more quickly. Second, the huge population growth in Kent County brought the same proportion of foreign-born as had been there before, but they

42 Vinovskis, "Social Historians," section entitled "Newburyport and the Civil War."
43 U.S. Census Office, *Population of the United States in 1860*, 218–19, 226, 247; U.S. Census Office, *Compendium: 1870*, 224, 418; U.S. Census Office, *Compendium: 1880*, 426.
44 U.S. Census Office, *Report on the Population: 1890*, vol 1, pt. 1, 434–5.

may have been newer to the country than in Essex County and may not have had the opportunity to fight in previous wars. Pension benefits in Kent County thus were paid to a select group of widows, most of whom were native-born, in a city where almost one-half of widows were foreign-born. As successive waves of immigration hit the United States in the late nineteenth and early twentieth centuries, widows receiving pensions in places where the population was rapidly expanding became an increasingly exclusive group.

Examining household composition and sources of support among widows who received pension payments and those who did not requires examining the data in a slightly different way. Household position and composition, as well as probability of working for wages, change as women age. For older women in the last half of the nineteenth century, widowhood increasingly meant the end of heading their own households as they aged,[45] although nearly one-half of widows in the United States over age 54 headed their own households in 1900.[46] For widows who had children, age made the difference between supporting minor children or living with adult children.

For the remainder of this section, we will compare an older and a younger group of widows. The younger group consists of widows under 65, and the older group consists of widows 65 and older.[47] There are compelling reasons to divide the sample this way. First, looking at older and younger widows will give us a glimpse of the impact of the pension legislation of 1890, which essentially created an old-age pension for widows and veterans, and enables us to see how it operated in the lives of older widows. Second, fewer older widows receiving pensions were linked to the census. Dividing the widows helps us to mitigate age biases that might be introduced by not finding those widows and also will minimize the effects of the different age distributions between pensioned and nonpensioned widows. Finally, widowhood is often thought of as a transition into old age, but almost 40 percent of widows in this study were below age 55, and over 60 percent were below age 65. Losing a spouse was a transition out of married life for many younger women as well as older women and may have had more dire consequences for younger

45 Howard P. Chudacoff and Tamara K. Hareven, "From the Empty Nest to Family Dissolution: Life Course Transitions into Old Age," *Journal of Family History,* 4 (Spring 1979); Daniel Scott Smith, "Life Course, Norms, and the Family System of Older Americans in 1900," *Journal of Family History,* 4 (Fall 1979), 290–1; Joyce Goodfriend, "The Struggle for Survival: Widows in Denver, 1880–1912," in *On Their Own,* ed. Scadron, 173.

46 Smith, "Life Course, Norms, and the Family System," 290.

47 The younger sample consists of 116 pensioned and 473 nonpensioned widows, and the older consists of 65 pensioned and 283 nonpensioned widows.

women. The experiences of younger widows are therefore worth studying.

Younger widows receiving pensions had fewer minor children to support than widows not receiving pensions, in all four communities.[48] This
difference was not significant in Salem, but in Grand Rapids 12 percent
more nonpensioned than pensioned widows lived with minor children.
Many widows with minor children also had adult children, who could
be sources of financial and emotional support, living in the household. In
Salem, 44 percent of pensioned widows and 38 percent of nonpensioned
widows living with minor children also lived with adult children. In Grand
Rapids, none of the pensioned widows who had minor children also lived
with adult children, while 36 percent of nonpensioned widows with minor children lived with adult children. Seventeen percent of pensioned
widows in rural Kent County who lived with minor children also had
adult children present, while 57 percent of nonpensioned widows did.
Regular pension payments in Kent County may have lessened the need
of women with minor children to retain adult children in the household,
even though fewer of them had minor children to support.

The presence of adult children in the household indicates a strategy for
support among older widows[49] and may indicate the same among younger
ones. Grand Rapids and Salem widows had adult children living with
them in similar proportions, regardless of pension status. About 56 percent of widows in Grand Rapids and 61 percent in Salem lived with adult
children. Differences between pensioned and nonpensioned widows were
pronounced and opposite in nonurban Kent and Essex counties. In rural
Kent County, 75 percent of nonpenisoned and 50 percent of pensioned
widows had adult children in their households. In nonurban Essex County,
60 percent of nonpensioned and 81 percent of pensioned younger widows lived with adult children. The age at which these women were widowed was important in determining whether they had older children
available to live with them. There were more pensioned than nonpensioned widows below the age of 35 in rural Kent County. Widows receiving pensions there probably had fewer adult children available to live
with them. In nonurban areas of Essex County, the opposite age difference occurred between pensioned and nonpensioned younger widows. A
slightly higher proportion of younger pensioned widows in nonurban
Essex County were above age 35 than nonpensioned widows.

48 Children under age 16 are defined as minor children for this study. This age is consis-
     tent with the federal government's definition of minor children for the purpose of
     pension payments. See Glasson, *History of Military Pension Legislation.*
49 Chudacoff and Hareven, "From the Empty Nest to Family Dissolution"; Smith, "Life
     Course, Norms, and the Family System."

Age alone does not explain the differences in living with adult children among younger widows. Salem pensioned and nonpensioned widows were about the same age, and they about equally lived with adult children, but all of Grand Rapids pensioned widows were above 35 years of age, and yet they lived with adult children in about the same proportions as nonpensioned younger widows. Also, the slight differences in age among Essex County widows is not enough to explain differences in the number of adult children living with them. Community of residence determined the context in which the consequences of widowhood played themselves out. Pensions, along with community of residence, mattered more than age in determining whether widows would live with adult children in nonurban Essex County and Grand Rapids. In many cases, pension payments helped widows who had fewer minor children than other widows in the community.

While more pensioned widows in outlying areas of Essex County lived with adult children, younger pensioned widows were more likely to head those households. The presence of adult children in the household suggests a strategy for economic support, but there are also reasons to believe that the presence of married children should indicate a loss of headship. Essex County women were using pension payments, along with the presence of adult children, to maintain independent households. In outlying areas of Essex County, 88 percent of pensioned widows headed their own households, while only 60 percent of nonpensioned widows did. The difference between the two groups was about evenly split between women living with relatives and women who were boarders or servants.[50] In Salem, where 81 percent of pensioned widows and 73 percent of nonpensioned widows headed their own households, the difference of 8 percent was entirely due to nonpensioned widows who were boarders (about 3 percent), servants, or dependents.[51] In Kent County, pension payments seem to have operated in a different way, contributing to the economic well-being of households headed by the children of widows. Younger widows who received pension payments in Kent County were slightly less likely to head their own households. Between 58 and 66 percent of all widows in Kent County headed their own households. Of these, about 7 percent more rural and 4 percent more urban nonpensioned widows headed their own households. More pensioned widows were likely to live with relatives, especially with children, in both rural

50 Women whose relationship to the household examined in the census was listed as that of servant of some kind were not included in this analysis unless they obviously also lived in the household.
51 Dependent women in this study most often lived in poor farms or homes for the aged or disabled, although some were boarded out with families. There were very few of them, and none received pensions.

and urban areas; in Grand Rapids a slightly higher percentage boarded, while in rural communities a slightly higher percentage were servants.

Pension payments also made a difference in visible sources of financial support among younger widows. Sources of support were divided into seven types by employment or family employment, taking in boarders, and dependency. For these purposes, women who were listed as keepers of boardinghouses were considered employed, to differentiate them from women who were merely taking a few boarders into their homes.[52] Table 7.4 shows sources of support for widows under 65 years of age. All younger widows receiving pensions, except in rural Kent County, were less likely to be employed than widows not receiving pensions, especially in non-urban Essex County and in Grand Rapids, although in Grand Rapids pensioned widows made up the difference by taking in boarders. In Essex County and rural Kent County, more pensioned widows had no visible means of support than nonpensioned widows, about one in three in Salem, suggesting that pension payments constituted an important financial supplement. Other sources of support for the widows who had no visible means of income could be varied, perhaps including accumulated savings or property, financial help from other family in town, or charity. The support of family members figured largely in the lives of many of these women; in most cases more than one-half appear to have been supported by family members. In turn, they may have been contributing to the household income through their pensions.

Women over 65 years of age and older experienced widowhood very differently from younger ones. Overall, older widows who received pensions were more likely to have adult children in their households than widows who did not receive pensions. The gap between pensioned and nonpensioned older widows was especially pronounced in Essex County, where 16 percent more pensioned than nonpensioned widows in Salem and 11 percent more pensioned widows in nonurban areas lived with adult children. Five percent more pensioned widows in Grand Rapids lived with adult children. Women receiving pensions in these areas were older than those not receiving pensions. In Salem, two in three pensioned older widows were age 75 years or more, while only two in five older nonpensioned widows were 75 or older. Age, not pension status, primarily determined whether older widows lived with adult children. Although older widows may have lost the support of a husband or son because of war, they still had children available to live with them in old age. For

52 Women who were employed also may have lived with family members who were employed, but since we are interested in whether the widow had to work, her employment is considered the first avenue of self-support. Women who took in boarders presumably had no other visible means of support.

Table 7.4. Source of support, pension status, and community of residence of younger war widows, 1880

Community	None visible (%)	Boarders (%)	Employed (%)	Employed, with boarders (%)	Family (%)	Family, with boarders (%)	Dependent (%)	Total (%)[a]	N
Kent County									
Grand Rapids									
Pensioned	18	7	18	4	36	18	0	101	28
Nonpensioned	20	1	26	1	47	5	0	100	147
Nonurban									
Pensioned	17	8	13	0	63	0	0	101	24
Nonpensioned	13	4	12	1	61	9	0	100	69
Essex County									
Salem									
Pensioned	34	0	18	0	42	5	0	99	38
Nonpensioned	19	1	20	2	51	5	2	100	187
Nonurban									
Pensioned	19	0	11	0	62	8	0	100	26
Nonpensioned	11	3	29	0	51	6	0	100	63

[a]Total percentages do not add exactly to 100, because of rounding.

children who lived with older mothers, pension payments probably eased the economic burden of the household.

Looking at older widows by their relationship to the head of household produces few patterns. Nonpensioned widows were more likely to be head of household in outlying areas of Essex County and in Grand Rapids, while pensioned widows were more likely to be head of household elsewhere. In Kent County, about 60 percent of all older widows were listed as mothers or mothers-in-law of the household head. In Salem, about 30 percent were listed as mothers, and in other areas of Essex County between 33 and 39 percent were mothers of the household head. Among older widows receiving pensions, Essex County women were more likely to be head of household, especially in Salem, where 62 percent of these women were head of household, even though the pensioned group there was much older. No pensioned older widows were servants or dependents, and boarding differed according to community of residence. Pension status did not determine whether an older widow headed her own household; community of residence did.

By the time most widows turned 65 they were either supported by family members, especially in Kent County, or had no visible means of support. Table 7.5 shows sources of support for widows aged 65 and older. A few pensioned widows took in boarders or worked, and more nonpensioned widows did so, but these means of support were much less important than living with relatives who worked. Several nonpensioned older widows were dependent on charity. Like younger widows, many still had no visible means of support, although in rural Kent County only 15 percent of older nonpensioned widows had no visible means of support. Losing a husband or son in war made little difference in an older widow's resources in terms of whether she had an adult child living with her or other relatives to help support her. Even though many of the older group of widows were mothers of Civil War soldiers and had declared themselves to be solely dependent upon their dead son for support, pension payments eventually added income to households of relatives who were in a position to support them. That about equal proportions of older widows lived with family regardless of pension status raises questions about whether financial need primarily determined whether older women lived with relatives or whether other concerns dominated the decision.

The Civil War widowed women who were mostly between the ages of 35 and 64 at the end of the war. Because communities differed demographically, women in different areas of the country were widowed at different ages. Civil War widows living in Michigan in 1880 were much younger than those living in Massachusetts communities. Since the ex-

Table 7.5. *Source of support, pension status, and community of residence of older war widows, 1880*

Community	None visible (%)	Boarders (%)	Employed (%)	Employed, with boarders (%)	Family (%)	Family, with boarders (%)	Dependent (%)	Total %[a]	N
Kent County									
Grand Rapids									
Pensioned	20	0	7	0	67	7	0	101	15
Nonpensioned	25	4	0	0	56	15	0	100	48
Nonurban									
Pensioned	20	10	0	0	60	10	0	100	10
Nonpensioned	15	6	6	0	67	2	4	100	48
Essex County									
Salem									
Pensioned	33	0	0	0	57	10	0	100	21
Nonpensioned	33	1	3	0	56	5	2	100	113
Nonurban									
Pensioned	33	0	11	0	44	11	0	99	18
Nonpensioned	29	6	6	0	54	4	1	100	70

[a]Total percentages do not add exactly to 100.0, because of rounding.

perience of widowhood differs dramatically according to the age of the person losing a spouse, the lifetime experiences of Civil War widows in Michigan were very different from those in Massachusetts. Because Civil war widows were concentrated between 35 and 64 years of age, their experiences were different from those of other widows in the community, some of whom were much younger and many of whom were much older. Civil War widows in each community were a more homogeneous group in terms of age.

Pensioned widows in Michigan and Massachusetts were more alike when we look at generation in the United States. They did not differ much from one another in the proportion that was foreign-born, although more Michigan widows who were native-born had foreign-born parents. While the generational mix of Massachusetts pensioned and nonpensioned widows was similar, pension benefits in Kent County were paid to a select group of widows, most of whom were native-born in a city where almost one-half of all widows were foreign-born. As immigration levels rose in the late nineteenth and early twentieth centuries, widows receiving pensions in places where the population was rapidly expanding became an increasingly exclusive group.

Younger widows receiving pensions in all communities had fewer minor children to support than widows who did not receive pension payments. Whether they also had adult children in the household who could help to support minor children depended upon community of residence. Pension payments to widows in Michigan may have lessened the need to keep adult children in households with minor children. Pension status, along with community of residence, mattered more than age in determining whether younger widows lived with adult children in nonurban Essex County and Grand Rapids.

Pension status also influenced strategies for maintaining an independent household, measured by whether a widow headed her own household. Essex County women used pension payments, along with the presence of adult children, to maintain independent households. In Kent County, pensions instead contributed to the economic well-being of households headed by adult children. Most younger widows receiving pension payments were less likely to be employed than those who did not, especially in nonurban Essex County and in Grand Rapids. Some made up the difference by taking in boarders, but many widows were supported by family members who worked. Widows receiving pensions in many cases may have been contributing to households in which relatives were employed.

Among widows who were older, 65 years of age or more, age primarily determined whether they lived with adult children, not pension status.

Although pensioned widows had lost one or more male relatives during a war, they still had children available to live with them in old age. For children who lived with older mothers, pension payments probably eased economic conditions in the household. While age determined whether older widows lived in the same household with adult children, community of residence determined whether they headed those households. In Essex County, pensioned widows were more likely to head their own households than nonpensioned widows, even though pensioned widows were older. Finally, neither community of residence, age, or pension status made much difference in visible sources of support of older widows. About equal proportions of older widows lived with family, raising questions about whether financial need primarily determined whether older women lived with relatives or other concerns dominated the decision.

Conclusion: War Widowhood in the Late Nineteenth Century

We know relatively little about how people experienced widowhood in the late nineteenth century. We do know that transition from married to widowed life has varied consequences, confronting the widow with overcoming grief and with new household and economic situations. The context in which a woman experiences widowhood has important implications for how she copes with her situation. Although we know little about the historical context, the evidence that exists suggests that widowhood in the nineteenth century was a very different experience from widowhood today.

First, because of higher birth rates, widows in the nineteenth century faced a greater probability of having to raise minor children. Over 98 percent of Utah widows under age 40 in the late nineteenth century had one or more children under the age of 16, and 64 percent of widows aged 40 to 59 still had minor children.[53] Women also had fewer opportunities for employment and fewer avenues of support. In Denver between 1880 and 1910, steady employment for widows was scarce.[54] Middle-class widows could rely upon fraternal associations set up by their husbands to look out for them after the death of their spouse; although financial benefits could be small, the men in these organizations may have taken on more of the responsibility for the widow's support.[55] Some charity was available as well, and even though many widows of the Civil War

---

53 Geraldine P. Mineau, "Utah Widowhood: A Demographic Profile," 151–2, in *On Their Own*, ed. Scadron, 140–65.

54 Goodfriend, "Struggle for Survival," 180.

55 Ibid., 171–2.

received regular pension payments, charitable organizations also were set up to help them.[56] Older widows often depended upon family for support; widowhood for older women in the early twentieth century, however, many times meant the loss of an independent household, unless they could remain employed.[57]

How women respond to widowhood not only depends upon the economic and demographic characteristics of their society but on the societal context as well. One aspect of the societal context is how death is viewed. Widows in the nineteenth century lived in a society in which death was more common and openly acknowledged, and they benefited from a better understanding of their situation.[58]

Although death may have been better understood, widows of the late nineteenth century still may have suffered from the image of widows as helpless. That idea is expressed, for example, in a list of the "Rights of a Woman" published in Newburyport in 1869, one of which is said to be "the right to comfort and to bless, The widow and the fatherless."[59] Similar images were found in a Grand Rapids newspaper. On Decoration Day (Memorial Day) in 1882, one speaker told the crowd that they must not forget "the helpless widows and orphans of our honored dead."[60]

While the people in a position to lend emotional support may have empathized with the widow's loss, the widow still lived in a society that first defined her by her relationship to her husband. A woman was identified by her relationship with her husband, and the death of her spouse did not remove that identification. Evidence of the strength of that perception can be seen in the way in which census takers listed the marital status and relationship to household head of some widows in the census. Men who had lost their spouses were not necessarily defined by that loss, while women were. One enumerator of a large section of Grand Rapids listed widowed men as "single" but listed women as "widowed." A rural enumerator listed all of his female widows who were heads of their own household as "wife" instead of "household head," reflecting their continued role even though their husbands were dead.

The Civil War itself heightened the communal nature of death. In 1868,

56 Ibid., 181.
57 Smith, "Life Course, Norms, and the Family System," 191–2.
58 Maris A. Vinovskis, "Death and Family Life in the Past," *Human Nature,* (1989), 109–22.
59 Ibid., September 2, 1869, 4.
60 *Daily Morning Democrat,* May 31, 1882, 1. The *Grand Rapids Democrat* went through several name changes during the last half of the nineteenth century. Issues quoted in this chapter – *Daily Morning Democrat, Daily Democrat,* and *Grand Rapids Democrat* – are referred to by their contemporary names. All may be found at the Bentley Historical Collections, University of Michigan, where they are listed under the unifying name *Grand Rapids News.*

the Grand Army of the Republic (GAR) designated May 30 as Decoration Day (now Memorial Day), to honor Union soldiers and sailors. Decoration Days were celebrated with parades, speeches, and the decoration of graves. An examination of the *Grand Rapids Democrat* on successive Decoration Days shows that celebrations in Grand Rapids were mostly reserved for honoring the dead. Surprisingly, widows and families of the war dead were rarely mentioned. A speaker in 1881 tells us why: There was hardly "a family or hearthstone" that had not lost a loved one, but "we are here to honor the dead, not to mourn."[61] A similar opinion was expressed in 1889: "Among those . . . assembled here . . . are the widows and children of those brave heroes. . . . They came here, not to mourn, but to bow down and worship before the shrine of liberty, and acknowledge the sacrifice which was made for them and all future generations."[62] The image of sacrifices on an altar of freedom or country was a common one, and appropriate, given the sheer number of soldiers who were killed in the war. From the writings of a wartime nurse emerges the same image: "There sleep our brothers and our sons – the best we had to give; the costliest sacrifice we could offer on the altar of our country."[63] That Decoration Day, or Memorial Day, lived on as a day of commemoration speaks to the great need of a society to recover from and continually justify a huge sacrifice.

War widowhood was a multidimensional experience. One dimension was personal: the loss of a husband or a son. Another was communal: The nation bore her sacrifice with her. Union war widows and families had made personal sacrifices of family members and themselves had paritcipated in a brave and noble war effort to save the nation from devastation. The nation repaid their sacrifices with honor, gratitude, and with pensions.

This chapter has briefly explored the impact of the Civil War pension upon widows of that war. A limited group of Union widows and dependent mothers received significant support from the government soon after the war, and many more women became eligible to receive that aid later, after 1890. The effect of the pension system was to aid financially two age cohorts of women: those who had been married to soldiers during the war, and those who were the mothers of soldiers. As these women aged, pension support became more widespread and became in effect an old-age pension, specialized in helping a unique but large group of women: two generations of widows, mothers, and wives. Pension aid was concentrated regionally as well, extending from east to west along the northern

61 *Daily Morning Democrat*, May 28, 1871, 5.
62 *Daily Democrat*, May 31, 1898, 2.
63 McKay, quoted in Moore, *Women of the War*, 299.

part of the nation. The effects of war included the death of male relatives and the payment of pensions, but the evolution of a national mourning rite may have helped to heal some of the damage. Clearly, the Civil War changed the course of the lives of many American individuals and families, and the consciousness of a nation. Pension income may have cushioned the damage caused by those changes for decades.

Index